Financial Systems, Central Banking, and Monetary Policy during COVID-19 Pandemic and After

Financial Systems, Central Banking, and Monetary Policy during COVID-19 Pandemic and After

Edited by Çağatay Başarır and Burak Darıcı

LEXINGTON BOOKS
Lanham • *Boulder* • *New York* • *London*

Published by Lexington Books
An imprint of The Rowman & Littlefield Publishing Group, Inc.
4501 Forbes Boulevard, Suite 200, Lanham, Maryland 20706
www.rowman.com

6 Tinworth Street, London SE11 5AL, United Kingdom

British Library Cataloguing in Publication Information Available

Library of Congress Cataloging-in-Publication Data Available

ISBN 978-1-7936-4555-5 (cloth: alk. paper)
ISBN 978-1-7936-4557-9 (pbk. : alk. Paper)
ISBN 978-1-7936-4556-2 (electronic)

Contents

List of Illustrations

FIGURES

TABLES

Acknowledgments

We would like to thank all the authors and researchers who are experts in their fields, for their devotion and diligence and we hope this work is of help to our readers. We are also grateful to their families and children who are the source of motivations for our authors withtheir support and patience during the creation of these valuable works.

Yours Truly,

Assoc. Prof. Çağatay Başarır
Prof. Burak Darıcı

Introduction

Financial crises have affected almost all the countries of the world and have been discussed in different economies under different conditions in the recent years. World economies have become highly integrated after the 1990s. As a result, money went beyond its traditional functions and leaped forward from the economies and economic systems where it was created both in real sector and financial sector, in other words, in every step people take. While the global production of goods and services was 250 billion dollars in the 1500s, it ascended to 86 trillion dollars in 2019. This enormous growth has taken place due to some major changes that have occurred in the last hundred years. However, it also brought financial crisis, speculative bubbles, and together with these new institutions aiming to solve the crisis. Central banks are the leader of these institutions that are seen as the saviors during the financial crisis. Therefore, central banking has a key function in the economy. In this context, the role of central banking in the management of the financial crisis that arose due to reasons such as pandemics has once again taken the center stage. In dealing with the financial crisis, all factors faced by the financial system, especially central banking, will be discussed in detail.

Infectious diseases that threaten the population simultaneously across the world are defined as pandemic. During a pandemic, governments change their policies and take measures to protect public health at first. However, in the globalizing world, pandemics seriously affect individuals' economic conditions and lives. Increase in inflation, unemployment rates, decline in economic growth rates, halt in production and consumption, and widespread poverty are considered as some of the potential effects of the epidemics. Countries announce economic packages to combat the epidemic, and central banks make necessary interventions to provide liquidity to markets. The purpose of this study is to investigate, from a historical perspective, how the pandemic period, especially COVID-19, affects the whole financial system, and what measures are taken and which policies are implemented to counter this menace.

Chapter 1

Analysis of the Impact of the COVID-19 Crisis on the Markets

Mustafa Kevser

INTRODUCTION

Since its existence, the world has had to struggle with various epidemics. Millions of people have died in many epidemics. For example, it is known that 25–50 million people died in Europe in the fourteenth century (1346–1350) due to the plague epidemic. It is estimated that nearly 20 million people died as a result of the epidemic known as the Spanish flu during the years of World War I (1918–1920). In recent history, similar to these epidemics, human beings have had to fight against HIV, SARS, and MERS viruses, and therefore many people lost their lives. The name of the last epidemic faced by the world and humanity is called COVID-19 (2019-nCoV).

The first official case of the new COVID-19 outbreak was seen on December 31, 2019, in Wuhan, China's Hubei province, according to the World Health Organization's statement, and it soon became a global crisis. On March 11, 2020, the virus affected more than 100,000 people in 100 different countries and caused many deaths (Albulescu 2021: 1). Upon this, the World Health Organization announced on March 12, 2020, that the epidemic turned into a pandemic. To date, the American continent has been seen as the region most and worst affected by the epidemic, followed by Europe and South Asia. From among the countries in the world, China, England, Italy, Spain, France, and the United States are the most affected by the epidemic (Ashraf 2020). According to the data of the World Health Organization, the total number of cases worldwide as on March 7, 2021, was 116,135,492 and the number of deaths was 2,581,976. Due to the rapid spread of the pandemic, countries have put social restrictions into effect. In this context, curfews and travel restrictions were imposed, schools were closed, and countries closed their borders. With the quarantine policies implemented, a sharp decline in social mobility, and the shrinkage in international trade caused the economies to weaken (Shen et al., 2020; Zeren and Hızarcı, 2020). In addition, the COVID-19 crisis can be described as a period of uncertainty, instability, and danger in many aspects (Karabağ 2020; Wojcik and Ioannou 2020; Al-Quadah and Houcine 2021). In this regard, COVID-19 significantly affected different markets and sectors negatively (Alfaro et al. 2020; Estrada et al. 2020; Zhang et al. 2020). While tourism, transportation, food and beverage industries are among the most adversely affected sectors (Albulescu 2020), there was a 30 percent decrease in major stock markets, especially in the S&P 500 index (Ali et al. 2020). When the daily decreases exceeded 7 percent in mid-March 2020 in U.S. stock markets, circuit breakers were applied and transactions were stopped for 15 minutes (Şenol, 2020: 81). The International Monetary Fund (IMF) announced its expectation of the global recession at the end of March 2020 (IMF, 2020). In this context, the IMF, World Bank, and OECD expected the gross domestic product to shrink between 3 percent and 7.5 percent globally in 2020, and predicted a growth between 2.8 percent and 5.8 percent in 2021 (World Bank 2020; IMF 2020; OECD 2020).

The VIX volatility index, which is an indicator of the global risk perception level and the fragility in the markets during the COVID-19 process, remained at a level close to the 2008 global financial crisis. While the uncertainties experienced in this respect had a negative impact on stock indexes as well as bonds, they also had an impact on commodity prices, such as gold and oil (Şenol, 2020; Anh and Gan 2020; Schoenfeld, 2020).

Many studies have examined the impact of COVID-19 on financial markets and the economy (So et al. 2021; Zhang et al. 2020; Tröster and Küblböck 2020; Sansa 2020; Demirgüç-Kunt, 2020; Fu and Shen, 2020). A significant portion of these studies have focused both on developed or developing countries, such as the United States, China, Germany, France, England, Italy, Spain, and Japan, and investigated the relationship between the number of cases and deaths and financial markets in the COVID-19 period. However, the research examining the causality relationships between bond markets, commodity markets, and indices is quite limited. In this context, an empirical analysis is also included in this study and the causality relationships between important financial indicators are examined. In this respect, the causality relationships between the VIX volatility index, Brent oil, gold, and U.S. 10-year bond prices and the USD/TRY exchange rate were examined in this study, and thus some contributions in these topics were made to the literature.

In the current study, daily data between the date of March 12, 2020, when it was announced that COVID-19 turned into a pandemic by the World Health Organization, and February 26, 2021, were used. The unit root was used as a method in the analyses, and the null hypothesis that the unit root is found in the time series was tested with the Augmented Dickey–Fuller (ADF) test. In addition, the direction of the relationship between variables was determined with the Pairwise Granger causality test. The results obtained in the current study have revealed the relationships between the VIX volatility index, gold and oil prices, US 10-year bond prices, and the USD/TRY exchange rate.

LITERATURE REVIEW

Toward the end of the twentieth century, the Asian crisis of 1997 and the Russian crisis of 1998 led to a financial contagion spreading to the world. The 2008 global financial crisis started in the United States spread globally at a great speed, and ravaged many countries, which shows the interlinking of world economies. In this respect, the spread of COVID-19 from China to the world and its financial effects being felt all over the world at the same time remind us of the previous global crises. Nations have intervened to reduce the effects of COVID-19. Arguments stating that trust in governmental practices and strong public response to the pandemic have a significant effect in reducing the negative impact of COVID-19 (Ashraf 2020; Anh and Gan 2020), which are important in combating the pandemic globally.

THE IMPACT OF COVID-19 ON FINANCIAL MARKETS

The effects of many different epidemics and pandemics, such as HIV, SARS, MERS, and finally COVID-19, on the financial markets in the twenty-first century have been examined in many studies, and as a result, it has been claimed that investors' concerns about their future incomes have led to economic losses in financial markets (Jiang et al., 2017; Liu et al., 2020). Al-Quadah and Houcine (2021) stated that investors' fears and insecurities function as a mediation and transmission mechanism and carry the effects of COVID-19 to stock markets. In this context, it is stated that the increasing number of COVID-19 cases and deaths negatively affect stock returns. On the other hand, Anh and Gan (2020) stated that the first period of COVID-19 had an adverse effect on the stock returns in the Vietnam stock market, but stated that the COVID-19 process positively affected the stock performance as a result of the measures taken by the Vietnamese government in the following periods. This situation experienced in the Vietnam stock exchange was explained by the trust the citizens had on their government as a welfare state. It is proven that the pandemic increases the risk of global financial markets. In particular, the risk factors specific to in each country and also the rate of spread of the pandemic have hit the stock markets accordingly. Zhang et al. (2020) draw attention to this issue and point out that the uncertainty brought about by the pandemic is related to economic losses, and within this framework, financial markets have become unpredictable, and volatility has increased. In addition to the increase in volatility in financial markets during the COVID-19 pandemic, systematic risks for securities have also increased. While the IMF stated that the impacts of COVID-19 could be deeper than the 2008 global financial crisis, So et al. (2021) stated that unlike previous crises, market factors cannot adequately explain the change in stock returns and draw attention to the systematic risks that arise. Sansa (2020) examined the effects of COVID-19 in terms of the Chinese and U.S. stock markets. In the study where regression analysis was used as the method, it was concluded that the number of deaths and positive cases between March 1, 2020, and March 25, 2020, had a statistically significant and encouraging effect on the Shanghai Stock Exchange and Dow Jones. In this respect, in contrast to the expected disadvantageous effects of COVID-19, it was found that stock markets continued to remain steady, which is an interesting finding. Although the whole world is affected by the COVID-19 pandemic, the extent to which each country is affected differs from country to country and from region to region. Countries such as the United States, England, Germany, Italy, Spain, and Japan were the first to be affected by the pandemic, and their financial markets experienced a rapid decline. Asian countries, on the other hand, faced abnormal negative returns during the pandemic.

Pessimism about the future and uncertainty in expected returns were highly influential in Asian countries. On the other hand, stock markets of Asian countries could react quickly to the pandemic and tended to recover in the next stage (Liu et al. 2021). Another negative effect of the COVID-19 pandemic on financial markets is that it has led to liquidity problems. Baig et al. (2020) stated that due to the increase in the number of cases and deaths, liquidity problem arose in U.S. capital markets, and at the same time, volatility increased. As can be seen in the examples given above, a significant part of the studies examining the impact of COVID-19 on financial markets have focused on short-term volatility. At this point, answering the question of what causes the volatility in financial markets will contribute to the evaluation of research findings from the COVID-19 perspective. In terms of financial markets, Hartwell (2018) explained the sources of volatility as follows:

- Change in economic conditions
- Institutional issues
- Uncertainty in the markets

When we evaluate the COVID-19 process around the world, it is justifiable to state that all the elements stated by Hartwell (2018) are strongly valid for the markets. In this respect, the fact that the pandemic caused high volatility in financial markets can be explained both theoretically and administratively.

In addition to causing significant losses, uncertainty, and risk in financial markets, the pandemic also had some consequences, especially on banks, which are the backbone of the economy. Banks are the fundamental institutions of economic growth and development, especially for developing countries. For this reason, the successful performance of the banking sector during the COVID-19 pandemic and the positive attitude of the banking sector toward the real sector's access to finance are important in terms of reducing the impact of the financial crisis. However, the banking sector is faced with a number of risks foremost being the loans disbursed to the population and their repayment. It is possible to group these risks under three main headings.

- **Credit risk**—failure to make repayment of the loans leads to this risk.
- **Market risk**—although the financial and administrative conditions of the corporates to which loans are granted are good, changes in loan prices or high fluctuations in the returns of the invested securities due to the adverse conditions of the markets in general indicate market risk.
- **Operational risk**—these are risks that cannot be classified either under credit or market risks.

It is possible to say that credit risk and market risk can be quite high for the banking sector during the COVID-19 pandemic. With the transformation of COVID-19 into a pandemic, many countries have devised policies to provide liquidity support to the markets through their central banks. In this context, it is seen that the loans provided by banks around the world are much higher than the loans provided in the 2008 global financial crisis. Demirguc-Kunt et al. (2020) examined the impact of COVID-19 on banking sector's stock prices. The research conducted on fifty-three countries showed that banks experienced decreases, especially in their stock returns during the pandemic. In addition, it has been determined that the negative impact of the pandemic on banks is more pronounced and longer lasting compared to corporates or other non-financial institutions. It was observed that financial expansion did not have a positive effect on banking sector's stock returns in developing countries. Borio (2020) stated that, although banks entered the crisis period with high equity, they operate with low profitability, and rating agencies tend to give low ratings due to increased non-performing loans. Aldasoro et al. (2020) also stated that the performance of banks in the stock and debt markets is at the same level as the 2008 global financial crisis. Especially, the increase in CDS (Credit Default Swap) premiums of banks entering the period of the

COVID-19 pandemic with high credit risk has created a negative impact. COVID-19 has also impacted the financial performance of companies operating in other sectors, as well as banks. The financial performances of firms can be affected by both internal and external factors. The COVID-19 pandemic is an external factor affecting the financial performances of corporates. Shen et al. (2020) stated that COVID-19 negatively affects the financial performance of corporates registered on the Chinese stock market. The decrease in total incomes and the reduction of the investment scale are suggested as the two main reasons for this negative effect. It is seen that especially small and medium-sized companies are affected more than large-scale companies during the pandemic (Rababah et al. 2020).

THE IMPACT OF COVID-19 ON COMMODITY MARKETS

In addition to its effects on financial markets, COVID-19 also has many effects on commodity prices. The rapid spread of the crisis led to a slow-down in economic activities, especially in developing countries, so nations that were commodity-dependent faced difficulties. Commodity prices reacted strongly to the crisis, and with the implementation of restrictions, commodity prices were re-determined in the newly emerged supply and demand conditions. Increasing risks and uncertainty during the spread of the pandemic brought about 30 percent shrinkage in the world stock markets in the first 100 days, and gold prices are plummeted, investors saw gold as a safer investment option compared to financial markets. On the other hand, it has been observed that gold prices are less volatile compared to other investment instruments in financial markets. Zeren and Hızarcı (2020) stated that the stock markets fluctuate with the number of deaths and recovery cases around the world, and therefore they are in co-integration for a long term, and that it would be appropriate for investors to avoid stock market investments and turn to gold investments. Ali et al. (2020) stated that oil prices have higher volatility than gold in this period, but attributes the reason for this volatility not only to the COVID-19 pandemic but also to the policies of oil-exporting countries. The decline in energy prices was quite striking in April and August 2020. Prices, which decreased by approximately 70 percent at the end of April 2020 compared to the beginning of 2020, still included a 30 percent loss in August 2020 compared to the beginning of the year. During the COVID-19 pandemic, oil as an asset caused the highest loss to its investors after the U.S. treasury bonds. The underlying reason for this decline is the worldwide pro-duction and consumption shrinkage, which in turn hit the commodity prices, in general.

The effect of COVID-19 on financial markets and commodity markets and the rapid spread of this effect across regions and countries is an important feature of pandemics or crises in general. This feature is the "contagion" feature in global markets. The combination of financial liberalization and the contagious environment created by globalization shows that the world has become much more vulnerable to economic crises compared to the past. Although many derivatives or new financial instruments are used to protect against the contagion effects of crises and pandemics, it cannot be claimed that the desired success has been achieved until now. In this respect, Corbet et al. (2020) stated that bitcoin is not a safe tool during the pandemic and does not serve as an adequate hedge mechanism in portfolio diversification and that bitcoin spreads contagion by increasing volatility. In addition, the joint action of the stock markets of developing countries and the stock markets of developed countries (Zeren and Hızarcı 2020) and the interdependence between the different stock markets increased the contagion effect during the pandemic. Malik et al. (2021) drew attention to the strategic and technological partnerships of Brazil and Russia and stated that the effects of the pandemic were transmitted from Brazil to Russia due to these loyalties and commercial partnerships.

During the COVID-19 pandemic, the micro and macro level economic conditions have changed, financial institutions have faced many problems, the risk has increased in the markets and an environment of uncertainty has prevailed. Firms have had to bear many business risks and suffered a loss of value. There occurred unprecedented changes in the job markets, and the volatility of stock, bond, and commodity prices has increased. The COVID-19 pandemic is expected to spread over a longer period, thus to further affect the global financial and commodity markets (Goodell 2020). Labor markets have contracted due to social distancing practices, school closures, individual isolation, and travel restrictions, and many people lost their jobs. The contraction of the labor market has weakened people's purchasing power, and the demand for goods and services has declined. On the other hand, the need for medical support has increased rapidly. The sharp rise in food demand along with the panic brought about by the pandemic has also emerged as a social problem caused by the pandemic (Nicola et al. 2020).

The effects of COVID-19 on financial markets and commodity markets, as well as its social effects, have given rise to many questions that need to be considered. The emerging results point to the depressing economic and social effects influencing the whole world. The food crisis that emerged within months is of vital importance and can be the subject of further research. The volatility of the markets, great value losses, fluctuations and losses in commodity prices, and high inflation rates have revealed the necessity of restructuring and regulating many economic issues.

THE IMPACT OF COVID-19 CRISIS ON
MARKETS: AN EMPIRICAL RESEARCH

Data

In this study, the effect of COVID-19 on financial markets and commodity markets was analyzed. In this context, the period from March 12, 2020, when World Health Organization announced that COVID-19 turned into a pandemic, to February, 26 2021, was selected as the sampling period. In the current study, the causality relationships between the VIX volatility index, U.S. 10-year bond prices, gold ounce price, Brent oil barrel price and USD/TRY exchange rate were examined. During the COVID-19 pandemic, the VIX volatility index is important in terms of showing the investment appetite and revealing the interaction between financial markets and commodity markets. In addition, as gold is considered as a reliable investment tool for protection against the effects of the crisis during financial crisis periods and as oil is one of the most important energy resources and one of the main inputs in production, they were included in the analysis. U.S. bonds, on the other hand, are preferred by investors due to the stability and confidence they offer. The U.S. central bank's interest rate decisions affect the whole world and investors shape their investment portfolios accordingly. In this respect, the causality relationship between bond prices and other investment and commodity prices during the pandemic is important. In developing countries, the exchange rate is extremely important for financial stability. Turkey is an important country as it is categorized as a developing country and also due to its dynamic structure. The relationship between the USD/TRY exchange rate and financial markets and commodity prices during the pandemic also serves as a testimony to the effects of the pandemic. The data were retrieved from the BIST datasore website (https://datastore.borsaistanbul.com) and the investing website (https://tr.investing.com).

METHODOLOGY

Since the data used in the study includes 11 months records belonging to five different variables, it has the characteristic of balanced panel data. Before performing the analysis for the panel dataset, it is necessary to investigate whether the series related to the analysis is constant over time, in other words, whether it is stationary or not. In an analysis made with non-stationary datasets, misleading results called spurious regression are encountered, so t, f, and R^2 values may give biased results. In this respect, the stability tests should be done first (Tatoğlu 2013, 199).

When testing the unit stationarity of the variables, the hypotheses are as follows:

- H_0: There is a general unit root in the series (H_0: pi = p = 1).
- H_1: There is no general unit root in the series (H0 = pi = p < 1).

In order to obtain significant results in the relationships between variables, the series must be stationary. If there is a trend in the time series of variables, a spurious regression problem is encountered. Therefore, the stationarity of the series shows that the relationships between variables are real. Panel unit root tests are divided into two as first-generation and second-generation tests. In this study, the ADF unit root test, one of the first-generation tests, which is an appropriate method in non-normally distributed (non-parametric) analysis and in cases where there is correlation between units, was used. The results obtained from the analysis show that the series are stationary. In this respect, the null hypothesis (H_0), which argues that the variables have unit root tests, is rejected because the series are stationary. Consequently, variables are suitable for conducting an econometric analysis.

When descriptive statistics are examined, it is seen that the VIX volatility index, also called the fear index, is 30.15 on average in the period under analysis. However, it is seen that the index increased up to 82.69 in the period examined. The VIX index is important in terms of showing the investment anxiety in the markets and hesitant position of investors. Brent oil price was 42.90 USD on average, during the period examined, and decreased due to the contraction in demand in this period but rose to the level of 67.04 USD afterward. The ounce price of gold, which is a safe haven for investors, was 1830.13 USD on average and decreased to 1487.1 USD during the COVID-19 pandemic, but also rose to 2069.40 USD in the same period. U.S. 10-year bond yield was 0.80 percent on average during the period under analysis. On the other hand, the mean USD/TRY rate was found to be 7.26 in Turkey during the period under analysis. However, in the same period, the exchange rate rose to 8.52, the highest level in history, and then declined to 6.20 with the measures taken and reform expectations.

When the correlation results are examined, it is seen that the most striking point is the presence of a negative relationship between the VIX volatility index, also called the fear index, and all the other variables. Accordingly, when the VIX volatility index increases, a decline occurs in securities and commodity prices. In addition, while bond prices are negatively correlated with gold prices, they are positively correlated with oil prices and the USD/TRY exchange rate. Especially, it can be mentioned that there is a strong and positive correlation between bond and oil. In addition, there is a positive correlation between gold prices and oil and also the USD/TRY exchange rate.

The correlation between gold and the USD/TRY is strong. Thus it can be concluded that there is a positive correlation between oil and the USD/TRY exchange rate.

FINDINGS

The relationships between the variables subject to current study were investigated with Granger causality test and results are presented in table 1.1. If the history of a random variable X provides a better prediction of another random variable Y, after taking into account all possible other factors and non-random information, then variable X is said to be the Granger-cause of Y (Atukeren 2011).

If $p < 0.10$ in table 1.1, the results obtained from the analysis are significant. When the results obtained are examined, it is seen that the p value between bond and gold is 0.0001, smaller than 0.10. Accordingly, there is a causality relationship between bond and gold, and this relationship is from gold toward bond. Correspondingly, changes in bond prices affect gold prices. When the relationship between gold and the USD/TRY exchange rate is examined, it is seen that the p value is 0.0630, and gold is the Granger cause of the USD/TRY exchange rate. Accordingly, the change in gold prices affects the USD/

Table 1.1   Pairwise Granger Causality Tests

	Obs. (N)	F-Statistic	Prob.
Petroleum to Gold	229	0.26343	0.7687
Gold to Petroleum		0.15230	0.8588
Bond to Gold	229	9.42125	0.0001
Gold to Petroleum		0.74177	0.4774
USD/TRY to Gold	229	0.73856	0.4790
Gold to USD/TRY		2.79969	0.0630
VIX to Gold	229	0.59842	0.5506
Gold to VIX		2.41897	0.0913
Bond to Petroleum	229	0.37127	0.6903
Petroleum to Bond		4.89318	0.0083
USD/TRY to Petroleum	229	0.13862	0.8706
Petroleum to USD/TRY		0.01225	0.9878
VIX to Petroleum	229	2.57765	0.0782
Petroleum to VIX		1.33530	0.2652
USD/TRY to Bond	232	0.46273	0.6302
Bond to USD/TRY		0.68917	0.5030
VIX to Bond	232	19.7020	1.E-08
Bond to VIX		0.81350	0.4446
VIX to USD/TRY	232	0.30678	0.7361
USD/TRY to VIX		0.52422	0.5927

Source: Calculated by Authors

TRY exchange rate, and this interaction is one-way and is directed to the USD/TRY exchange rate from gold. Another result obtained from the analysis of the relationships between the variables is the relationship between oil and bond. The p value between oil and bond is 0.0083. Accordingly, the change in oil prices affects bond prices and oil is the Granger cause of bond, and this relationship is one-way and is from oil to bond. Finally, a significant correlation was found between the VIX volatility index and oil prices. In the analysis, the p value between the VIX volatility index and oil prices was found to be 0.0782. In this respect, the volatility in the VIX volatility index affects oil prices, and the VIX volatility index is the Granger cause of oil prices, and this relationship is one-way and is derived from the VIX volatility index to oil prices.

CONCLUSION

Economic and financial crises occur for different reasons and in different periods. Although many authors define high inflation, recession, or deflation as a crisis, there is no clear definition of crisis per se. Cases such as epidemics, illnesses, and earthquakes that are not caused by structural economic problems and that occur at unexpected moments can also be the cause or the beginning of crises. The 1929 depression, the oil shock in the 1970s, the Asian crisis in 1997, and the global financial crisis in 2008 can be cited as examples of crises based on economic reasons. However, the plague epidemic experienced in the fourteenth century, the Spanish flu experienced during World War I, diseases caused by HIV, SARS, and MERS viruses or the earthquake experienced in Turkey in 1999 are examples of crises not based on economic reasons. Even though crises have occurred for different reasons, their results are similar. The most obvious consequences of crises are a decline in consumer demand, a fall in the production and investments of the firms, and an increase in unemployment, and accordingly, a decrease in living standards. In addition, the environment of increasing uncertainty in times of crisis also affects the financial markets. As a result of the increasing uncertainty, there is high volatility in world and country indices, sharp declines are experienced in stock prices and national currencies face significant depreciation against foreign currencies.

Financial liberalization brought about by globalization also increases the contagion effect of crises, and a crisis in one country can easily spread to other countries.

COVID-19 was seen on December 31, 2019, in Wuhan, China's Hubei province, and it significantly affected the whole world in economic, financial, social, social, and especially medical terms. After the World Health

Organization (WHO) declared COVID-19 as a pandemic on March 12, 2020, the virus spread rapidly all over the world. As a result , countries have implemented many measures, in addition to restricting socio-cultural activities, they suspended education and imposed curfews. With the implementation of travel restrictions between countries, the economies of countries were seriously affected, and tourism, transportation, logistics services, and international trade were seriously and adversely affected. COVID-19 has also had negative effects on financial markets. The sharp falls in the world stock markets have been accompanied by the decline in the value of stocks and assets. Volatility in stock markets, asset prices, and exchange rates have added to the uncertainty, and the investment climate has deteriorated accordingly.

In this study, the relationships between gold and oil prices, which are the basic commodities of investment and production, and the U.S. 10-year bond prices, USD/TRY exchange rate, and the VIX volatility index were investigated with Granger causality test. A causality relationship was determined between bond prices and gold prices, and the direction of this relationship was found to be from bond prices to gold prices. Besides, causality was determined from gold prices to USD/TRY exchange rate, from oil prices to bond prices, and from the VIX volatility index to oil prices. The results obtained show that commodity prices, assets, and exchange rates can have a domino effect on each other during crisis periods. In addition, the effect of the VIX volatility index on oil prices explains the shrinking production volume during the crisis period and consequently the decline in demand for energy. The current study has a number of limitations. The COVID-19 pandemic has completed its first year in early 2021. In this context, the sample of the study covers the period from March 12, 2020, to February 26, 2021, and constitutes the basic limitation of the study. The economic and financial consequences of the pandemic will be more evident in the medium and long term. In this respect, analyzing the relations between commodity prices, financial assets, and exchange rates with a broader dataset and different models will provide a clearer understanding of the relations.

In addition to its negative effects, the COVID-19 pandemic has necessitated a self-assessment by world economies and communities. Late restriction decisions in the crisis period accelerated the spread of the virus, so the economic effects became more devastating. The necessity of adopting more serious and rapid approaches and practices against health care has been understood more clearly. The fact that world production is concentrated in certain countries has revealed that irreparable consequences may arise in terms of the supply chain. Distance education and work-from-home have become the new norm. The most prominent effect of the crisis is the emergence of the need to improve health systems. The serious problems that even the developed countries of the world have faced in the patient admission and treatment processes during the crisis period revealed the need for countries to reconsider healthcare and restructure their healthcare systems without wasting time. The COVID-19 crisis continues to be felt strongly around the world, and after the first two waves, a third wave is expected. In the following days, governments have to take and implement rational economic and social decisions so that economic activities do not suffer, production does not decline, and individuals do not lose their basic living rights and minimum subsistence standards.

REFERENCES

Albulescu, Claudiu, Tiberiu. 2020. "Coronavirus and financial volatility: 40 days of fasting and fear." *Working Papers*, hal-02501814, HAL. https://hal.archives-ouve rtes.fr/hal-02501814. Accessed at 08.03.2021.

Albulescu, Claudiu, Tiberiu. 2021. "COVID-19 and the United States financial markets' volatility." *Finance Research Letters*, 38, 101699.

Aldasoro, Iñaki; Fender, Ingo; Hardy, Bryan; Tarashev, Nikola. 2020. "Effects of COVID-19 on the banking sector: The market's assessment." *BIS (Bank for International Settlements)*, No.12, 1–7.

Alfaro, Laura; Chari, Anusha; Greenland, Andrew N; Schott, Peter K. 2020. "Aggregate and firm-level stock returns during pandemics, in real time." *Working Paper No. w26950, National Bureau of Economic Research,* Massachusetts.

Al-Qudah, Anas, Ali; Houcine, Asma. 2021. "Stock markets' reaction to COVID-19: Evidence from the Six WHO regions." *Journal of Economic Studies.* DOI 10.1108/ JES-09-2020-0477.

Ali, Mohsin; Alam, Nafis; Rizvi, Syed Aun R. 2020. "Coronavirus (COVID-19)-An epidemic or pandemic for financial markets." *Journal of Behavioral and Experimental Finance.* 27, 100342, 1–9.

Anh, Dao Le Trang; Gan, Christoper. 2020. "The impact of the COVID-19 lockdown on stock market performance: Evidence from Vietnam." *Journal of Economic Studies.* DOI 10.1108/JES-06-2020-0312, 836–851.

Ashraf, Badar, Nadeem. 2020. "Stock markets' reaction to COVID-19: Cases or fatalities?" *Research in International Business and Finance*, 54, 101249, 1–7.

Atukeren, Erdal. 2011. "Granger-nedensellik sınamalarına yeni yaklaşımlar." *Atatürk Üniversitesi İİBF Dergisi,* 10. Ekonometri ve İstatistik Sempozyumu Özel Sayısı 137–153.

Borio, Claudio. 2020. "The prudential response to the COVID-19 crisis." *BIS (Bank for International Settlements),* 1–6.

Baig, Ahmed, S.; Butt, Hassan, Anjum; Haroon, Omair; Rizvi, Syed, Aun R. 2020, "Deaths, panic, lockdowns and US equity markets: The case of COVID-19 pandemic." *Finance Research Letters.* DOI 10.1016/j.frl.2020.101701, 101701, 1–9.

Corbet, Shaen; Larkin, Charles; Lucey, Brain. 2020. "The contagion effects of the COVID-19 pandemic: Evidence from gold and cryptocurrencies." *Finance Research Letters*, 35, 101554, 1–7.

Demirguc-Kunt, Aslı; Pedraza, Alvaro; Ortega, Claudia, Ruiz. 2020. "Banking sector performance during the COVID-19 crisis." *Policy Research Working Paper;No. 9363*. World Bank, Washington, DC, https://openknowledge.worldbank.org/hand le/10986/34369, 1–49.

Fu, Mengyao; Shen, Huayu. 2020. "COVID-19 and corporate performance in the energy industry." *Energy Finance Letters*, 1, 1–5. DOİ:10.46557/001c.12967.

Goodell, John, W. 2020. "COVID-19 and finance: Agendas for future search." *Finance Research Letters*, 35, 101512, 1–5.

Hartwell, Christopher, A. 2018. "The impact of institutional volatility on financial volatility in transition economies." *Journal of Comparative Economics*, 46, 598–615.

https://datastore.borsaistanbul.com

https://tr.investing.com

IMF. 2020. (Accessed 10 April 2020) Available at: www.imf.org/en/News/Articles /2020/03/23/pr2098-imf-managing-directorstatement-following-a-g20-ministerial -call-on-the-coronavirus-emergency.

IMF. 2020. "World economic outlook, April 2020: The great lockdown." International Monetary Fund, Washington.

Jiang, Yan; Zhang, Yi; Ma, Chunna; Wang, Quanyi; Xu, Chao; Donovan, Connor; Ali, Gholam; Xu, Tan; Sun, Wenjie. 2017. "H7N9 not only endanger human health but also hit stock marketing." *Advances in Disease Control and Prevention*, 2, 1, 1–7. DOİ 10.25196/adcp201711.

Liu, Hai, Yue; Manzoor, Aqsa; Wang, Cang, Yu; Zhang, Lei; Manzoor, Zaira. 2020. "The COVID-19 outbreak and affected countries stock markets response." *International Journal of Environmental Research and Public Health*, 17, 8. DOI 10.3390/ijerph17082800, 1–19.

Malik, Kunjana; Sharma, Sakshi; Kaur, Manmeet. 2021. "Measuring contagion during COVID-19 through volatility spillovers of BRIC countries using diagonal BEKK approach." *Journal of Economic Studies*, DOI 10.1108/JES-05-2020-0246.

Nicola, Maria; Alsafi, Zaid; Sohrabi, Catrin; Kerwan, Ahmed; Al-Jabir, Ahmed; Iosifidis, Christos; Agha, Maliha; Agha, Riaz. 2020. "The socio-economic implications of the coronavirus pandemic (COVID-19): A review." *International Journal of Surgery,* 78, 185–193.

OECD. 2020. "OECD economic outlook, June 2020—Preliminary Version." OECD Publishing, Paris. https://doi.org/10.1787/0d1d1 e2e-en.

Rababah, Abedalqader; Al-Haddad, Lara; Sial, Muhammad, Safdar; Chunmei, Zheng; Cherian, Jacob. 2020. "Analyzing the effects of COVID-19 pandemic on the financial performance of Chinese listed companies." Academic Paper, Wiley. DOI: 10.1002/pa.2440, 1–6.

Ruiz Estrada, Mario Arturo; Koutronas, Evangelos; Lee, Minsoo. 2020. "Stagpression: The economic and financial impact of COVID-19 pandemic." Contemporary Economics, 15, 1, 19–33.

Sansa, Nuhu, A. 2020. "The impact of COVID-19 on the financial markets: Evidence from China and USA." *Electronic Research Journal of Social Sciences and Humanities* 2, 2, 29–39.

Schoenfeld, Jordan. (Accessed 27 July 2020) "The Invisible Business Risk of the COVID-19 Pandemic." Available at: https://voxeu.org/article/invisible-business-risk-covid-19-pandemic, 2020.

Shen, Huayu; Fu, Mengyao; Pan, Hongyu; Yu, Zhongfu; Chen, Yongquan.2020. "The Impact of the COVID-19 Pandemic on Firm Performance." *Emerging Markets Finance and Trade*, 56 (10), 2213–2230.

So, Mike, K.P.; Chu, Amanda, M.Y.; Chan, Thomas, W.C. 2020. "Impacts of the COVID 19 pandemic of financial market connectedness." *Finance Research Letters*, 38, 101864, 1–8.

Şenol, Zekai.2020. "COVID-19 krizi ve finansal piyasalar." *Para ve Finans*. IKSAD Publishing House, 75–124.

Tatoğlu, Ferda, Yerdelen .1993. "Panel veri ekonometrisi." İstanbul: Beta Yayınevi, 2. Baskı.

Tröster, Bernhard; Küblböck, Karin.2020. "Unprecedented but not unpredictable: effects of the COVID-19 crisis on commodity-dependent countries." *The European Journal of Development Research*, 32, 1430–1449.

Zeren, Feyyaz; Hızarcı, Atike Elanur. 2020. "The impact of COVID-19 coronavirus on stock markets: evidence from selected countries," *Bulletin of Accounting and Finance Reviews*, 3(1), 78–84.

Zhang, Dayong; Hu, Min; Ji, Qiang. 2020. "Financial markets under the global pandemic of COVID-19." *Finance Research Letters*, In press, p. 101528. DOI: 10.1016/j.frl.2020.101528, 1–6.

Chapter 2

Effect of COVID-19 on Financial Markets

Mustafa Bilik and Üzeyir Aydın

INTRODUCTION

COVID-19, identified as a new coronavirus type in 2019, emerged in Wuhan, China, and quickly spread across the globe. The number of cases tested positive as well as the rising number of deaths had an enormous global consequence. With the spread of the epidemic from China, countries have begun to conduct research and find remedies for eradicating the virus. In the meantime, many people were infected and even lost their lives. The disease, which spreads quickly, has been declared a global pandemic. Many epidemics with significant consequences have existed throughout human history. The plague, cholera, typhus, smallpox, Ebola, and flu are the most well-known. In 1347, the plague, which emerged in China and Central Asia, impacted nearly a third of Europe's population, while cholera originated as an intestinal infection caused by the bacterium *Vibrio cholerae*. The Spanish flu between 1918 and 1920 is known as the flu epidemic caused by a deadly subtype of the H1N1 virus, and it spread worldwide toward the end of World War I. Typhus is an infectious disease caused by lice and fleas and was effective during World War II. Ebola, which was seen in a small village in Guinea in 2014 and spread to West Africa, causes complications such as viral hemorrhagic fever. Some 17–50 million people died due to the Spanish Flu, which had the worst impact among the epidemic diseases. COVID-19 has taken place in history as the first infectious disease of this extent and size that the world faced after the Spanish Flu (TÜBA 2020, 25). The official name of coronavirus, which is a new viral respiratory tract disease defined by high fever and shortness of breath, is defined as SARS CoV 2 (Severe Acute Respiratory Syndrome-Coronavirus-2) by the World Health Organization (WHO). The WHO uses the term COVID-19 to describe the disease caused by the virus. The new coronavirus is an infection that causes respiratory tract infection and can be transmitted from person to person. There are also other types of coronavirus that can be transmitted from person to person. It was first discovered in 1965 with the name 229E. The SARS-COV-1 type is the cause of the SARS epidemic in 2003. It is seen as a common cold. The NL63 type was discovered in Holland in 2004, the type defined as the name HKU1 was detected in Hong Kong in 2005 and is known to cause respiratory infections. The MERS-COV type is the kind that emerged in 2012 and has been defined as the deadliest of the coronavirus family. It resulted in 37 percent mortality across the world (TÜBA 2020).

When coronavirus types are compared across history, while various types appeared at different times and in different places, they always produce the same effect. In a short period of time, diseases can turn into epidemics, wreaking havoc on social and economic life and resulting in mass mortality. The first case of COVID-19 in Turkey was detected on March 11, 2019. According to the data by the Presidency of the Republic of Turkey Digital Transformation, total number of cases in the world is 104.6 million, number of people recovered is 58.1 million and number of deaths is 2.3 million as of February 6, 2021. In Turkey, 2.5 million cases were reported, 2.4 million people recovered, and 26,467 people died from the day the first case was reported. The highest number of cases was detected in the United States, followed by India, Brazil, England, and Russia. While in China, 100,305 cases were tested positive, 93,342 patients recovered and 4,821 patients died. China, the country where the first case emerged, surprisingly, had the least number of cases among other countries (https://corona.cbddo.gov.tr/).

Numerous efforts have been made by governments to combat the COVID-19 pandemic, which continues to cause chaos on many countries throughout the world. Limiting and subsequently stopping overseas travel, enforcing work-from-home norms, vacationing schools, minimizing the risk of contamination caused by congested places, vaccine development, lockdowns, curbing public transportation, stay-at-home restrictions, quarantine rules, wearing masks, and social distancing laws, all of which differ from country to country, are among these strategies. In this context, upscaling the country's healthcare system is crucial. Sufficient funds should be allocated to promote research and treatment. It is known that people infected with COVID-19 were found to have chronic illness and health problems that come with increasing age; this population failed to respond to the treatment. However, it was observed that the negative effects of the epidemic can be reduced if the obligated measures are followed, and vice versa.

It has been observed throughout history that the measures taken during an epidemic brought about important economic consequences. For example, in studies examining the effects of the SARS virus epidemic on the economy that started in 2003, it was determined that the epidemic changed the expectations in terms of supply and demand, led to lesser consumption, and in addition to the risk caused by the increase in company costs, it caused serious impacts on economies by re-evaluation of country risks (Eryüzlü, 2020, 3). The COVID- 19 outbreak caused the death of many people and has also seriously affected social and economic life on a global scale. The uncertainty about the end date of the pandemic has affected the economy in many ways. As it is understood from the literature review, unemployment has increased, many companies and businesses have closed, and the production of most commodities has been interrupted. The income loss of households along with the increasing unemployment caused demand curve to fall. Therefore, the worldwide spread of the COVID-19 epidemic affected production, supply chains, and consumption, and it has also significantly contracted the economic activities of the world, bringing some industries to a standstill. Financial problems caused by the epidemic, unemployment, reduced demand, difficulties in production and uncertainty have caused several negative effects to every economy; global crisis became inevitable (Adıgüzel, 2019, 192).

Countries affected by the epidemic have also taken monetary and financial measures in order to reduce the damage caused by the effects of the epidemic on their economies. The financial and technical measures implemented by Turkey are the regulations made in terms of tax law, opportunity of working from home, R&D support, applications and procedures related to customs for international trade to be transferred to digital environment, import applications on demand, removal of taxes on breathing apparatus for COVID-19. Within the context of monetary measures, various applications such as interest discounts, asset purchases, liquidity increase, and loan support programs are implemented. In this scope, first measure taken by the Central Bank of Turkey (CBT) during this period is the decrease of interest rates from 10.75 percent to 9.75 percent in the Monetary Policy Committee meeting dated March 17, 2020. Additionally, to lower the interest rate, on three different occasions, that is March 17, March 31, and April 17, 2020, some stimulus packages were announced. With these measures, the government aimed to grant flexibility in the Turkish Lira (TL) and foreign currency liquidity management of banks and to increase predictability to support credit flow to the real sector and to provide subsidy to the exporting companies, to support exporters with rediscount loan arrangements and to increase the market liquidity with Government Domestic Borrowing Notes (GDS) (CBRT 2020).

Each country has experienced various social and economic consequences because of the COVID-19 outbreak. Therefore, the measures taken and the time intervals vary from country to country. For example, following an increase in cases and deaths in the United Kingdom, a curfew was imposed across the country on March 24, 2020, and a lockdown was announced in Belgium on April 4, 2020. Oxford University researchers developed an index that depicts the range of actions taken in each country as a result of the use of various tactics at various times in the fight against the pandemic. The Stringency Index assesses the frequency with which countries acted in the pandemic. The frequency score ranges from 0 to 100. As a result, the Netherlands has the highest index score, followed by Cuba, Lebanon, and other countries. China, the first country to be infected with the virus, had a score of 69.9. China has implemented measures such as lockdown limitations, quarantine, prohibition of admission to confined areas, disruption of education, shutdown of workplaces, lockdown of public transportation, and international travel prohibitions. Turkey and the United States scored 68 in the index. Similar to China, Turkey has taken the measures such as stay home, lockdowns, restriction of public transport, prohibition of collective activities, domestic and international travel barriers, shut down applications for businesses after the first case COVID-19 (Government Stringency Index, Worldometers).

Health and economy must be integrated in order to maximize the welfare of the society. The risks created on the world economies in addition to the health dimension of the pandemic show that the economic impacts of the measures should be taken into account along with medical and public health measures to control the pandemic (ULİSA 2020, 1). Recovering from the stagnation caused by the COVID-19 in social and economic life and returning to normal flow of life depend substantially on the successful performance of the health systems of the countries in reducing the number of cases and death rates.

The pandemic era had led to a market environment of uncertainty. Uncertainty leads to risk and panic; in this situation, policy makers devise policies on the face of this uncertainty. This in turn affects the price of financial products. Investors have the tendency to choose financial instruments with relatively lower risks while investing in times of uncertainty. COVID-19 caused mass deaths and affects social and economic life within in a short time. In this study, a partial dimension of this effect has been analyzed. The effect of the case and death numbers due to COVID-19 and its impact on the returns of stocks, gold, and United States dollar and interest rates is investigated using GARCH (generalized autoregressive conditional heteroskedasticity) models. In the study, first the literature is reviewed. Next, goals and hypotheses are set up and dataset and models are included. Finally, empirical findings are analyzed, and the study ends with the conclusion section.

LITERATURE REVIEW

On January 30, 2020, COVID-19 was announced as a global health emergency by the WHO. On March 11, 2020, the virus was declared as a pandemic, in other words, a global pandemic. Therefore, COVID-19, whose effects are accepted globally after these dates, has been and continues to be the subject of scientific and academic studies in many aspects. This section includes the literature review of the researches and analysis about the effects of COVID-19 on economy and finance. The mentioned literature can be summarized as follows.

Adıgüzel (2020) analyzed the effects of COVID-19 pandemic on Turkish economy with a macroeconomic approach. Main economic indicators of Turkey are evaluated in the study between 2015 and 2019, and changes in economic indicators are examined in March 2020 when the pandemic had started. In the study, it is found that COVID-19 has caused recession in Turkish economy by affecting production, employment, personal and business income, exports, current account deficit, budget deficit and central government total debt burden negatively. In addition, it was predicted that 400–675 billion TL loss will occur in GDP depending on the duration of the pandemic. It was stated that even if the pandemic period is over, there will be obstacles, such as the shrinkage of domestic and foreign demand and the decrease in production, unemployment, foreign exchange costs in the structured debts of companies borrowing with foreign currency for the healthy functioning of the economy. It was stated that the budget deficit would increase further and this would affect the economy negatively.

Baker et al. (2020) investigated the effects of COVID-19 on the U.S. stock market volatility comparing the COVID-19 outbreak with the epidemic diseases experienced in previous periods. They determined that historical outbreaks such as the Sars Outbreak, Ebola Outbreak, Spanish Flu, Avian Flu and Swine Flu have had a modest effect on the U.S. stock market volatility, but news about COVID-19 has had a significant impact over the U.S. stock market since February 24, 2020.

Barut and Kaygın (2020) analyzed the impact of COVID-19 on financial markets in their studies. In this context, eleven countries where the disease spread widely, based on the total number of cases and the total number of deaths from the first appearance of the cases until April 8, 2020, have been examined. In the study, Bayer and Hanck (2012) used the co-integration analysis to determine the relationship between the total number of COVID-19 cases and the closing prices of the most important indices of the said countries. The indices of the following eleven countries were studied: China (Shanghai), the United States (DOW 30), the United Kingdom (FTSE 100), Italy (FTSE MIB), Spain (IBEX 35), Germany (DAX), France (CAC 40),

Belgium (BEL 20), Netherlands (AEX) , Switzerland (SMI), and Turkey (BIST 100). As a result of the analysis, it was concluded that there was integration between the total number of COVID-19 cases and the BIST100, FTSE MIB, IBEX35, AEX, and Shanghai indices, while there was no integration between the DAX, CAC 40, BEL 20, SMI, FTSE 100, and DOW 30 indices. In the analysis, it was determined that there was a long-term and negative relationship between BIST100, FTSE MIB, IBEX35, AEX, and Shanghai stock market indices and COVID-19 cases.

Gürsoy et al. (2020) investigated the effect of Covid-19 on international investment instruments. In the study, the causal relationship between the financial market instruments, which are often preferred after global crises, and the Chinese stock market was examined by Toda-Yamamoto (1995) analysis. A comparative study was conducted between January 3, 2017, before the pandemic, and March 10, 2020, after the pandemic. In the study, the coefficients for the pre- and post-covid periods were obtained for the analysis. While determining the variables used in the study, the effect of the SSEC index, which is the benchmark stock market in China, where the coronavirus (COVID-19) emerged, on gold, Brent oil, Bitcoin, and VIX fear index was examined. It has been determined that the causality relationship is one-way from SSEC index to gold and bidirectional from SSEC index to the VIX index. Additionally, it is concluded that there is no relationship between Brent oil and Bitcoin. During the time periods of the study, it was determined that a change in the Chinese Equity market, which was directly affected by the coronavirus (Covid19), had an effect on gold prices and the VIX fear index, and this interaction increased even more for gold prices.

Kaçak and Yıldız (2020) compared the five European countries against Turkey with regard to the severity of the measures and the first consequences of measures taken against COVID-19. Comparison of pandemic prevention policies in terms of severity, due to the date when interventions were first implemented and investigation of its effects on cases and deaths, were analyzed for Italy, Spain, France, the United Kingdom, and Germany against Turkey. For comparison, the Administrative Measure Strictness Index, which was developed to measure the rigidity of government measures against COVID-19, was used. Country frequency data were aggregated into time series and combined with the number of cases and deaths in order to compare the policies of countries and their effects on case and death statistics.

Kılıç (2020) analyzed the effect of the coronavirus emerging in China on Borsa Istanbul sector using the event study method. Kılıç found negative abnormal returns in most of the indices as a result of the analysis. He concluded that the highest negative returns based on sectors were in the tourism and textile sectors, while the positive returns were found in the trade sector.

Mckibbin (2020) examined the macroeconomic effects of COVID-19 using seven different scenarios. The first three scenarios are about how the isolation measures in China affected the economies of other countries. The other three scenarios are based on the fact that epidemiological shocks do not affect countries to the same degree. In the last scenario, it was assumed that the epidemic could repeat every year in consequence of the uncertainty related to the upcoming period. In the results of the scenarios related to COVID-19, it was found that there has been a significant decline in the gross domestic product (GDP)

In his study, Onali (2020) searched the effect of COVID-19 cases and deaths related to the U.S. stock market. In the study, the effect of the changes in the number of cases and deaths on the U.S. stock market return was examined using the GARCH (1,1) model in the period between April 08, 2019, and April 09, 2020. In the study, Italy (11591), Spain (7340), China (3309), the United States (3170), France (3024), Iran (2757), and the United Kingdom (1408), countries with at least 1,000 COVID-19 reported deaths as of March 31, 2020, has been included in the analysis. Results based on GARCH (1,1) models show that changes in the number of cases and deaths in the United States and other countries heavily affected by the COVID-19 crisis (China, Italy, Spain, United Kingdom, Iran, France) in the first three months of 2020 had no effect on the U.S. stock market returns except for the number of cases reported for China. However, it can be concluded that it had a positive effect on the conditional variances of Dow Jones and S&P returns. According to the VAR models used in the study, it was found that the number of deaths reported in Italy and France had a negative effect on Dow Jones returns and a positive effect on the VIX. The study also concluded that in Markov-switching models, the size of the negative impact of VIX on stock market returns tripled at the end of February.

Özatay and Sak (2020), studied the effects and potential economic consequences of COVID-19. In the current situation, attention was drawn to the initiation of necessary measures to eliminate the effects of the pandemic and to ensure the maintenance of the activities of companies and enterprises in this process.

Sansa (2020) analyzed the impact of COVID-19 on financial markets through the examples of China and the United States. In the analysis, the effect of COVID-19 on Shanghai Stock Exchange in China and New York Dow Jones in the United States between March 1, 2020, and March 25, 2020, was examined using a regression model. In the study, it was determined that all the confirmed cases affect the stock prices positively.

Sarı and Kartal (2020) investigated the relationship between the COVID-19 pandemic and gold price, oil price, and the VIX index. The ARDL Boundary Test was used for examining data between the period of January 22, 2020, and April 20, 2020. Accordingly, the direction of the correlation between both gold prices and the VIX index and the number of cases was pointing to the same direction. However, there was no correlation between the number of cases and oil prices. However, the gold price and VIX index were significantly affected by the number of cases.

Şit and Telek (2020) investigated the effects of the COVID-19 on the gold ounce price and dollar index in their studies. In the study, the daily number of cases and deaths, gold ounce prices and dollar index data for the period from March 1, 2020, to May 7, 2020, were analyzed. In order to determine the correlation between variables, the Hatemi-J co-integration test was applied. As per the results, a correlation was determined between the variables and the causality relationship was examined using the Hatemi-J Asymmetric causality test. Result of the analysis showed that there was a correlation between the number of deaths and positive cases and the dollar index. The causality test determined that the rise in the number of cases and deaths caused shocks on the dollar index and gold ounce price .

OBJECTIVES AND HYPOTHESIS

The effect of the volatility in the number of cases and deaths related to COVID-19 in Turkey on gold, U.S. dollar returns, and interest rates was examined for the period March 12, 2020, to November 30, 2020. Within the framework of the study, the following hypotheses were created.

Hypothesis 1: COVID-19 pandemic has a significant effect on the financial markets.

Hypothesis 2: COVID-19 pandemic caused an increase in permanence in the markets against the shock to the markets.

Hypothesis 3: COVID-19 caused an increase in risk in the markets.

DATASET AND MODEL

Within the framework of the aforementioned purpose, daily data including the period March 03, 2020, and November 30, 2020, are used in the study. Definitions and descriptive statistics of the dataset used in the study are included in table 2.1:

The summary of table 2.1 shows that the highest return is found in dollars and the interest rate. According to the values of skewness and kurtosis, none

Table 2.1   Definitions and Descriptive Statistics of the Dataset

Variable	Definition	Data Source
GBIST100	Return series of the closing prices of BIST100	investing.com
GDOLAR	Return series of USD/TL exchange rate	investing.com
GGOLD	Return series of ounce gram gold	investing.com
GRATE	Indicative interest rate	investing.com
LCASES	Logarithm of the active case numbers in Turkey related to Covid-19	https://corona .cbddo.gov .tr/
LDEATHS	Logarithm of the active death numbers in Turkey related to Covid-19	https://corona .cbddo.gov .tr/

	GBIST100	GDOLAR	GGOLD	GRATE
Mean	0.000393	0.001027	0.000247	0.002987
Median	0.000268	0.000190	0.000538	0.000216
Maximum	0.001267	0.025627	0.017563	0.191105
Minimum	0.000000	-0.034080	-0.022210	-0.155902
Standard Deviation	0.000278	0.008010	0.005349	0.040797
Skewness	1.477657	-0.574758	-0.551422	0.536724
Kurtosis	4.588812	7.374939	5.567040	8.607850
Jarque-Bera	83.49834	151.7559	57.89418	241.7853

Source: Calculated by authors

of the data has a normal distribution. They show a pointed and thick tail. In other words, they have a leptokurtic distribution.

In the study, IGARCH (1, 1) (Integrated Generalized Autoregressive Conditional Heteroskedasticity) model was used to examine the effects of COVID-19 on stock, gold, and dollar returns, and interest rates. For analyzing the effect of COVID-19, the volatility of the number of active cases and number of death in Turkey have been examined. The following models have been created for this purpose:

$$y_t = \theta_0 + \sum_{i=1}^{q}\theta_i y_{t-i} + \sum_{i=1}^{p}\varphi_i e_{t-i} + \gamma LCASES + \delta LDEATHS + e_t$$

$$\sigma_{,t} = \sum_{i=1}^{q}\alpha_i \varepsilon_{t-i}^2 + \sum_{i=1}^{p}\beta_i \sigma_{t-i} + \varepsilon_t$$

$$\sigma_t : f\left(\sigma_{GBIST100,t}, \sigma_{GDOLAR,t}, \sigma_{GGOLD,t}, \sigma_{GRATE,t}\right)$$

$$y_t : f\left(y_{GBIST100,t}, y_{GDOLAR,t}, y_{GGOLD,t}, y_{GRATE,t}\right)$$

ε_i shows the stochastic process. In the model, θ_i stands for AR parameter, φ_i for MA parameter, α_i for ARCH (autoregressive conditional heteroscedasticity) parameter, and β_i for GARCH parameter. In the GARCH (p, q) model, in order for the conditional variance of the process to be stationary, the condition $\alpha(1) + \beta(1) = \sum_{i=1}^{p} \alpha_i + \sum_{i=1}^{q} \beta_i < 1$ should be fulfilled. At the same time, the condition $\alpha_0 > 0$, $\alpha_i \geq 0$, $\beta_i \geq 0$ must be satisfied in order to ensure that the variance is positive (Bollerslev 1986, 308-309). If $\alpha_i + \beta_i = 1$ in the GARCH model, it indicates that the shock to the system is permanent and the unconditional distribution of the error term has infinite variance. If $\alpha_i + \beta_i = 1$, GARCH (p, q) model turns into IGARCH (p, q) model. The IGARCH (p, q) model tests whether the conditional variance has a unit root or not. If $\alpha_i + \beta_i < 1$ in the IGARCH (p, q) model, it indicates that the model is covariance stationary. Thereby, shocks must be permanent in the long-term for volatility to have an effect on prices. If the shocks are not permanent, the market will not make any adjustments for the future discount rate. If the shocks are not permanent, the market will not make any adjustments to the future discount rate. In other words, if volatility shocks are temporary, expected return values are not affected by volatility movements. The closer the sum of α_i ve β_i is to one, the bigger the persistence of volatility shocks will be (Choudhry 1995).

EMPIRICAL FINDINGS

In the study, first, the data was tested for its stationary position. For this purpose, the ADF unit root test and the Zivot–Andrews unit root test, which measures single structural break, are applied to the dataset. The results are enlisted in table 2.2.

As it can be seen from table 2.2, according to the ADF unit root test, all variables except death rates (LDEATHS) are stationary at 5 percent significance

Table 2.2 Unit Root Test Results

	ADF	Zivot Andrews	Break dates
GBIST100	−9.8785 (2)	−14.9043 (2)	26.05.2020
GGOLD	−13.7086 (1)	−14.0904 (1)	08.05.2020
GDOLAR	−10.6945 (0)	−10.9813 (0)	29.07.2020
GRATE	−9.7357 (3)	−10.4759 (3)	29.05.2020
LCASES	−2.9406(6)	−6.4924(0)	16.06.2020
LDEATHS	−2.3033(6)	−5.6354(2)	25.06.2020

Note: For all the variables, Unit root test with constant terms was applied. While the critical value for the ADF test at the 5 percent significance level is −2.8770, the critical value for the Zivot Andrews unit root test at the 5 percent significance level is −4.93. Values in parentheses indicate lag lengths. Lag lengths were determined according to the Akaike information criteria.
Source: Calculated by authors

level, however, considering the unit root test result with structural break, it can be stated that all series are stationary at 5 percent significance level.

These evaluations can be made by comparing the economy on a regular day, that is before the pandemic, the developments from the date of outbreak of the pandemic, that is, after the pandemic. Due to the decline in the number of cases as a result of the safety measures taken for COVID-19, the normalization process has started in a phased manner from May 11, 2020. The second phase of the normalization process is believed to have started from May 26, 2020, and continued gradually until August 31, 2020. It can be said that during the break-up dates that coincide including the post-Bairam period, especially the aviation sector stock values decreased due to the epidemic, while the general course of the stock market continues. As per a news flow on May 26, 2020, a study conducted in the Netherlands revealed that the duration of immunity against coronavirus did not exceed six months. Similarly, in this period, the same news flow announced that U.S. companies have given up investing in China due to the pandemic. However, after the start of the normalization process, the expectation of the economy has been positively affected. Although the number of cases and deaths continued as on June 16, 2020, the general course of the economy continues.

Credit demand by companies and individuals increased as a result of the affected cash flows due to the COVID-19 pandemic. Central Bank of the Republic of Turkey (CBRT) has taken a number of measures on June 20, 2020, in order to meet the increasing demand. In this context, in order to provide flexibility to banks to meet credit demand specific to this period, the condition that the adjusted real loan growth rate should be less than 15 percent for the banks with an annual real loan growth rate above 15 percent has been decided not to be applied for a temporary period until the end of the year to benefit from reserve requirement incentives. It has been announced that the amendment will be valid from the obligation period of June 12, 2020, which will start on June 26, 2020, until the obligation period of December 25, 2020 (CBRT, 2020). In the news flow on July 27, 2020, second wave of the epidemic was forewarned in Spain. On July 29, 2020, the CBRT published the Monetary Policy Committee meeting summary about inflation rates. The Committee issued a press release regarding the reduction of a-week repo auction interest rate, which is the policy rate, from 8.75 percent to 8.25 percent to be published within five working days.

After examining the fluctuations, the IGARCH (1,1) model was estimated to determine the volatility structures of the variables representing each market. For the model determination, the significance of the Akaike and Schwarz information criteria coefficients and the stationary assumptions were taken into account. The IGARCH (p, q) model is estimated by the GED distribution which takes the effect of asymmetry into account. The results are shown in table 2.3.

Table 2.3 Results of the IGARCH Models for the Volatility Structure of the Variables

	GBIST100		GGOLD		GDOLAR		GRATE	
Mean Equation								
θ_0	-5.03E-03 (0.1726)	0.00025*** (0.0000)	0.013844*** (0.0092)	0.004421*** (0.0029)	-0.002962 (0.1553)	0.001081** (0.0250)	-0.007403 (0.7780)	-0.001023 (0.9290)
Γ	5.01E-05*** (0.0000)		-0.0017** (0.0287)		0.000450 (0.1336)		0.001785 (0.5985)	
Δ		6.14E-06*** (0.0000)	—	-0.000978*** (0.0044)		-0.000293 (0.0767)		0.001803 (0.5234)
θ_1	-0.082414 (0.8837)	-0.038143*** (0.0000)	—	—	-0.104071 (0.6077)	-0.32807*** (0.0000)	-0.115671 (0.7065)	-0.120104 (0.6968)
θ_2	-0.111676 (0.9107)	-0.108279*** (0.0000)	—	—	-0.170285 (0.3573)	-0.000259 (0.5185)	0.027454 (0.9179)	0.025762 (0.9222)
θ_3	-0.013608 (0.9568)	-0.035082*** (0.0000)	—	—	-0.030418 (0.4539)	-0.014398 (0.3586)	-0.72933*** (0.0003)	-0.72663*** (0.0003)
θ_4	-0.017929 (0.3337)	-0.038149*** (0.0000)	—	—	0.041810 (0.1565)	-0.04297** (0.0290)	—	—
θ_5	0.995070*** (0.0000)	0.979340*** (0.0000)	—	—	0.17347*** (0.0000)	0.17201*** (0.0000)	—	—
θ_6	0.079680 (0.8870)	0.040946*** (0.0000)	—	—	0.013386 (0.3563)	0.04332*** (0.013)	—	—
θ_7	0.111718 (0.9103)	0.113062*** (0.0000)	—	—	0.045224 (0.3246)	0.08207*** (0.0000)	—	—
θ_8	0.009846 (0.9687)	0.041119*** (0.0000)	—	—	-0.007426 (0.5547)	0.05125*** (0.0014)	—	—
θ_9	0.017594 (0.2928)	0.040791*** (0.0000)	—	—	-0.11757*** (0.0000)	-0.08686*** (0.0000)	—	—
φ_1	0.129935 (0.8172)	0.092284*** (0.0000)	—	—	-0.043923 (0.17500)	-0.12217*** (0.0000)	—	—

PARAMETER	(1)	(2)	(3)	(4)	(5)	(6)	(7)	(8)
φ_2	0.151381 (0.8800)	0.108111*** (0.0000)	—	—	0.354415* (0.0749)	0.60408*** (0.0000)	0.058163 (0.8667)	0.061038 (0.8605)
φ_3	-0.012781 (0.9496)	0.000451*** (0.0000)	—	—	0.268879* (0.0790)	0.24987*** (0.0000)	-0.229649 (0.4288)	-0.231554 (0.4196)
φ_4	0.001033 (0.9583)	0.006820*** (0.0000)	—	—			0.557392 (0.0170)	0.55244*** (0.0199)
φ_5	-0.016606 (0.6944)	-0.028160* (0.0813)	—	—				
φ_6	-0.012173 (0.4746)	-0.012795*** (0.0000)	—	—				
φ_7	-0.003589 (0.7533)	-0.014403*** (0.0083)	—	—				
φ_8	-0.001229 (0.8753)	-0.003680 (0.003741)	—	—				
Variance Equation								
α_1	0.457039* (0.0974)	0.487273* (0.1071)	0.0168809* (0.0971)	0.019949** (0.0539)	0.11101*** (0.0000)	0.09208*** (0.0000)	0.04959*** (0.0000)	0.05007*** (0.0000)
$\beta 1$	0.530687*** (0.0000)	0.497566*** (0.0000)	0.983111*** (0.0000)	0.980051*** (0.010348)	0.88898*** (0.0000)	0.90792*** (0.0000)	0.95040*** (0.0000)	0.94992*** (0.0000)
GED PARAMETER	0.406151*** (0.0000)	0.333085*** (0.0000)	1.031514*** (0.0000)	1.055022*** (0.0000)	0.628901*** (0.0000)	0.57366*** (0.0000)	0.523736*** (0.0000)	0.524237*** (0.0000)
Arch(5)	0.1267 (0.9862)	0.0579 (0.9978)	1.5268 (0.1840)	1.5131 (0.1883)	1.4471 (0.9524)	2.6069 (0.7677)	0.433603 (0.9947)	0.408506 (0.9954)
Q(50)	41.152 (0.157)	41.212 (0.184)	51.830 (0.402)	52.970 (0.360)	40.292 (0.369)	40.285 (0.369)	35.775 (0.807)	35.941 (0.801)

Note: ***, **, * denotes the significance levels at 1 percent, 5 percent and 10 percent respectively. Values in parentheses show probability values.
Source: Calculated by authors

Table 2.4   Results of ARCH Effect and Autocorrelation Tests

	GBIST100		GGOLD	
ARCH-LM(5)	0.1267	0.0579	1.5268	1.5131
	(0.9862)	(0.9978)	(0.1840)	(0.1883)
Q(50)	41.152	41.212	51.830	52.970
	(0.157)	(0.184)	(0.402)	(0.360)
	GDOLAR		GRATE	
ARCH-LM(5)	1.4471	2.6069	0.433603	0.408506
	(0.9524)	(0.7677)	(0.9947)	(0.9954)
Q(50)	40.292	40.285	35.775	35.941
	(0.369)	(0.369)	(0.807)	(0.801)

Note: Values in parentheses show probability values.
Source: Calculated by authors

In table 2.4, the ARCH-LM test was applied to assess the presence of ARCH effect for IGARCH (1,1) models the data of the stock, gold, and money market, while the Ljung-Box Q statistical values were applied to test the presence of high-order autocorrelation in parameters and residuals. ARCH-LM test is an LM test generated for the autoregressive conditional heteroskedasticity. ARCH-LM statistics are calculated from the auxiliary regression equation. The auxiliary regression equation can be expressed as follows:

$$\varepsilon_t^2 = \beta_0 + \left(\sum_{s=1}^{q} \beta_s \varepsilon_{t-s}^2 \right) + v_t$$

The LM statistic is calculated by multiplying the number of observations by R^2, with reference to the auxiliary regression above.

When ARCH-LM test statistics and Ljung-Box statistics results are examined from table 2.4, it is seen that the IGARCH (1,1) model established for BIST100 stock return, gold ounce return, dollar return, and interest yield provide the necessary assumptions. Thus, in order to examine whether there is an ARCH effect in the models, ARCH test was applied at the 5th lag and it was revealed that the ARCH effect disappeared in the models. Similarly, in order to examine whether there is autocorrelation between high-order error terms in the model, Ljung-Box Q statistics at the 50th lag were analyzed and it was seen that there was no high-order autocorrelation problem in the model. In addition, in order to satisfy the stationary assumptions of the model, the sum of the ARCH and GARCH parameters must be less than 1, and these parameters must be positive. When the models are examined, it can be stated that this assumption is also satisfied.

Accordingly, the IGARCH (1,1) model estimation results in table 2.4 can be interpreted. ARCH and GARCH parameters are statistically significant in the model. While the ARCH parameter shows the effect of the first shock in the models, the GARCH parameter provides information about the permanence of the shock. Hereunder, shocks in the gold market (gold ounce return) and money market (dollar return and interest yield) are permanent. However, it is observed that the volatility in the gold market is higher than the money market. It can be stated that the stock market has a lower volatility during the COVID-19 period, although the effect of the first shock was higher.

When the findings are evaluated in terms of the duration of the shocks to the system, it can be observed that the duration against a shock is the longest in the gold market, followed by the money market (dollar and interest returns). The market with the lowest duration of the shocks is the stock market. These results show that investors can make rapid decisions in the stock market, can change their behavior immediately against incoming news, and therefore change their decisions quickly against a shock. However, against a shock to the dollar exchange rate, investors are reluctant to change their dollar-denominated deposits. Therefore, when there is a shock to the dollar exchange rate, it takes longer for the shock to disappear. Although the similar situation is valid for gold, it can be said that the effect lasts much longer. This result shows that gold is perceived as a safe haven by investors. Although the volatility in the number of cases and deaths in Turkey increases the volatility of returns BIST100, the size of this effect is very limited. On the other hand, an opposite relationship is found between the ounce of gold return volatility and the increase in volatility in the number of cases and deaths. However, the volatility of the number of cases and deaths does not have a significant impact on the dollar return and interest yield. These findings reveal that COVID-19 has effects on the gold and the stock market, while it has no effects on the money market.

CONCLUSION

The COVID-19 pandemic has turned from a health crisis into an economic crisis by causing the deterioration of supply and demand channels in the economy. In order to reduce and control the spread of the pandemic, governments continue to implement lockdown and strict measure policies even after one year of the pandemic. This situation has added severely to the uncertainty in the economy. In this study, the effects of the COVID-19 pandemic on stock, gold, and money markets were examined. In this context, ARMA-IGARCH model was used. The model evaluates the persistence in variance. In this way, the effect of the shock against the markets and the duration of the shock can be determined.

When the results are evaluated due to the hypotheses, it is seen that Hypothesis 1 is valid for stock market and gold market. In other words, while the COVID-19 pandemic affects the stock and gold market in a statistically significant extent, it does not have a significant effect on the money market. Hypothesis 2 is valid in the gold and money market. While the persistence of the shock is high in the gold and money markets in the COVID-19 period, the duration of the shock in the stock market is very short. Similarly, hypothesis 3 is valid for the gold and money market. In the analysis period, the effects of past conditional variance in gold and money markets are higher, while the effect of the first shock in the stock market was greater.

When the findings of the analysis are evaluated together, COVID-19 is effective on stock and gold markets but does not have a significant effect on the money market. While the persistence of the shocks is high in terms of the duration, the effect of the first shock is high on the stock market.

REFERENCES

Adıgüzel, Muhittin.2020. "Macro-Economic Analysis of the Effect of the COVID-19 Pandemic in Turkey." *Istanbul Commerce University Journal of Social Science, 19*(37), 191–221.

Scott R. Baker, Nicholas Bloom, Steven J. Davis, Kyle J. Kost, Marco C. Sammon, & Tasaneeya Viratyosin. 2020. *The unprecedented stock market impact of COVID-19.* No. w26945. National Bureau of Economic Research.

Barut, Abdulkadir, & Kaygın, Ceyda Yerdelen. 2020. "COVID-19 Pandemisinin Seçilmiş Borsa Endeksleri Üzerine Etkisinin İncelenmesi." *Gaziantep Üniversitesi Sosyal Bilimler Dergisi. 19* (COVID-19 Special Issue). 59–70.

Bollersev, Tim. 1986. "Generalized Autoregressive Conditional Heteroskedasticity." *Journal of Econometrics.* 31(3). 307–627.

Choudhry, Taufig. 1995. Integrated- GARCH and Non-Stationary Variances: Evidence from European Stok Markets During the 1920s and 1930s. *Economics Letters.* 48. 55–59.

Eryüzlü, Hakan. 2020. "COVID-19 Economic Impact and Measures: In Turkey "Helicopter Money" Application." *Journal of Economics Public Finance Business.* 3(1). 10–19. Doi: 10.46737/emid.745621

Gürsoy, Samet, Tunçel, Mert Baran, & Sayar, Burak. 2020. "Koronavirüsün (COVID-19) Finansal Göstergeler Üzerine Etkileri." *Ekonomi Maliye İşletme Dergisi. 3*(1). 20–32.

https://www.haberler.com/26-mayis-2020-haberleri-13262586-haberi/.

https://www.investing.com/, Şubat 2021.

Ekonomik Sonuçları Yönetebilmek İçin Ne Yapılabilir? Politika Notu. Mart 2020. N202006. Türkiye Ekonomi Politikaları Araştırma Vakfı (TEPAV). https://www.tepav.org.tr/upload/files/1585023057-6.Covid_19un_Ekonomik_Sonuclarini_Yonetebilmek_Icin_Ne_Yapilabilir.pdf

Kaçak, H., & Yildiz, M. S. (2020). Stringency of government responses to COVID-19 and initial Results: A comparison between five European countries and Turkey.

Turkish Bulletin of Hygiene & Experimental Biology/Türk Hijyen ve Deneysel Biyoloji, 77(2). 233–242.

Kılıç, Yunus. 2020. "Borsa İstanbul'da COVID-19 (Koronavirüs) Etkisi. *JOEEP: Journal of Emerging Economies and Policy*. 5(1). 66–77.

McKibbin, Warwick, and Roshen Fernando. (2021) "The global macroeconomic impacts of COVID-19: Seven scenarios." *Asian Economic Papers 20*(2).1–30.

Onali, Enrico. 2020. *COVID-19 and Stock Market Volatility*. Available at SSRN 3571453.

Our World in Data. 2021. COVID-19: Government Stringency Index, Feb 9, 2021, https://ourworldindata.org/grapher/covid-stringency-index?stackMode=absolute &region=World

Özatay, Fatih, and Sak, Güven. 2020. COVID-19 'un Ekonomik Sonuçlarını Yönetebilmek, TEPAV Politika Notu, 202005.

Sansa, Nuhu A. 2020. The Impact of the COVID-19 on the Financial Markets: Evidence from China and USA. March 27, 2020. Available at SSRN: https://ssrn .com/abstract=3562530 or http://dx.doi.org/10.2139/ssrn.3562530

Sarı, Salim Sercan, and Kartal Taha. 2020. "COVID-19 Salgının Altın Fiyatları, Petrol Fiyatları ve VIX Endeksi İle Arasındaki İlişki." *Erzincan Üniversitesi Sosyal Bilimler Enstitüsü Dergisi.* 13(1). 93–109.

Şit, Ahmet, and Telek, Cebrail. 2020. "COVID-19 Pandemisinin Altın Ons Fiyatı Ve Dolar Endeksi Üzerine Etkileri" Gaziantep University Journal of Social Sciences. Cilt 19 COVID-19 Özel Sayısı. 1–13.

TCMB. 2020. "Koronavirüsün Ekonomik Ve Finansal Etkilerine Karşı Alınan Tedbirler." 20 Ocak 2021. https://www.tcmb.gov.tr/wps/wcm/connect/TR/TCMB +TR/Main+Menu/Duyurular/Koronavirus

TÜBA (Turkish Academy of Sciences).2020. *The Assessment Report on COVID-19 Global Outbreak,* Turkish Academy of Sciences Publications, TÜBA Report No: 39, July 2020, Ankara.

Türkiye Cumhuriyeti Dijital Dönüşüm Ofisi. 2021. *Koronavirüs COVID-19 Dünya Haritası.* Şubat 2021, https://corona.cbddo.gov.tr/

ULİSA12, Institute for International Relations and Strategic Research (IIRSR). 2020, Kovid-19 (Koronavirüs) Salgınının Ekonomik Etkileri, Politika Notu, Ankara Yıldırım Beyazıt Üniversitesi Uluslararası İlişkiler ve Stratejik Araştırmalar (ULİSA) Enstitüsü, Nisan 2020. https://aybu.edu.tr/yulisa/contents/files/ULI%CC %87SA12_Kovid_19_Ekonomik_Etkiler.pdf

Chapter 3

Investigation of the Contagion Effect of COVID-19 Pandemic in Financial Markets

İnci Merve Altan and Metin Kılıç

INTRODUCTION

The twenty-first century witnessed SARS (2002–2003), Swine Flu-H1N1 (2009), Polio and EBOLA (2014), Zika (2016), and finally Corona virus (COVID), which originated in Wuhan, China, on December 31, 2019. The sudden deaths and large population losses, the upset of daily life as a result of the safety measures announced, the disruption of production activities caused by the COVID-19 virus, which was declared as a pandemic by the World Health Organization (WHO) on March 11, 2020, and continued to mid-2021 ravaged world economies and financial markets (Barut and Yerdelen Kaygın, 2020:61; Gürsoy et.al., 2020:21; Duran and Acar, 2020:55).

The world economy was also devastated by financial crises such as 1929 Great Economic Depression, 1973 Oil crisis, 1992 European Exchange Mechanism crisis, 1994 Mexico crisis, 1997 Asian crisis, 1998 Russia Crisis, 1999 Brazil crisis, 2001 Argentina crisis, and 2008 Global crisis. In 2021, the world economy crumbled as a result of COVID-19, a pandemic. A microscopic virus endangered human lives and crushed the economies of even developed nations. According to the IMF, the reasons that distinguish the COVID-19 crisis from other crises are explained in three headings (IMF, 2020):

1. The economic and financial shock is enormous. Production losses as a result of quarantine and restrictions applied as measures against the virus that threatens human life are much more than other global crises.
2. Similar to the war or political crisis, duration and intensity of the crisis are uncertain.
3. Pandemic conditions make it difficult to apply regulatory policies for the economy.

Other characteristic of the COVID-19 crisis can be identified as the negative effects of supply and demand simultaneously, throwing employees out of work, non-production of enterprises, artificial demand for food, and fear of investments by individuals and enterprises (Loayza and Pennings, 2020).

As a result of globalization, the boundaries between markets have disappeared and the financial markets of countries have become integrated. Thereby, domestic markets are affected not only by internal factors but also by the events that occur in the markets of other countries it interacts with. This interaction between financial markets has been advantageous to investors, such as increasing investment alternatives and diversity, but it also created an important risk in terms of contagion of a negative situation in one market to another. Financial contagion effect, which is defined as the same directional change process that occurs in financial markets under conditions of uncertainty, cannot be explained by economic integration and becomes stronger over time, which has become an important factor to be taken into account for investors, as it weakens the stability of nations. Determination of the contagion of the crisis is very important for both countries and investors in terms of measures to be taken (Altan and Yıldırım, 2020: 260). Therefore, pandemic conditions and the impact of the COVID-19 crisis on financial markets are important issues for researchers. In this context, this study aims to examine the effect of contagion between the financial markets of the United States, Brazil, India, the United Kingdom, and Russia, which are the top five countries with the highest number of cases, according to the data of China and WHO (2020), and to provide evidence to guide financial market actors.

The study consists of four parts. General information about the COVID-19 crisis and financial contagion is given in the first part. Studies on biological and financial contagion in the literature are reviewed in the second part. In the third part, in order to examine the presence of the contagion effect of the COVID-19 crisis between the financial markets of China and the United States, Brazil, India, the United Kingdom, and Russia having the top five countries with the highest number of cases; the daily indices of MSCI between December 31, 2019, that is, the day of first COVID-19 case reported, and December 31, 2020, are examined with the Auto Regressive Distributed Lag(ARDL) method and the findings of the analysis are presented. Finally, findings are interpreted in the fourth part.

LITERATURE REVIEW

The disruptions in the production and operations of enterprises as a result of the measures taken by countries in order to prevent the pandemic have directed the attention of the researchers to the effects of the COVID-19 virus on the economy and financial markets. In this direction, many studies are carried out to examine the impact of the crisis caused by the COVID-19 pandemic on financial markets. When the studies in the area of economy and finance are analyzed, it is seen that the effects of COVID-19 can be felt on the monetary policy (Cochrane, 2020), labor supply, risk premium of countries, production by sector, consumption demand, government spending, loss of GDP (McKibbin and Fernando, 2020), oil prices, tourism and travel (Çıtak and Çalış, 2020; Arezki and Nguyen, 2020), supply and demand in trade, trade (Baldwin and Tomiura, 2020), economic anxiety (Fetzer et al., 2020), banks (Ersoy et al., 2020 ; Cecchetti and Schoenholtz, 2020), and financial markets (Şenol, 2020; Zeren and Hizarci, 2020; Barut and Yerdelen Kaygın, 2020; Zhang et al., 2020; Feng et al., 2020; Acar, 2020; Avşarlıgil, 2020).

Few studies examine the impact of epidemics on financial contagion. Financial contagion is generally studied in terms of financial crises (King and Wadhwani, 1990; Lee and Kim, 1993; Eichengreen, 1996; Baig ve Goldfajn, 1999; Kaminsky and Reinhard, 2000; Walti, 2003; Gray, 2009; Alou et.al ., 2011; Çetinkaya, 2011; Samarakoon, 2011; Mollah et.al., 2011; Cherif and Gammoudi (2012); Çelik, 2012; Erdem, 2012; Monder and Gammoudi, 2012; Kenourgios et.al., 2013; Kıraç, 2015; Budak Yalçındağ, 2017; Altan, 2019). However, studies examining biological and financial contagion can be summarized as follows:

Peckham (2013) aimed to create a model to explain the dynamics of financial shocks and the spreading infections by evaluating the global crisis that emerged in the United States at the end of 2007 and the influenza (H1N1) epidemic in 2009. In addition, the effects of financial crises are formulated by presenting the results, and also the study has raised important questions in how the financial system is designed and represented.

Corbet et al. (2020) examined the effect of contagion between financial markets by analyzing the volatility relationship between the stock markets of China, where COVID-19 pandemic emerged, and Bitcoin. It is observed that during the pandemic period, the relationship between Chinese stock markets and Bitcoin was getting stronger.

Kaya (2020) aimed to examine whether the COVID-19 pandemic, which occurred in China and rapidly spread all over the world, caused the contagion effect on the financial markets. For this purpose, the correlation between the number of cases belonging to sixteen countries and their stock market indices are examined, a negative correlation was found between the number of COVID-19 cases and stock market index variables in all countries.

Financial and biological contagion has an important role in understanding the global effects of risk. It is very beneficial to understand the effects of financial contagion so that investors can minimize their portfolio risks in times of crisis. Therefore, this chapter studies the financial contagion effect of the COVID -19 crisis between the financial markets of China and the financial markets of the United States, Brazil, India, the United Kingdom, and Russia, which are the top five countries with the highest number of cases according to WHO (2020), in order to guide both investors and countries during the pandemic period, which is full of uncertainties.

MODEL AND FINDINGS

The literature review on the financial and biological contagion effect has been presented in the previous chapters and a theoretical framework has been introduced in this context. In this section, the presence of contagion effects between the financial markets of China and the related countries is examined by using Autoregressive Distributed Lag-ARDL method, with the econometric model built by taking into account the definition of crisis conditional contagion and the monsoon effect from the date when the first COVID-19 case was reported, that is, from December 31, 2019, to December 31, 2020. The main reasons for using the ARDL method instead of traditional co-integration approaches, such as Engle and Granger (1987) and Johansen (1991, 1995), is that it provides statistically more reliable results and includes information about short- and long-term dynamics between variables with error correction model (Uçak et.al.., 2018: 206; Akel and Gazel, 2014: 21).

The econometric model used in the study is given by equation (1).

$$XP_t = \propto_0 + \propto_1 CHIP_t + \varepsilon_t, \text{ X = USA, BRA, IND, ENG, RUS.} \quad (1)$$

Here ε_t is the error term and both the short-/long-term correlation of countries and the contagion effect can be interpreted using the model given by equation (1).

In the econometric model, MSCI Stock Index data, which is the standardized version of the market indices of each country, is taken as the variable. Variables used in models are $USAP_t$; MSCI USA Stock Index, $BRAP_t$; MSCI Brazil Stock Index, $INDP_t$; MSCI India Stock Index, $ENGP_t$; MSCI England Stock Index, $RUSP_t$; MSCI Russia Stock Index, $CHIP_t$; MSCI China Stock Index and data is obtained from MSCI (Ethics committee approval is not required for data obtained from databases). Since trend can be affected by cyclical and seasonal movements in economic time series; they generally have non-stationary processes (Johansen and Jesulius, 1990: 171). The problem of spurious regression can be observed in analyses using non-stationary time series (Granger and Newbold, 1974). In order to eliminate this problem, a difference can be taken; however, this process can both cause loss of information and eliminate the existing relationship between the series (Pamuk and Bektaş, 2014: 81). The most important advantage of the ARDL limit test method is the applicability of variables regardless of whether they are at I (0) or I (1) stationary level (Pesaran et al., 2001: 290). Therefore, against the probability of the series being I (2), it is necessary to determine whether all variables are stationary in order of I (0) and I (1) for the reliability of estimation results. For this purpose, unit root tests are carried out with Augmented Dickey Fuller (ADF), Phillips Perron (PP) tests. When the stationarities of variables are analyzed, it was observed that the series are stationary at I (1) according to both ADF and PP tests. Thus, the existence of correlation should be investigated for the model given by equation (1) to apply the ARDL test. In order to test the existence of the correlation, the F test is applied to the first lags of dependent and independent variables (Karagöl et al., 2007: 76). For the basic hypothesis defined as H_0: "There is no co-integration between variables," the F statistic is compared with Pesaran lower and upper critical values. If the calculated F statistic is less than the Pesaran lower critical value, there is no correlation between the series. If the calculated F statistic is between the lower and upper critical value, a certain interpretation cannot be made, and other correlation test approaches should be applied. After determining the correlation between series, ARDL models are established to determine long- and short-term relationships. Accordingly, bound test results for the United States, Brazil, India, the United Kingdom, and Russia are given in table 3.1.

Bound values are obtained as 4.04 and 4.78 from the analyses made according to the estimated models. The F statistic for the United States is 4.969673 and the H_0 hypothesis is rejected because it is bigger than the upper boundary. Thus, there is correlation between the United States and Chinese stock market indices in the long run. Brazil's F statistic is 3.694384, India's F statistic is 3.776115, the United Kingdom's F statistic is 2.713828, and Russia's F statistic is 1.967248, and these values are smaller than the lower boundary value of 4.04 so H_0 hypothesis is accepted. Thus, there is no correlation between the stock market indices of Brazil, India, the United Kingdom, Russia, and China. Accordingly, since there is only a correlation between the United States and China, the ARDL bound test can be used.

Table 3.1   Bound Test Results

	USA	Brazil	India	England	Russia
Pesaran I(0) & I(1)	4.04 & 4.78	4.04 & 4.78	4.04 & 4.78	4.04 & 4.78	4.04 & 4.78
F-Statistic	4.969673	3.694384	3.776115	2.713828	1.967248

Source: Calculated by authors

Two asymptotic limit values are used when applying the bound test. ECM is used to determine the short-term relationship and demonstrate the short-term correction mechanism because of moving away from the long-term balance. Accordingly, error correction model is given in equation (2).

$$\Delta USAP_t = \beta_0 + \sum_{j=1}^{p} \beta_{1j}\Delta USAP_{t-j} + \sum_{j=0}^{q} \beta_{2j}\Delta CHIP_{t-j} + \theta\epsilon_{t-1} + \varepsilon_t \quad (2)$$

Here Δ denotes the change in variables. In addition, if it is statistically significant $0 < \theta < 1$, it provides the correction of the long-term error in the short term by including the lagged value of a long-term deviation.

The long-run equation for the ARDL model is obtained by including it into the error correction model with lag. Thus, the first lag of equation (1) is rearranged and added to equation (2), and as a result of this operation, equation (3) is derived, which shows both short- and long-term relationships. The ARDL (p, q) model is expressed with the derived equation (3).

$$USAP_t = \psi + \eta_0 USAP_{t-1} + \eta_1 CHI_{t-1} + \sum_{j-1}^{p} \beta_{1j}\Delta USAP_{t-j}$$

$$+ \sum_{j-0}^{q} \beta_{2j}\Delta CHI_{t-j} + \varepsilon_t \quad (3)$$

Here, $\psi = \beta_0 - \theta\alpha_0$, $\eta_0 = \theta$. In addition, the coefficients in the ARDL model are determined as $\eta_0, -\eta_1 / \theta$.

The most appropriate lag length used for the estimation of the model that analyzes the effect of financial contagion between the United States and China is determined as ARDL (4,1) using the Akaike information criterion and using maximum 4 lags. The summary of the estimations results of the both ARDL model and the Error Correction Model is shown in table 3.2.

Table 3.2.a shows that the US MSCI index is affected by the Chinese MSCI index at 1 percent significance level in the long run. The US MSCI index is positively affected by the value of China in the t period and the value of the United States in the t-1 and t-2 periods, while it is negatively affected by the t-1 period of China. In short, a statistically significant long-term relationship is detected between the United States and China.

In table 3.2.b, ECM (-1) value is −0.007823 ϵ (−1, 0) at 5 percent significance level and it is observed that it monotonously approaches the long-term balance value. In addition, when the results of the error correction method in table 3.2.b are examined, a 1 percent increase in the Chinese MSCI index causes an increase of 1.918588 percent in the U.S. MSCI index in the short term. Accordingly, a positive and significant relationship has been obtained between the United States and China in the short term.

Table 3.2   ARDL Model and the Error Correction Model Estimations Results

Variable	Coefficient	Standard Deviation	t-Statistic	Probability
a. ARDL Model Estimation Results				
USA(-1)	0.668357*	0.055110	12.12765	0.0000
USA(-2)	0.440547*	0.065994	6.675546	0.0000
USA(-3)	−0.077591	0.065699	−1.181015	0.2387
USA(-4)	−0.088387	0.053754	−1.644279	0.1014
CHI	12.06435*	1.265741	9.531456	0.0000
CHI(-1)	−11.04289*	1.310120	−8.428915	0.0000
C	17.46138	27.96114	0.624487	0.5329
b. Results of the Error Correction Model				
DUSA(-1)	0.625730	0.005984	1.045710	0.2983
DUSA(-2)	0.275865	0.057990	4.756740	0.8976
DCHI	1.918558*	0.434390	0.416680	0.0164
ECM(-1)	−0.007823*	0.001245	1.512689	0.0112
C	7.216648	1.937114	0.225960	0.1100

NOTE: * denotes 1 percent significance level.
Source: Calculated by authors

CONCLUSION

Borders between markets have disappeared with globalization, and the financial markets of the nations have become integrated. Thus, a domestic market is affected not only by internal factors but also by the events that occur in the markets of other countries that it interacts with. While this interaction between the financial markets provides investors some significant advantages, such as increasing investment alternatives and international-scale diversity, it has also generated an important risk in terms of spreading the negative effects of one market to another.

Unlike the financial crises which resulted due to economic reasons, COVID-19 crisis is a pandemic which devastated world economies. Other features of the COVID-19 crisis are it adverse impact on the supply and demand, unemployment, non-productivity of enterprises, artificial demand created for food, and insecurity of investors.

In addition to the biological contamination effects of the COVID-19 virus under pandemic conditions, the contagion effect of the crisis on the financial markets has been an important issue for researchers. In this context, the study aimed to examine the effect of contagion between the financial markets of China and the United States, Brazil, India, the United Kingdom, and Russia, which are the top five countries with the highest number of cases, according to WHO (2020) data, and also to guide financial market actors with empirical evidence.

In the econometric model built for this study purpose, MSCI index data, which allows consistent and complete analysis by avoiding mismatch of references, is taken as independent variables and analyzed with ARDL. As a result of the analysis, no correlation was observed between the financial markets of China and Brazil, India, the United Kingdom, and Russia. Short-term and long-term correlation has only been determined between the United States and China.

REFERENCES

Acar Yusuf. 2020. "New Coronavirus (COVID-19) Outbreak and Its Impact on Tourism Activities." *Current Journal of Tourism Research*, 4 (1), 7–21.

Aloui, Riadh, Mohamed Safouane Ben Aïssa, and Duc Khuong Nguyen. (2011). "Global Financial Crisis, Extreme Interdependences, and Contagion Effects: The Role of Economic Structure?" *Journal of Banking and Finance*, 35, 130–141.

Altan, İnci Merve. 2019. "The Contagion Effect on International Financial Markets: Investigation of the Relationship Between the USA and Developing Countries." Karabuk University Graduate Education Institute, PhD Thesis.

Altan, İnci Merve, and Yıldırım, Murat. 2020. "Current Researches in Money and Capital Markets: The Contagion Effect in International Financial Markets: Investigation of the Relationship Between The USA and Turkey," Gazi Bookstore, 257–284.

Arezki, Rabah, and Nguyen, Ha. 2020. "Novel Coronavirus Hurts the Middle East and North Africa Through Many Channels: Economics in the Time of COVID-19." London: CEPR (Centre for Economic Policy Research) Press, 53–58.

Baig, Taimur, and Goldfajn, Ilan. 1999. Financial Market Contagion in The Asian Crisis. *IMF Staff Papers*, 46(2), 167–195.

Baldwin, Richard, and Weder di Mauro, B. 2020. *Economics in the Time of COVID-19*. London: CEPR (Centre for Economic Policy Research) Press.

Barut, Abdulkadir, and Yerdelen Kaygın, Ceyda. 2020. "Investigation of the Effect of COVID-19 Pandemic on Selected Stock Market Indices," Gaziantep University Journal of Social Sciences 2020 Special Issue 59-70.

Budak Yalçındağ, H. Zeynep. 2017. "Financial Contagion and Turkey in Stocks and Bonds Market Investigation of Financial Contagion." Istanbul: Istanbul University Institute of Social Sciences. Doctoral Thesis.

Cecchetti, Stephen G., and Kermit L. Schoenholtz. 2020. "Contagion: Bank Runs and COVID-19." *Economics in the Time of COVID-19*. (pp. 77–80). London: CEPR (Centre for Economic Policy Research) Press.

Cherif, Monder, and Gammoudi Mouna. (2012). Impact of the U.S Subprime Crises on MENA Stock Markets: New Empirical Investigation. La Revue Du Financier. 34, 120–128.

Cochrane, J. H. (2020). *Coronavirus monetary policy. İçinde: Economics in the Time of COVID-19 (s.105-108)*. London: CEPR (Centre for Economic Policy Research) Press.

Corbet, Shaen, Charles Larkin, and Brian Lucey. 2020. "The Contagion Effects of the COVID-19 Pandemic: Evidence from Gold and Cryptocurrencies." *Finance Research Letters* 3,101554.

Çelik, Sibel. 2012. The More Contagion Effect on Emerging Markets: The Evidence of DCC-GARCH Model. *Economic Modelling, 29*(5): 1946–1959.

Çetinkaya, Engin. 2011. "The Contagion Effect of Major Global Crises in the World Economy After 1990 on the ISE." Istanbul: Istanbul University Institute of Social Sciences. Master Thesis.

Duran, M. S., and Acar, M. 2020. "What a Virus Worldwide: Macroeconomic Effects of the COVID-19 Pandemic." *International Journal of Social and Economic Sciences*, 10(1): 54–67.

Eichengreen, B., Rose, A., and Wyplosz, C. 1996. "Contagious Currency Crisis: First Tests." *The Scandinavian Journal of Economics*, 98(4), 463–484.

Erdem, N. 2012. "Similar Crises, Different Geographies: Mexico and South Korea." *Ankara: Journal of Ankara University Social Sciences Institute,* 3(1), 60–96.

Ersoy, H., Gürbüz, A. O., and Fındıkçı Erdoğan, M. 2020. "Effects of COVID-19 on Turkish Banking and Finance Sector, Measures to be Taken." Istanbul Commerce University Journal of Social Sciences, COVID-19 Social Sciences Special Issue (Special Supplement), 19(37): 46–173.

Feng, J., Bao, Y., Wang, Y., Meng, S., Xia, J., and Zhang, Q. 2020. "Coronavirus VS Market: Investment Opportunities Lies Underneath the Epidemic." SSRN: https://ssrn.com/abstract=3563059

Fetzer, T., Hensel, L. Hermle, J., and Roth, C. 2020. "Coronavirus Perceptions and Economic Anxiety." arXiv:2003.03848.

Gray, D. 2009. "Financial Contagion Among Members Of The Eu-8 A Cointegration and Granger Causality Approach." *International Journal of Emerging*, 4, 299–314.

Gürsoy, S., Tunçel, M. B., and Sayar, B. 2020. "Effects of Coronavirus (COVID-19) on Financial Indicators." *Economy Finance Business Journal*, 3(1): 20–32.

IMF. 2020. https://www.imf.org/en/Topics/imf-and-covid19

IMF. 2020a. Global Financial Stability Report. April 2020

Kaminsky, G. L., and Reinhard, C. M. 2000. "On Crises, Contagion and Confusion." *Journal of International Economics,* 51, 145–168.

Karagöl, E., Erbaykal, E., and Ertuğrul, H. M. 2007. "Economic Growth and Electricity Consumption Relations in Turkey: Bound Testing Approach." *Dogus University Journal*, 8(1): 72–80.

Kaya, A. 2020. "Did COVID-19 Cause Contamination?" *ETÜ Synthesis Economic and Administrative Sciences Journal,* 1(1), 1–12.

Kıraç, F. 2015. "Contagion Effect of Global Crisis: An Application on Stock Exchanges." Kütahya: Dumlupınar University Institute of Social Sciences. Doctoral Thesis.

King, M. A., and Wadhwani, S. 1990. "Transmission of Volatility Between Stock Markets." *The Review of Financial Studies*, 3(1), 5–33.

Lee, S. B., and Kim, K. J. 1993. "Does the October 1987 crash Strengthen the Co-Movements Among National Stock Markets?" *Review of Financial Economics,* 3, 89–102.

Loayza, N. V. and Pennings, S. 2020. "Macroeconomic Policy In the Time of COVID19: A Primer for Developing Countries." World Bank Group.

McKibbin, W. and Fernando, R. 2020. "The Global Macroeconomic Impacts of COVID-19: Seven Scenarios." CAMA Working Paper, The Australian National University.

Monder, C., and Gammoudi, M., 2012. "Impact Of The U.S Subprime Crises On MENA Stock Markets: New Empirical Investigation." Conference Organisee Par La Sfaf Sur Les Actifs Immateriels.

MSCI, www.msci.com/end-of-day-data-search, 05.01.2021.

Peckham, R. 2013. "Economies of Contagion: Financial Crisis and Pandemic." *Economy and Society*, 42, 226–248.

Samarakoon, L. P. 2011. "Stock Market Interdependence, Contagion, and The U.S. Financial Crisis: The Case of Emerging and Frontier Markets." *Journal of International Financial Markets, Institutions & Money*, 21, 724–742.

Sarı, S. S., and Kartal, K. 2020. "The Relationship Between COVID-19 Outbreak Gold Prices, Oil Prices and VIX Index," Erzincan University Journal of Social Sciences Institute 2020-13 (1), 93–109.

Şenol, Zekai. 2020. "COVID-19 Crisis and Financial Markets." *Money and Finance*, İksad Publishing House, Ankara, 75–124.

Uçak, Sefer, and Usupbeyli, Akın. 2015. "Causality Between Oil Consumption and Economic Growth in Turkey." *Ankara University Faculty of Political Sciences Journal*, 70(3): 769–787.

Walti, Sebastien. 2003. "Testing For Contagion In International Financial Markets: Which Way To Go?." FAME- International Center for Financial Asset Management and Engineering, Research Paper No. 92.

WHO. 2020. https://covid19.who.int/region/amro/country/br, 09.01.2021.

Zhang, D., Hu, M., and Ji, Q.2020. "Financial Markets Under the Global Pandemic of COVID-19." *Finance Research Letters*. https://doi.org/10.1016/j.frl.2020.101528.

Zeren, Feyyaz, and Hizarci, Atike.2020. "The Impact of COVID-19 Coronavirus on Stock Markets: Evidence from Selected Countries." *Bulletin of Accounting and Finance Reviews*, 3(1), 78–84.

Chapter 4

The Impact of COVID-19 on Stock Market Volatility

Evidence from Impulse Response Analysis

Ramazan Ekinci

INTRODUCTION

On March 11, 2020, the World Health Organization (WHO) officially declared the coronavirus (COVID-19) epidemic to be a global pandemic. Starting from January 20, 2020, the daily detected number of cases and deaths in China and regions outside of China started reporting and were published by the WHO. With the epidemic spreading rapidly around the world, more than 8 million COVID-19 cases were detected worldwide together with more than 436,000 deaths until mid-June. This pandemic is not only a global health problem but is also the cause of a significant global economic contraction. According to the International Monetary Fund (2020), approximately 4.9 percent contraction in the global economy is expected for 2020. However, the contraction is expected to be much severe than the 2008–2009 Global Financial Crisis. Governments have begun to implement many control measures, such as closure of workplaces and schools, travel restrictions, home isolations, mandatory quarantines, social distance, and wearing masks in order to prevent the worldwide spread of the COVID-19 epidemic (WHO 2020). The total loss in the world economy because of the strict quarantine policies applied against the epidemic in the short term is expected to be 0.5 percent of global GDP (Ayittey et al. 2020, 475). All these measures affected not only global economic activities (Yılmazkuday 2020, 3) but also worldwide financial markets significantly (Cao et al. 2020, 4-5; Ramelli and Wagner 2020, 68-69). Due to fear and uncertainty in China, the Shanghai stock market crashed by 8 percent on February 3, 2020, and afterward the shock quickly spread to the financial markets of all countries. Baker et al. (2020, 1-2) presented some evidence that the impact of the current crisis in the United States is close to the Great Depression level.

Stock market indices, exchange rates, and interest rates of the countries are important indicators in observing the negative situations and risk in financial markets (Demirhan 2020, 2). The researchers assert that the volatility in stock market returns is largely related to the market uncertainty, and therefore it is a key parameter in most investment/portfolio management decision. High volatility shows that there is significant change in stock prices in the short term. With the increase in volatility, the risk also rises. Besides, low volatility means that stock prices change at a constant rate without showing any high volatility in the short term (Glosten, Jagannathan and Runkle 1993, 1781). On the other hand, unexpected events, such as global epidemics, are expected to directly affect the financial assets of countries. The panic environment created by the exit of investors looking for safer instruments from country's stock markets caused the prices to decrease and volatility to increase (Hoque and Zaidi 2019, 997). The emergence of the COVID-19 pandemic as a new global risk factor caused a sudden fall in stock prices due to the quick and simultaneous sales of investors. While many shocks wave were experienced in the markets since February 2020, because of the fear and panic, financial volatility has continued to increase in the context of COVID-19 uncertainty. This increase in volatility in financial markets was recorded to be close to or higher than the 2008/9 financial crisis (Fernandes 2020, 2-3).

In this study, the effect of COVID-19 pandemic on stock markets of Turkey and the United States are analyzed. The reason for limiting the sample to only two countries is to make a better analysis of the interaction between markets together with the approaches used. The highest number of cases was detected in the United States by April 1, 2020, and therefore it is chosen as a sample considered to be a good indicator in comparisons. Unlike other studies, the effect of COVID-19 on volatility is tested using two different approaches in this study. First, similar to Chaudhary, Bakhshi, and Gupta (2020), the effect of COVID-19 on volatility was tested by adding the COVID-19 variable to the conditional variance equation of the EGARCH model. Chaudhary, Bakhshi, and Gupta (2020) investigated the relationship between coronavirus and market volatility by including the COVID-19 dummy variable in the conditional variance equation of the GARCH model. Unlike Chaudhary, Bakhshi, and Gupta (2020), the EGARCH model with the asymmetric effect is used in this study. In addition, the logarithmic values of the COVID-19 case numbers are used in this study instead of the COVID-19 dummy variable of 0 and 1 values. Second, multivariate volatility models are estimated considering the volatility spillover between markets, and the impact of COVID-19 is tested using the volatility impulse response function (VIRF) obtained from this model. Here, the date March 11, 2020, when COVID-19 was declared as "global epidemic" is added to the model as a shock variable at the forecast stage. Thereby, it is examined whether or not there is a significant difference in the stock market volatility of the countries in the post-epidemic period compared to the pre-epidemic period. In this respect, this chapter first analyzes the impact of the COVID-19 crisis on financial markets using the VIRF of Hafner and Herwartz (2006). Considering that there are only a limited number of studies analyzing the impact of COVID-19 on financial volatility, this study is expected to contribute to existing literature. The following parts of the study are planned as follows. In the second part, empirical literature about the impact of COVID-19 on stock market volatility is summarized. In the third and fourth sections, the dataset and the approaches followed are explained, respectively. In the fifth section, empirical findings are included. In the last part, general findings and evaluations are presented.

LITERATURE REVIEW

Although the financial and economic effects of COVID-19 have recently started to be studied in the literature, few studies analyze the relationship between the COVID-19 epidemic and financial market volatility. Alber (2020, 9) investigated the impacts of COVID-19 on stock markets of China, France, Germany, Italy, Spain, and the United States and concluded that stock market returns are more sensitive to COVID-19 cumulative case numbers. The study also determined that COVID-19 had no negative impact on stock market returns of Italy and the United States. Baker et al. (2020, 12–13) examined the response of U.S. stock to COVID-19 and found that there was a jump in U,S. stock exchange volatility due to COVID-19. The authors also concluded that the impact of COVID-19 on U.S. stock volatility is much greater than the past epidemics, especially due to the economic consequences of shutdown policies. Zaremba et al. (2020, 6) examined the impact of the government's measures against COVID-19 on international stock market volatility. The authors revealed that strict measures taken by governments caused a significant increase in stock market volatility.

Onali (2020, 9) investigated the impact of the number of deaths and cases reported by the United States and other countries (China, Italy, Spain, United Kingdom, Iran, and France) on U.S. stock market returns and volatility. Findings show that U.S. stock market responds in the form of increased volatility to the reports of COVID-19 cases and deaths for more than one country. Haroon and Rizvi (2020, 2–3) investigated the impact of COVID 19 news on the volatility of twenty-three industry indices traded in Dow Jones (USA). The authors found that the biggest impact was on the transport, automobile, energy, and travel and entertainment sectors together with the change in volatility. However, most of the industries that were included in the analysis did not show a change in volatility against COVID-19 news. A similar study was done by Albulescu (2020) for the United States. In this study, the author investigated the impact of official announcements of new infection and death rates of COVID-19 on the volatility in U.S. financial markets. In the study, S&P500 realized volatility values were used to represent the volatility of financial markets, and the effect of global and U.S.-based COVID-19 news on volatility were also analyzed. The author concluded that health-related crises increase the volatility of the S&P500 index. It has also been confirmed that globally published COVID-19 data were more effective on volatility than data published for the United States. Gunay (2020, 13-14) examined the effect of COVID-19 on the stock market in China, Italy, Spain, Turkey, the United Kingdom, and the United States, and determined that the relations between Turkey and China stock market increased more than other exchanges due to the spillover effects of COVID-19. The author analyzed the impact of COVID-19 on the stocks of the countries with variance break tests. According to the test results, a structural break was detected in variance in the Chinese stock index on January 30, 2020, the first periods of the epidemic. However, an interesting conclusion was reached for Turkey, and during the outbreak period, no structural break was observed in Turkey stock index. Chaudhary, Bakhshi, and Gupta (2020, 13) analyzed the impact of COVID-19 on financial markets for the top 10 countries that make up 66 percent of the world's GDP. The authors reveal that using the GARCH $(1,1)$, it was proved that COVID-19 has significant positive effect on conditional variance for all indices. This result shows that the virus increases the volatility of the stock indices of the countries addressed. Bai et al. (2020, 4) analyzed the impact of the infectious disease pandemic on the financial markets for the United States, China, the United Kingdom and Japanese stock markets. In order to measure the impact of the pandemic, they used the Infectious Disease Equity Market Volatility Tracker (EMV-ID) index developed by Baker et al. (2020). Result of the analysis using the GARCH-MIDAS model showed that the infectious disease pandemic has significant and strong effects on the volatility of four international stock markets.

DATASET

Dataset includes the daily closing prices of BIST100 and S&P500 index that are the main market indices for Turkey and U.S. stock market. The time period spans from January 1, 2014, to September 8, 2020, and consists of 1,745 observations in total. The dataset used in the study is compiled from Bloomberg database. Series are transformed into return series by taking their logarithmic differences with the help of the formula below and included in the analysis.

$$r_t = 100 \times \left[\ln\left(P_t\right) - \ln\left(P_{t-1}\right) \right]$$

Table 4.1 summarizes the main statistical characteristics of stock returns. The table contains information about the period before and after COVID-19, as well as the entire period. The average return of both stock indices is positive. However, a significant increase in average returns is seen for the period after COVID-19 (especially for S&P500). On the other hand, for both return series, a negative skewness and a left-skewed distribution are observed. The high kurtosis values in the table (greater than 3) show that the distribution has a leptokurtic characteristic. In addition, the Jarque–Bera test strongly rejects the null hypothesis that stock returns are normally distributed. Accordingly, both return series show a strong deviation from the normal distribution.

Correlation analysis was conducted in order to determine the degree of the relationship between the return series used in the study. Calculated correlation coefficients are included in table 4.1. The correlation coefficient differs significantly before epidemic period and during the epidemic period. Especially in the COVID-19 period, the positive correlation coefficient between BIST 100 and S&P500 stock indices increased from 0.25 (before

Table 4.1 Descriptive Statistics

	Entire Period		Before COVID-19		COVID-19 Period	
	BIST100	S&P500	BIST100	S&P500	BIST100	S&P500
Panel A: Descriptive Statistics						
Mean	0.02	0.03	0.02	0.02	0.06	0.11
Min	−8.41	−12.76	−7.34	−7.90	−8.41	−12.76
Max	5.81	8.96	5.25	4.84	5.81	8.96
Std. Dev.	1.32	1.10	1.28	0.87	1.78	2.64
Skewness	−0.56	−1.09	−0.38	−0.81	−1.41	−0.79
Kurtosis	6.35	26.57	5.14	11.32	9.25	9.53
Jarque–Bera	909.35[a]	40742.87[a]	348.57[a]	4839.10[a]	255.37[a]	245.35[a]
Observations	1745	1745	1615	1615	130	130
Panel B: Unconditional Correlations						
BIST100	1.00	0.31	1.00	0.25	1.00	0.57
Panel C: Unit Root Tests						
ADF I(0)	−41.648[a]	−12.828[a]				
PP	−41.663[a]	−49.969[a]				
Panel D: ARCH-LM Test						
F-statistic	12.581[a]	118.001[a]				
LM statistic	751.599	125.871[a]				

[a] Denotes statistical significance at 1 percent level. The 1 percent critical values are −3.432 and −3.961 for the ADF and PP tests, respectively.
Calculated by authors

COVID-19) to 0.57. This result means that markets react similarly to shocks. Accordingly, the degree of dependency between markets increases during the epidemic period. This result provides a basis for the application of multivariate volatility models, which will be discussed in the next section.

METHODOLOGY

In the study, the effect of COVID-19 on stock volatility is tested against univariate and multivariate volatility models. In this section, EGARCH model and DCC-GARCH models are examined, respectively. In addition, the impact of COVID-19 on financial markets as an exogenous shock is analyzed with VIRFs.

UNIVARIATE VOLATILITY MODEL: EGARCH

Nelson developed the EGARCH approach in 1991, considering the signs of negative and positive shocks and demonstrating the effects of these parameters. The EGARCH approach was developed against the situations where conditional variance may take negative values (Nelson 1991). In this way, the condition that variance should not be negative in estimations is provided. The functional equation of the EGARCH technique is as follows:

Mean equation: $r_t = \mu + \varepsilon_t$
Variance equation:

$$\ln\left(\sigma_t^2\right) = \omega + \beta \ln\left(\sigma_{t-1}^2\right) + \alpha\left|\frac{\varepsilon_{t-1}}{\sigma_{t-1}}\right| + \gamma_1 \frac{\varepsilon_{t-1}}{\sigma_{t-1}} + \gamma_2\left(\left|\frac{\varepsilon_{t-1}}{\sigma_{t-1}}\right| - E\left|\frac{\varepsilon_{t-1}}{\sigma_{t-1}}\right|\right) \quad (1)$$

The coefficients of the parameters in this equation were obtained by using Oxmetrics 7 and GARCH module. In this equation, γ_1 and γ_2 show the sign and magnitude effects, respectively. γ_1 is the leverage parameter that captures the asymmetric effect in the model. If $\gamma_1 < 0$, this means that negative shocks (bad news) increase volatility more than positive shocks (good news). However, if $\gamma_1 > 0$, it can be said that positive news causes more volatility increase than negative news. The parameter γ_2 is the magnitude effect of shocks showing the effect of the actual shocks and the expected shocks. If the parameter γ_2 is positive, this indicates that the actual situations are more effective on the volatility than the expected situations. On the contrary, the expected situations are more effective on volatility. The EGARCH approach is a technique that enables the analysis of the effect of positive and negative news in the economy on volatility, especially with the data represented by high frequency series. As long as the data used have high frequency, the effects that are accepted as news here can also be defined as economic shocks. The EGARCH approach provides the decomposition of the effects that are defined as news or shocks and at the same time gives information about the asymmetry of these effects.

As it is stated in the introduction section, the main purpose of this study is to analyze the impact of COVID-19 on financial markets. For this purpose, the EGARCH model is expanded by including the number of COVID-19 cases into the conditional variance equation.

$$\ln\left(\sigma_t^2\right) = \omega + \beta\ln\left(\sigma_{t-1}^2\right) + \alpha\left|\frac{\varepsilon_{t-1}}{\sigma_{t-1}}\right| + \gamma_1\frac{\varepsilon_{t-1}}{\sigma_{t-1}} + \gamma_2\left(\left|\frac{\varepsilon_{t-1}}{\sigma_{t-1}}\right| - E\left|\frac{\varepsilon_{t-1}}{\sigma_{t-1}}\right|\right) + \delta COVID_t$$

The COVID variable was created by taking the logarithmic values of the number of cases announced for the current coronavirus period and taken as 0 for the pre-coronavirus period. Thus, in the conditional variance equation, while a negative and statistically significant COVID coefficient means a decrease in market volatility, a positive and statistically significant COVID coefficient indicates an increase in market volatility.

MULTIVARIATE VOLATILITY MODEL: DCC-GARCH

In the study, the change of the correlation between stock returns over time is examined by Engle's (2002) dynamic conditional correlation model (DCC-GARCH). The DCC model is a generalized version of Bollerslev's (1990) constant condition correlation model (CCC). The model is estimated in two stages: First, univariate GARCH models are estimated in order to generate standardized residuals. Second, the correlation coefficients are calculated using the residuals obtained from GARCH model. The multivariate DCC-GARCH model can be expressed as: $r_t = \mu_t + \varepsilon_t$ where, $\varepsilon_t \mid \Omega_{t-1} \to N\left(0, H_t\right)$ is the information set of the period Ω_{t-1} t-1 and H_t (N×N) is the dimension covariance matrix. For the estimation of the parameters, the covariance matrix should be decomposed from GARCH models with one variable to a diagonal matrix consisting of conditional standard deviations varying with time $D_t = diag\left\{\sqrt{h_t}\right\}(NxN)$ and a time-varying conditional correlation matrix $R_t\left(NxN\right)$. The conditional variance-covariance matrix (Ht) in the DCC model can be expressed as: $H_t = D_t R_t D_t$. Here, $D_t = diag\left(h_{ii,t}^{1/2} \ldots h_{kk,t}^{1/2}\right)$ is defined as $h_{ii,t} = \omega_i + \alpha_i \varepsilon_{i,t-1}^2 + \beta_i h_{ii,t-1}$ and $R_t = \left(diag\left(Q_t\right)\right)^{-1/2} Q_t \left(diag\left(Q_t\right)\right)^{-1/2}$. In equation, Qt is defined under the DCC model and the time varying ($N \times N$) dimensional covariance matrix of u_t is written as $Q_t = (1 - \alpha - \beta)\bar{Q} + \alpha \varepsilon_{t-1} \varepsilon'_{t-1} + \beta Q_{t-1}$ where $\bar{Q} = E\left[u_t u'_t \right]$ is the unconditional covariance matrix of u_t (NxN). The α and β parameters show the effects of previous shocks and previous dynamic conditional correlations on current dynamic conditional correlations. Moreover, these parameters should not be negative and ensure the similar condition ($\alpha + \beta$ <1) in the GARCH model.

In the study, the VIRF developed by Hafner and Herwartz (2006) is used to measure the effects of shocks on conditional variance and to observe the effects of independent shocks on volatility over time. In line with Hafner and Herwartz (2006), the BEKK model is transformed in its vector notation (vech) so as to generate volatility impulse response functions. Hafner and Herwartz (2006) define VIRF as the difference between an initial shock and expectation of past volatility and a basic expectation based only on past conditions. Equation is shown as follows:

$$V_t(z_0) = E\left[\text{vech}(H_t) \big| z_0, \Omega_{t-1} \right] - E\left[\text{vech}(H_t) \big| \Omega_{t-1} \right],$$

where z_0 is a specific initial shock coming to the system at zero. Ω_{t-1} shows the observed past until time (t-1) and the effects of the conditional variance-covariance matrix components of z_0 with $N^* = N(N+1)/2$ vector identical and independent shock components effect up to the distance. Using the BEKK (1, 1) model followed by the vech notation, the one-step ahead VIRF is obtained as follows:

$$V_1(z_0) = R_1 \times \left\{ \text{vech}\left(H_0^{1/2} z_0 z_0' H_0^{1/2} \right) - \text{vech}(H_0) \right\}$$

$$= R_1 D_N^+ \left(H_0^{1/2} \otimes H_0^{1/2} \right) D_N \text{vech}(z_0 z_0' - I_N),$$

where H_0 is the conditional variance-covariance matrix at the initial time of 0, D_N is the replication matrix for any symmetric ($N \times N$) Z matrix defined by the $\text{vec}(Z) = D_N \text{vech}(Z)$, I_N is the identity matrix, $\otimes$ is the Kronecker factor, and R_1 represents parameter matrices.

EMPIRICAL RESULTS

Whether the return series in the study meets the stationarity condition is examined using augmented Dickey–Fuller test (ADF) and Phillips–Perron test (PP) and the test results are shown in table 4.1. According to the results of ADF and PP unit root test in Panel C of table 4.1, the null hypotheses are rejected and the return series are found to be stationary. Also, the ARCH LM test is used to determine whether the time series in the study have constant variance (Engle 1982).

ARCH LM test results are included in Panel D of table 4.1. The ARCH LM test shows that all stock returns have ARCH effect. This result means that nonlinear processes should be included in the model with variance (Hsieh 1989). Thus, GARCH model is convenient for model estimation.

In the next section, estimation results of EGARCH and DCC-GARCH models are given, respectively. Finally, the empirical findings section is completed with the volatility impulse response analysis.

EGARCH ESTIMATION RESULTS

Table 4.2 contains the estimation results of the EGARCH model calculated with different distributions. AR (p) and MA (q) lag lengths (orders) (p = q = 0 for BIST100 and p = 1, q = 1 for S&P500) are determined by examining partial autocorrelation (PACF) and autocorrelation functions, respectively. In addition, a common view in financial modeling (Hansen and Lunde 2005; Bollerslev, Chou and Kroner 1992) is that the GARCH (1,1) specification is sufficient to capture autocorrelation in squared returns. Therefore, EGARCH (1,1) model is used in the study.

The constant coefficient (c) in the conditional mean equation is positive and statistically significant for both markets (BIST100 and S&P500) (except for the estimated GED distribution for BIST100). While the constant term coefficient (ω) in the variance equation is positive and statistically significant for the BIST100 index, the sign of the coefficient for the S&P500 index is negative (for Gaussian and Student's t distribution) and is significant. The coefficient is positive and significant only for the GED distribution. ARCH parameter in the table is not statistically significant. The fact that the ARCH parameter (α) is not statistically significant indicates that there is a shock effect within the market due to the effects of positive and negative shocks (Kahyaoğlu 2015). On the other hand, the GARCH parameter (β) is significant and close to each other for both markets. The GARCH (β) parameter is approximately 0.92 for BIST100. Accordingly, a change of 1 percent in past volatility will increase the current volatility by 0.92 percent. For the S&P500 index, this value varies between 0.92 and 0.94 for different distributions. Furthermore, the high GARCH coefficient for both markets shows that shocks for conditional variance take a long time to disappear and are therefore it is *persistence*. Also, the fact that the sum of ARCH and GARCH coefficients is less than one ($\alpha + \beta$ <1) indicates that shocks are not permanent in the market. Consequently, it can be said that the variance is constant, and the system is stable with a mean-reverting process. Negative

Table 4.2   EGARCH (1,1) Model Estimation Results

	S&P 500			BIST100		
	Gaussian	Student's t-test	GED	Gaussian	Student's t	GED
c	0.0420[a]	0.0588[a]	0.0466[a]	0.0336[a]	0.0599[b]	0.0396
	(0.0062)	(0.0126)	(0.0052)	(0.0110)	(0.0274)	(0.0350)
ϕ_1	−0.0693[a]	−0.0381	0.0073	(NA)	(NA)	(NA)
	(0.0280)	(0.4929)	(0.0154)			
θ_1	0.0019	−0.0265	−0.0750[b]	(NA)	(NA)	(NA)
	(0.0246)	(0.4869)	(0.0311)			
ω	−0.6474[a]	−0.8950[a]	0.1565[a]	0.5364[a]	0.4479[a]	0.4587[a]
	(0.1283)	(0.1570)	(0.0239)	(0.0933)	(0.0802)	(0.0851)
α	0.0340	0.0057	0.0198	0.4838	0.2363	0.2490
	(0.1740)	(0.1592)	(0.1596)	(1.1834)	(0.69200)	(0.7100)
β	0.9289[a]	0.9454[a]	0.9369[a]	0.9273[a]	0.9256[a]	0.9227[a]
	(0.0117)	(0.0110)	(0.0110)	(0.0450)	(0.0392)	(0.0400)
γ_1	−0.2263[a]	−0.2451[a]	−0.2403[a]	−0.0712	−0.0949[b]	−0.0924[c]
	(0.0426)	(0.0443)	(0.0417)	(0.0578)	(0.0472)	(0.0485)
γ_2	0.1885[a]	0.1879[a]	0.1896[a]	0.0563[c]	0.0707[b]	0.0694[b]
	(0.0460)	(0.0359)	(0.0374)	(0.0331)	(0.0278)	(0.0294)
COVID	0.1586[a]	0.1470[a]	0.1565[a]	0.0119	0.0133	0.0122
	(0.0277)	(0.0230)	(0.0239)	(0.0188)	(0.0198)	(0.0185)
Shape	(NA)	4.8173[a]	(NA)	(NA)	5.7495[a]	(NA)
		(0.6387)			(0.8099)	
Skew	(NA)	(NA)	1.1531[a]	(NA)	(NA)	1.2405[a]
			(0.0627)			(0.0756)
LB (10)	6.79	6.46	6.66	3.87	3.27	3.76
	(0.55)	(0.59)	(0.57)	(0.95)	(0.65)	(0.95)
LB2 (10)	10.92	10.15	10.26	7.79	7.44	7.55
	(0.20)	(0.25)	(0.24)	(0.45)	(0.48)	(0.47)
ARCH-LM	0.94	1.16	1.02	0.46	0.58	0.61
	(0.38)	(0.31)	(0.35)	(0.62)	(0.55)	(0.53)
Log-likelihood	−1962.69	−1896.87	−1889.50	−2897.58	−2844.88	−2841.59
AIC	2.261[3]	2.186[2]	2.178[1]	3.330[3]	3.271[2]	3.267[1]
BIC	2.289[3]	2.218[2]	2.209[1]	3.352[3]	3.296[2]	3.292[1]

Notes: [a, b, c] Denote statistical significance at 1 percent, 5 percent, and 10 percent level, respectively. Standard errors reported in parentheses. AIC and BIC are Akaike information criteria and Bayesian information criteria, respectively. LB (10) and LB2 (10) are the Ljung–Box statistics for the standardized and squared standardized residuals using 10 lags, respectively. Numbers in parentheses below the LB statistics and ARCH coefficients are the p-values. Superscripts for AIC and BIC denote the rank of model.
Source: Calculated by author

and significant coefficient of γ_1 in the table shows the presence of asymmetric effect. This means that during the period under review, negative shocks (bad news) have higher impact on the volatility of the following period than positive shocks of the same magnitude (good news). In the real world, the volatility spillover mechanism is asymmetrical for the reason that the investors are more sensitive to negative news than positive news. On the other hand, the coefficient γ_2 is positive and statistically significant. Accordingly, it can be said that the actual shocks are more effective on the volatility than the expected shocks.

The COVID variable in the model is added to the conditional variance equation of the EGARCH model as an exogenous shock in order to investigate the effect of the epidemic on the volatility of stock markets. In the table, the COVID coefficient estimated for the S&P500 index is positive and statistically significant. Therefore, the COVID 19 has a positive effect on the conditional variance of the S&P500 index. Accordingly, the COVID 19 is a risk factor that increases volatility in the U.S. stock market. In the table, the COVID coefficient in the BIST100 equation is not statistically significant. Accordingly, it can be stated that COVID-19 has no significant effect on the volatility of the BIST 100 index. These results coincide with the results of Gunay (2020) that determined there is no structural break in Turkey stock index during the epidemic period.

The diagnostic test results performed to evaluate model fit show that the models are correctly specified. ARCH-LM tests show that conditional variance in return series has been successfully captured. In addition, since Ljung-Box Q statistics for standard errors (LB 10) and squares of errors (LB2 10) are not significant, it can be stated that all the models are correctly determined. AIC and BIC values are used for the selection of GARCH specifications suitable for the data. Model selection criteria show that models using the GED distribution fit the data better than models using Student's t-test and Gaussian distribution.

DCC-GARCH ESTIMATION RESULTS

Although univariate GARCH models explain variance and asymmetry in volatility, they do not give information on the characteristic of correlation. However, according to Kroner and Ng (1998), if the expected return of an asset changes according to the effect of asymmetric volatility, then the correlation between the return of that asset and the returns of other assets must change as long as other assets are not affected by the volatility effect. Despite these limitations of GARCH models, Cappiello, Engle, and Sheppard (2006) expanded the DCC-GARCH model (Engle 2002) in order to take the asymmetric effect between correlations into account and introduced the new Asymmetric Dynamic Conditional Correlation-GARCH (ADCC) model. Thereby, the effect of COVID-19 on stock volatility and stock correlation can be analyzed over time.

The estimation of the DCC-GARCH model is done in three stages. First, standardized residues are obtained by estimating the series using VAR analysis, up to 12 lags with the mean. Second, the lag value with the smallest AIC test value for each series of returns is selected to be used in the DCC model. The lag length in the model is determined as zero according to the minimum AIC value. Finally, the Ljung–Box Q test is performed at the selected lag length to verify that there is no serial correlation in the residuals.

Estimation results of the symmetric and asymmetric DCC-GARCH model are shown in table 4.2. In order to determine the existence of volatility spillover, first, the ARCH effect on model residuals must be investigated. The null hypothesis suggesting no ARCH effect in residuals with the selected lag length is rejected for both variables (BIST100 and S&P500) (Panel D of table 4.1). This shows that the selected specification can be estimated using the DCC-GARCH method. In order to test the volatility spillover, it is necessary to determine whether the series are stationary or not. According to the unit root test results, it is determined that the series are stationary (Panel C of table 4.1). When the estimation results are analyzed, it is seen that the variance parameters of both models are significant. It is obvious from these results that each index is significantly and positively affected by its own past shocks or news

Table 4.3 DCC Model Estimation Results

	Symmetric DCC-GARCH		Asymmetric DCC-GARCH	
	Coeff	p-value	Coeff	p-value
Conditional Mean Equation				
μ	0.0901^a	0.0027	0.0813^a	0.0043
δ	0.0828^a	0.0000	0.0842^a	0.0000
Conditional Variance Equation				
C_{11}	0.1655^a	0.0000	0.2107^a	0.0005
C_{22}	0.0416^a	0.0000	0.0459^a	0.0000
A_{11}	0.0759^a	0.0000	0.0662^a	0.0000
A_{12}			0.0233^c	0.0602
A_{21}			-0.0047^b	0.0134
A_{22}	0.2327^a	0.0000	0.2354^a	0.0000
B_{11}	0.8315^a	0.0000	0.8001^a	0.0000
B_{22}	0.7369^a	0.0000	0.7413^a	0.0000
DCC(α)	0.0244^c	0.0557	0.0298^c	0.0513
DCC(β)	0.8992^a	0.0000	0.8952^a	0.0000
Ljung–Box Test for Autocorrelation				
LB (5)	29.86		30.14	
p-Value	0.07		0.06	
LB (10)	44.91		44.87	
p-Value	0.27		0.27	
Lagrange Multiplier (LM) Test for ARCH Residuals				
LM (5)	30.48		29.06	
p-Value	0.95		0.96	
LM (10)	56.58		55.50	
p-Value	0.99		0.99	

Notes: [a,b,c] Denote statistical significance at 1 percent, 5 percent, and 10 percent level, respectively.
Source: Calculated by author

(ARCH effect). In addition, each index is affected by its own past volatility (GARCH effect). The DCC parameters, DCC (α) and DCC (β), in the table show the effects of past shocks and past period correlations, respectively. The estimated DCC (α) parameter for both models (symmetric and asymmetric) indicated that the effect of past shocks on current conditional correlations is quite low (0.024 and 0.029). The coefficient of the lagged conditional correlation matrix DCC(β) is of high value (0.899 and 0.895) and statistically significant for all models. Accordingly, past correlations have a higher effect on current conditional correlations when compared to past shocks. In other words, it is understood that there is a volatility clustering in both markets, and volatility has a permanent effect on the markets. On the other hand, the A_{12} parameter, which expresses the presence of the interaction from S&P500 volatility to BIST100 volatility, is statistically significant at the 10 percent level. Accordingly, a 1 percent shock that increases volatility in S&P500 increases BIST100 volatility by 0.02 percent. A_{21} parameter, indicating the presence of volatility interaction from BIST100 to S&P500, is statistically significant at the 5 percent significance level, but it is negative. Accordingly, a 1 percent shock that increases BIST100 volatility reduces S&P500 volatility by 0.004 percent. Finally, according to the Ljung-Box Q-statistic, it is understood that there is no serial correlation problem in residuals up to 5 and 10 lags. ARCH-LM test shows that there is no heteroskedasticity problem in the model. Therefore, the necessary criteria for model fit are provided.

VARIANCE IMPULSE RESPONSE ANALYSIS RESULTS

In this section, we will examine the persistence of volatility shocks in stock markets using Hafner and Herwartz's (2006) VIRF. For this purpose, the date March 11, 2020, when COVID-19 was declared as *global epidemic* by the WHO, is included in the model as a shock variable. The global epidemic period has increased the risk level of all countries significantly creating a global uncertainty. Studies show that the risk levels of all countries increased remarkably in March, with the spread of COVID-19 to more than 200 countries. This risk and uncertainty, emerging from the epidemic, had significant effects on the financial markets of countries since early March 2020. The aim of this study is to test this effect empirically within the framework of volatility analysis. For this purpose, estimated volatility impulse response analysis results are given in figure 4.1.

When the VIRFs are analyzed, it is observed that COVID-19 (March 11, 2020, and after) has a positive effect on the expected variance of both stock markets. Moreover, the impulse response function shows a gradually decreasing trend during the period starting from a high positive value. Especially the

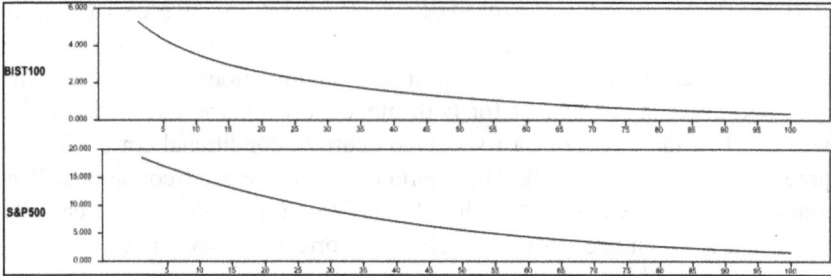

Figure 4.1   Volatility Impulse Response Function. *Source:* Calculated by Author.

initial impact of the shock caused an increase in the volatility of both stock markets at the same level. However, after the initial impact of the shock, the impact on the BIST100 index quickly decreases, while the impact on the S&P500 shows a longer and slower declining trend. This result supports the findings previously reached with the EGARCH model. Accordingly, it can be said that the COVID-19 shock has a stronger and longer-term effect on the volatility of the S&P500 index.

Our empirical findings contribute to the literature in different aspects. First, the empirical results, the U.S. and Turkey stock markets are close to each other in the context of the volatility. Second, we saw the COVID-19 shock intensify the volatility spread between U.S. and Turkey stock markets. The magnitude of volatility shows that an unexpected shock increases correlation not only in its own assets or market but also in other assets or markets. Moreover, the magnitude and persistence of volatility impulse responses differ from market to market, as investors react differently to shocks. Generally, these findings have important implications for policy makers, regulators, and market investors in terms of volatility transfer and market stability techniques in volatile market periods.

CONCLUSION

This study aims to empirically test the effect of the COVID-19 pandemic on financial markets. In this research, responses of Turkey and U.S. stock markets to COVID -19 pandemic are analyzed comparatively. Unexpected events such as global epidemics are supposed to directly affect the financial assets of countries. For this reason, in this study, different techniques are used to investigate the effect of such events on volatility, which is an important parameter in monitoring country risk.

In the study, the effect of COVID-19 on the volatility of stock markets is tested using two different approaches. In the first approach, volatility is calculated using the return series. EGARCH approach is used to calculate the volatility. Although the GARCH (1,1) model is the most common method of volatility estimation in the literature, in the study EGARCH (1,1) model is used to consider the asymmetric effect. Then, by adding the COVID-19 shock as an exogenous variable to the conditional variance equation of the EGARCH model, the effect of the epidemic on the volatility of stock markets was tested. Subsequently, as a result of adding the COVID-19 shock to the conditional variance equation of the EGARCH model as an exogenous variable, the effect of the epidemic on the volatility of the stock markets is tested. As a result of the analysis, it is concluded that the COVID coefficient estimated for the S&P500 index is positive and statistically significant. These results show that the coronavirus pandemic has an increasing effect on volatility in the U.S. stock market. On the other hand, the COVID coefficient estimated for the BIST100 index is positive but not statistically significant. According to this result, it can be stated that COVID-19 had no significant effect on the volatility of the BIST100 index.

The world economies are becoming more and more integrated as globalization and international trade continuously grow. A similar process is seen in the financial markets of countries. Financial integration refers to the process of integrating the financial system of a country more closely with the financial systems of other countries in the world. The consequences of integration generally occur in the form of an increase in capital flows of a country. Or, it can be defined as a tendency of the asset prices and returns to equalize across countries as investors look for the best current returns. This situation causes the gradually increasing positive correlation between world stock markets and as a result decreasing the benefit of investors from portfolio diversity. This integration process seen in the financial markets of the countries, as a country being integrated into the global market, Turkey is affected from the international fluctuations like the countries that are also integrated to the system. The global dependency caused by financial integration is also a fundamental reason of the volatility spillover between financial markets. This effect is controlled by multivariate volatility models in the second stage within the scope of the study.

Therefore, the effect of COVID-19 on the volatility spread of markets is analyzed using the VIRF developed by Hafner and Herwartz (2006). The results obtained by including the date March 11, 2020 when the epidemic was declared as "global pandemic" as a shock variable show that the response of the BIST100 and S&P500 indices to the COVID-19 shock is different. Accordingly, while the effect of COVID-19 on BIST 100 decreases rapidly after the first impact of the shock, its effect on the S&P500 is longer and more permanent. This result supports the findings that are previously obtained with the EGARCH model. Accordingly, it can be concluded that the COVID-19 shock has a stronger and longer-lasting effect on the volatility of the S&P500 index when compared to the BIST100 index.

In the study, while volatility spillover between the stock markets of the United States and Turkey is examined under the influence of COVID-19 shock, it is too complicated to explain the transmission mechanism under the assumption that the markets affected by many factors. Related studies suggest that financial factors such as exchange rates, interest rates, speculation, and derivative markets can play a determinant role on the dynamics of stock volatility. Therefore, the effects of different factors on the volatility of stock markets should be investigated using different practices and techniques.

Our findings show that the S&P500 index responds permanently against COVID-19 shock. The effect of the shock on the BIST100 is shorter when compared to the S&P500. However, considering that the S&P500 is the leading indicator of the world economy, it can be said that the COVID-19 effect is an external shock for the United States. From this point, it can be stated that the sectors in the S&P500 in the United States are highly affected by the shock. The most effective measure to be taken to prevent the spread of this shock to the world economy is to give priority to the policy coordination between countries rather than the policies at the country level.

REFERENCES

Alber, Nader. "The Effect of Coronavirus Spread on Stock Markets: The Case of the Worst 6 Countries." *SSRN Electronic Journal* 1–11. http://ssrn.com/abstract =3578080.

Albulescu, Claudiu Tiberiu. 2020. "COVID-19 and the United States financial markets' volatility." *Finance Research Letters* (In Press).

Ayittey, Foster K., Matthew K. Ayittey, Nyasha B. Chiwero, Japhet S. Kamasah, and Christian Dzuvor. 2020. "Economic impacts of Wuhan 2019-nCoV on China and the World." *Journal of Medical Virology* 92: 473–75.

Bai, Lan, Yu Wei, Guiwu Wei, Xiafei Li, and Songyun Zhang. 2020. "Infectious disease pandemic and permanent volatility of international stock markets: A long-term perspective." *Finance Research Letters* 1–9 (In Press).

Baker, Scott R., Nicholas Bloom, Steven J. Davis, Kyle J. Kost, Marco C. Sammon, and Tasaneeya Viratyosin. 2020. "The Unprecedented Stock Market Impact of COVID-19 ." *NBER Working Paper* 1–22. No. 26945. Cambridge, MA: National Bureau of Economic Research.

Bollerslev, Tim, Ray Y. Chou, and Kenneth F. Kroner. 1992. "ARCH modeling in finance: A review of the theory and empirical evidence." *Journal of Econometrics* 52 (1–2): 5–59.

Bollerslev, Tim, Robert F. Engle, and Jeffrey M. Wooldridge. 1988. "A capital asset pricing model with time-varying covariances." *The Journal of Political Economy* 96: 116–131.

Cappiello, Lorenzo, Robert F. Engle, and Kevin Sheppard. 2006. "Asymmetric Dynamics in the Correlations of Global Equity and Bond Returns." *Journal of Financial Econometrics* 4(4): 537–572.

Chaudhary, Rashmi, Priti Bakhshi, and Hemendra Gupta. 2020. "Volatility in International Stock Markets: An Empirical Study during COVID-19." *Journal of Risk and Financial Management* 13(9): 1–17.

Demirhan, Ecem. 2020. *COVID-19 Küresel salgınının Türkiye CDS primlerine ve BİST 100 endeksine etkisi.* Türkiye Ekonomi Politikaları Araştırma Vakfı (TEPAV) Değerlendirme Notu. https://www.tepav.org.tr/tr/yayin/s/1475

Engle, Robert F. 1982. "Autoregressive conditional heteroscedasticity with estimates of the variance of United Kingdom Inflation." *Econometrica* 50: 987–1007.

Engle, Robert F. 2002. "Dynamic Conditional Correlation: A Simple Class of Multivariate Generalized Autoregressive Conditional Heteroskedasticity Models." *Journal of Business & Economic Statistics* 20(3): 339–350.

Fernandes, Nuno. 2020. "Economic effects of coronavirus outbreak (COVID-19) on the world economy." *SSRN Working Paper* 1–29. https://ssrn.com/abstract=3557504

Gunay, Samet. 2020. "A new form of financial contagion: COVID-19 and stock market responses." *SSRN Working Paper 1–16.* http://dx.doi.org/10.2139/ssrn.3584243

Glosten, Lawrence R., Ravi Jagannathan, and David E. Runkle. 1993. "On the relation between the expected value and the volatility of the nominal excess return on stocks." *The Journal of Finance* 48: 1779–1801.

Hafner, Christian M., and Helmut Herwartz. 2006. "Volatility impulse response for multivariate GARCH models: An exchange rate illustration." *Journal of International Money and Finance* 25(5): 719–740.

Hansen, Peter R., and Asger Lunde. 2005. "A forecast comparison of volatility models: does anything beat a GARCH(1,1)?" *Journal of Applied Econometrics* 20: 873–889.

Hsieh, David A. 1989. "Testing for nonlinearity in daily foreign exchange rate changes." *Journal of Business* 62(3): 339–368.

Haroon, Omair and Syed Aun R. Rizvi. 2020. "COVID-19: Media coverage and financial markets behavior—A sectoral inquiry." *Journal of Behavioral and Experimental Finance* 27: 1–5, 100343.

Hoque, Mohammad Enamul and Mohd Azlan Shah Zaidi. 2019. "The impacts of global economic policy uncertainty on stock market returns in regime switching environment: Evidence from sectoral perspectives." *International Journal of Finance & Economics* 24(2): 991–1016.

IMF. (2020). "A crisis like no other, an uncertain recovery." *IMF World Economic Outlook Update*, June 2020.

Kahyaoğlu, Sezer Bozkuş. 2015. "Optimal ve Etkin Korunma Oranına Yönelik Çok Değişkenli Oynaklık Yaklaşımları: Türkiye ve İngiltere Elektrik Piyasaları Üzerine Bir Analiz." PhD diss., Dokuz Eylül University.

Kang Hua Cao, Qiqi Li, Yun Liu & Chi-Keung Woo (2021) Covid-19's adverse effects on a stock market index, *Applied Economics Letters* 28(14): 1157–1161.

Kroner, Kenneth F., and Victor K. Ng. 1998. "Modelling Asymmetric Comovements of Asset Returns." *The Review of Financial Studies* 11(4): 817–844.

Nelson, Daniel B. 1991. "Conditional heteroskedasticity in asset returns: a new approach." *Econometrica* 59(2): 347–370.

Onali, Enrico. 2020. "COVID-19 and stock market volatility." *SSRN Electronic Journal* 1–24. https://doi.org/10.2139/ssrn.3571453.

Ramelli, Stefano and Alexander Wagner. 2020. "What the stock market tells us about the consequences of COVID19?" In *Mitigating the COVID Economic Crisis: Act Fast and Do Whatever It Takes*, edited by Baldwin, Richard and Beatrice Weder di Mauro, 63–70. CEPR Press, London.

Yilmazkuday, Hakan. 2020. "Coronavirus Disease 2019 and the Global Economy." *SSRN Working Paper*, 1–31. Available at SSRN 3554381.

World Health Organization (2020). "Coronavirus disease 2019 (COVID-19)." Situation report. Report No:59.

Zaremba, Adam, Renatas Kizys, David Y. Aharon, and Ender Demir. 2020. "Infected markets: novel Coronavirus, government interventions, and stock return volatility around the Globe." *Finance Research Letters* 35: 1–7.

Chapter 5

Cryptocurrency and Crypto Money Markets in COVID-19 Period

İbrahim Külünk

INTRODUCTION

As the cryptocurrency market is a rather new subject for academic literature, there isn't much work yet. The studies at hand are about the differences of the cryptocurrency market from other markets, market shares and competitive conditions, and price volatility. Dwyer (2014), Bartos (2015), Carrick (2016), Caporale and Plastun (2019), and Bariviera et al. (2017) emphasized the difficulty of making an exact definition of cryptocurrency. The uncertainties about whether it is an investment instrument or a currency make it difficult to define the crypto money market exactly. Plasaras (2013) states that the cryptocurrency market, where transactions are made without being connected to a center and for investment instruments and commercial transactions, has a security weakness caused by the lack of regulation. However, according to Zhang and Wang (2020), there is a positive relationship between investor interest and cryptocurrencies. Apart from these, there are also some studies analyzing the relationship between price volatility and investments in crypto money markets. In these studies, there is generally some evidence that price volatility is related to investment behavior (Fry and Cheah, 2016, Bouri et al., 2017, Schilling and Uhlig, 2018, Liu and Serletis, 2019).

DEVELOPMENT, PRODUCTION, AND TRANSFER OF CRYPTOCURRENCIES

Cryptocurrency is virtual money that works with some kind of encryption system. For example, Bitcoin and Altcoins are independent currencies, in the sense that they are not a currency belonging to any country.

After the 2008 financial crisis that emerged in the United States and spread around the world rapidly, pseudonymous person or persons called Satoshi Nakamato published an article titled "Bitcoin: A Peer-to-Peer Electronic Cash System." This article describes the working principle of Bitcoin. In the introduction of the article, it is explained that in this end-to-end system, there is no need for financial institutions, and the system provides online money transfer from one side to the other in an environment where there is no third party (Nakamoto, 2008). The first successful cryptocurrency is Bitcoin. Bitcoin, which is described as the first-generation Block-Chain and is a public payment network, went into operation in 2009 with an end-to-end electronic payment system that third parties could not intervene. The operation principle that does not allow any financial regulation and control underlies the rapid rise in the market value of Bitcoin. This rise was achieved by an enormous jump that no currency or security could reach before. So that in 2009, when Bitcoin started operations for the first time, the stock exchange named New Liberty Standard determined the first BTC/Dollar rate as 1.309/1 in October 2009, while 1 Bitcoin is priced as 31.733 dollars in the market today as of January 11, 2021. This tremendous rise has revealed Altcoins. Altcoin is the common name for currencies other than Bitcoin. While it is continuously changing, there are 4,312 Altcoins in the market and the value of the crypto money market today, including Bitcoin, is approximately $891 billion. About $617 billion of this value belongs to Bitcoin solely. At this point, it should be emphasized that these numbers vary highly on a daily basis. For example, a week before this chapter was written (as of January 7, 2021), while the total cryptocurrency market exceeded $1 trillion, Bitcoin lost 13 percent in the last 24 hours (as of January 12, 2021).

The widely known name of the crypto money production and transfer process is mining. Mining, which is one of the two ways of having the crypto money, is solving specific problems and transferring money between wallets, depositing it into the transaction pool before being included in the blockchain, blocking and confirming transactions here, and getting crypto money as a reward for these transactions. Some mining methods are ASIC (Application-Specific Integrated Circuits), GPU (Graphics Processor Unit), CPU (Central Processing Unit), and Cloud Mining.

The legal regulations of cryptocurrencies are not completely clarified yet. However, the unconventional working principle of the crypto money market that excludes the financial system and the rapid increase in demand for the market have prompted countries to develop both legal regulations and currencies in this field. However, despite this, no net taxation can be made in the consequence of the working principle of the crypto money market.

DEVELOPMENTS IN THE CRYPTO MONEY MARKET IN THE COVID-19 PERIOD

The crypto money market, which has a financial ecosystem outside the traditional financial system, is an active market that has achieved high goals in terms of value increase with its ups and downs, and expanding as a result of the rapid proliferation of Altcoins.

The crypto money market has begun to attract more attention with the advertisements in social media and websites. In Table 5.1, seen that the interest in economic value in the crypto money market has increased particularly during the pandemic period. It is obvious that many small investors turned to Altcoins during this period and that there has been a possible manipulation for these currencies on social media.

Before the pandemic (in the last quarter of 2019), there were sharp falls in the market which can be defined as bottom, especially in Bitcoin. Bitcoin, which has the value of $34,000 as on February 1, 2021, increased its value to $35,000 levels from $7,000 levels on April 22, 2020.

The relationship between the increasing interest in cryptocurrencies and COVID-19 can be seen from many open sources. However, since this subject is very new, it is beneficial to examine some scientific findings obtained with only a few studies. During the pandemic period, studies on crypto currencies have focused on the reasons of the valuations in the market and the confidence in the market. The common view is that interest in these markets increased during the pandemic. On the other hand, these studies also state that the market is in a state that cannot be seen as a safe haven (Kristoufek, 2020, Yarovaya et al., 2020, Goodell and Goutte, 2020, Conlon and McGee, 2020, Corbet et al., 2020). Crypto currencies that do not depend on a certain central authority are traded in a market that is open to manipulation with this characteristic. Cryptocurrencies, which have no certain definition, have been valued during the pandemic period. Among these, Ether, which is the second largest cryptocurrency, has become the most valued currency. Among these, Ether, which is the second largest cryptocurrency, is the most valued currency.

Table 5.1   Crypto Money Movements before and after COVID-19

	January 1, 2018	January 1, 2019	January 1, 2020	June 1 2020	August 1, 2020	February 3, 2021
BTC	10,231	3,527	9,284	9,282	11,698	36.347
ETH	1,106	105	175	223	434	1,556
LTC	162	31	67	45	60	150
XRP	1.11	0.31	0.23	0.17	0.27	0.39
Bitcoin (BTC), Ethereum (ETH), Litecoin (LTC), Ripple (XRP),						

Source: www.tradingview.com (Approximate values are taken)

The interest in Ether is explained by the fact that, after the pandemic, Ether (ETH) compensates for its sharp fall after reaching a peak in January 2018. Although not as much as Ether, Bitcoin has experienced significant acceleration with the pandemic. Although the main factor in this is the incentive to protect savings, profit opportunities affect the investors to a degree that cannot be ignored. Especially in the first months of 2021, after the manipulations of cryptocurrencies, the interest of many small investors turned into this market. The inclusion of institutions making individual transactions in the market and increasing number of the central banks studies accordingly give some ideas about the future of the Crypto Money market. According to IMF President Lagarde (2018), central banks should take action on digital currency. Naci Ağbal, the head of the CBRT, stated that in the second half of 2021, pilot implementations on digital money will begin. FED chairman Powell said that the FED has years ahead for a digital currency. Certainly, the baseline of this statement is that the US dollar is currently the global reserve currency. China is more active than other countries in the production of digital money and crypto money. The Chinese central bank has developed the Digital Currency Electronic Payment (DCEP) system. The head of the UK central bank, Bailey, made announcements similar to Powell. Nabiullina, the head of the Russian central bank, stated that pilot implementations will be completed before the end of 2021. European Central Bank (ECB) president Christine Lagarde explained the goals in an online conference, saying, "Banknotes will continue to exist, but eventually we will have a digital euro surely." Much more examples can be cited on this. Except U.S. and UK central banks, it is seen that countries, especially PBoC (People's Bank of China), are taking action about digital money. Certainly, these examples give some predictions about the future of the crypto money market. It can develop into a safer and more widely used market. Cryptocurrencies, which can be manipulated even on social media in their existing form, can transform into a less uncertain and less risky area as a result of the applications of central banks.

CONCLUSION

Particularly, the COVID-19 epidemic triggered a rapid digitization process. This compulsory and rapid transformation has put e-commerce, digital media consumption, screen addiction, and credit cards at the center of life.

The interest of crypto currencies in this period can be seen as a part of this rapid digitalization. However, the main reasons for the rising interest in the market are the profit opportunities offered by the market rather than the wind of digitalization. Today, while the remarkable manipulation of cryptocurrencies on digital platforms poses a high risk for many small investors, it also involves the desire for high profits. It seems that cryptocurrencies will be an even more sought-after investment instrument in post-covid19. Two problems arise here. First, how can the fields of manipulation be narrowed? Second, what will be the universal answer to the question of what is crypto money? When these two important issues are revealed, the crypto money market will be able to have a much larger transaction volume with a value exceeding \$1 Trillion. The world stock exchange market, approaching \$100 trillion, gold funds and valuable papers, which offered very generous profit opportunities to the investors during the pandemic, were perceived as a security blanket. Cryptocurrencies also owe some of their attention to this. However, it seems difficult to define digital currencies as safe haven, thus they do not have a counterpart. Cryptocurrencies may not be able to fulfill this function as yet due to their vulnerabilities.

REFERENCES

Bariviera, Aurelio F., María José Basgall, Waldo Hasperu´e, Marcelo Naiouf. 2017. "Some stylized facts of the Bitcoin market." *Physica A: Statistical Mechanics and its Applications* 484: 82–90.

Bartos, Jakub. 2015. "Does Bitcoin follow the hypothesis of efficient market." *International Journal of Economic Sciences* 4.2: 10–23.

Bouri, Elie, Georges Azzi, and Anne Haubo Dyhrberg. 2016. "On the return-volatility relationship in the Bitcoin market around the price crash of 2013." *Available at SSRN 2869855*: 1–16.

Caporale, Guglielmo Maria, and Alex Plastun. 2019. "The day of the week effect in the cryptocurrency market." *Finance Research Letters* 31: 258–269.

Carrick, Jon. 2016. "Bitcoin as a complement to emerging market currencies." *Emerging Markets Finance and Trade* 52.10: 2321–2334.

Conlon, Thomas, and Richard McGee. 2020. "Safe haven or risky hazard? Bitcoin during the COVID-19 bear market." *Finance Research Letters* 35: 101607.

Corbet, Shaen, Charles Larkin, and Brian Lucey. 2020. "The contagion effects of the COVID-19 pandemic: Evidence from gold and cryptocurrencies." *Finance Research Letters* 35: 101554.

Dwyer, Gerald P. 2015. "The economics of Bitcoin and similar private digital currencies." *Journal of Financial Stability* 17: 81–91.

Fry, John, and Eng-Tuck Cheah. 2016. "Negative bubbles and shocks in cryptocurrency markets." *International Review of Financial Analysis* 47: 343–352.

Goodell, John W., and Stéphane Goutte. 2020. "Co-movement of COVID-19 and Bitcoin: Evidence from wavelet coherence analysis." *Finance Research Letters* 38: 101625,

Kristoufek, Ladislav. 2020. "Grandpa, grandpa, tell me the one about Bitcoin being a safe haven: Evidence from the COVID-19 pandemics." *arXiv preprint arXiv:2004.00047.*

Lagarde, Christine. 2018. "Winds of change: The case for new digital currency." *Speech at the Singapore Fintech Festival* 14: 2018.

Liu, Jinan, and Apostolos Serletis. 2019. "Volatility in the cryptocurrency market." *Open Economies Review* 30.4: 779–811.

Nakamoto, Satoshi. 2008. *Bitcoin: A peer-to-peer electronic cash system.* Decentralized Business Review, 21260.

Plassaras, Nicholas A. .2013. "Regulating digital currencies: bringing Bitcoin within the reach of IMF." *Chicago Journal of International Law* 14: 377.

Schilling, Linda, and Harald Uhlig. 2019. "Some simple bitcoin economics." *Journal of Monetary Economics* 106: 16–26.

Yarovaya, Larisa, Roman Matkovskyy, and Akanksha Jalan. 2020. "The effects of a 'Black Swan' event (COVID-19) on herding behavior in cryptocurrency markets: Evidence from cryptocurrency USD, EUR, JPY and KRW Markets." *EUR, JPY and KRW Markets (April 27, 2020).*

Zhang, Wei, and Pengfei Wang. 2020. "Investor attention and the pricing of cryptocurrency market." *Evolutionary and Institutional Economics Review* 17.2: 445–468.

Chapter 6

Global Financial System and the Monetary Crisis of 2020

Arzu Alvan

INTRODUCTION

Currently, we are witnessing a world that is about to enter the biggest monetary crisis faced in the history. It is at a turning point of a systemic transformation of the world's monetary and economic system. We have been living in a real sector for nearly 300 years; therefore, examining the cyclical processes of the world's economy during a pandemic is the first step to understanding the transformation. Accordingly, the aim of this study is to evaluate the causes and possible consequences of the current monetary and economic crisis, in which the system reset (Big Reset) has begun to be more pronounced.

The monetary system is an important component of the entire economic system. However, we do not understand the significance of this phenomenon today. We don't ask ourselves how it works and whether it is the best solution or it needs a transformation. Therefore, in order to understand and interpret this situation, which can be defined as a money and credit crisis, we first have to understand the economic system, money, and industrial economy we have been living with for the last three centuries. It is important to examine how economic, social, and political factors have progressed in history, for which a statistical approach is necessary. Although monetary systems seem stable, they have been fluctuating periodically in the last century. Especially in economic studies, analyzing the historical cycles of statistical data can be useful in predicting future conditions roughly. In the historical process, it has been observed that the economic cycles shaped the living conditions of the societies. Therefore, it can be said that the economic order is one of the most important factors that shape the lifestyles of societies.

The money and industrial economy that we live in, started in England in the second half of the eighteenth century, and by means of the Industrial Revolution, the scattered and small-scale structures of production systems began to be centralized on a large scale, this can be defined as a system in which money, that is, capital, is the guiding factor. Money and industrial economies started to decline in countries such as Europe, Japan, and the United States since 1950s. Digitalization started for the first time in the 1950s. When we look at the world economy, we see that money transforms from a limited (solid) form to an unlimited form, and this is a cyclical process. It is observed that generally crises occur in case of the transition from limited money to unlimited money. In economies with robust industries and production, money is the strength and it is limited. Limited money is reasonable because currency cannot be printed easily. If the production in an economy does not increase or increases only slightly, but the amount of money increases more, the structure of the monetary system will deteriorate in that economy and inflation is inevitable. This causes the social segment that controls money to become richer and wealth transfer occurs, which is called resource transfer. This situation also results in unfair distribution of income and increase of direct/indirect taxes (Maloney 2008).

In line with the purpose of the study, in the first part, money economy and the structure of the current system will be discussed under the sub-headings of limited and unlimited money, the gold standard, and Fiat (fiduciary, representative) money. In the second part, the bond/stocks exchange markets, real estate markets, and partial reserve money system, which are the leading indicators of the probable biggest financial crisis of the world that we are about to face, will be examined.

MONEY ECONOMY

Money economy is basically a network of economic relations based on money, which is the engine of the current production system. Currently, the economic system is largely centralized and focused on capital, that is, money. This form of production model started to occur during the Industrial Revolution. The Industrial Revolution started around 1760 in Great Britain, but the main impact of this transition began to be seen in the late 1800s, and economies largely dependent on agriculture and small-scale production began to shift to the industrial form. The increasing interdependence associated with the Industrial Revolution also created the need for a reliable commodity in trade. The commodity money system, consisting of valuable assets such as gold and silver, was already in use, but there were also major limitations in this system. In a relatively isolated or primitive society, almost any commodity could function as money; however, as trade became more sophisticated, most of the commodities failed. In the course of time, as technology costs declined, the infrastructure demands of large factories, such as canals and railways began to increase. The need for capital started to arise in order to put the infrastructure projects into operation. With the commodity system of the time, it was not possible to meet the ever-increasing demand for money instantly. Thus, the banking system started to take form. Expert banks, having information about specific industries and areas, have grown to take full advantage of this situation. Banks also began to make profits by holding cash reserves and lending sums to earn interest (Wilde August 27, 2020).

In 1944, the Bretton Woods Agreement was negotiated by delegates from forty-four countries at the United Nations Money and Finance Conference held in Bretton Woods, New Hampshire. The aim of the agreement was to create an efficient foreign exchange system, prevent competitive devaluations of currencies, and promote economic growth. Moreover, under the Bretton Woods system, the nominal values of foreign currencies were pegged to U.S. dollars, the value of which is traditionally expressed as gold, which is US $35 per ounce (Bordo and Eichengreen 1993). Since the Bretton Woods Agreement, U.S. dollar is the reserve currency in the global economy, so the United States, the country of origin of the dollar, leads the money economy.

On August 15, 1971, Nixon linked the country to the world economy in a new economic policy called "Nixon Shock," aiming to fix the balance of payments, but also to stop inflation and lower the unemployment rate. As a first measure, he broke the bond between gold and the dollar. Foreign governments could no longer convert their dollars into gold. Thus, the semi-solid monetary system created with the dollar, which is almost half of gold has been terminated and a new global unlimited money experiment has started where dollars could be issued unlimitedly. The Bretton Woods system thus came to an end soon (Meltzer 1991, Bordo, Humpage, and Schwartz April 2011). The collapse of Bretton Woods led to the creation of the petrodollar system, in which the United States and Saudi Arabia agreed to set oil prices in U.S. dollars. This meant that any country that bought oil from the Saudi government had to convert its currency to U.S. dollars before completing the transaction. This caused the remaining OPEC countries to follow other member-countries and led them to price their own oil in U.S. currency. By 1975, all oil-producing countries of OPEC decided to price their oil in dollars and agreed to invest excess oil revenues in U.S. government debt securities. Thanks to this agreement, the petrodollar system was born with the transition from fixed exchange rates and gold-backed currencies to unsupported, floating exchange rate regimes (Historian).

LIMITED/UNLIMITED MONEY

This device (money) circulates and sustains its power mostly from its amount, not its content.
                      —Julius Paulus, Roman Jurist, A.C. second century.

Before talking about the monetary crisis, it is necessary to define cash money, which is the engine of the system we are in. The money mentioned here, which we will discuss in more detail later, is Fiat (fiduciary, deposit) money that is not backed by any precious commodity. One of the economic definitions of money is "the commodity of all commodities." Goods produced for sale are called commodities. In this case, money is a widely accepted commodity that can be exchanged for all commodities.

The coin was first used by the Lydians in the city of Sardes by King Alyattes. It was produced in 600 BC by mixing silver and gold. This is the first official coin. Alyattes' son, Krezus, produced pure gold coin for the first time in history. Thus, limited (solid) money was produced for the first time. After that, there came a period when the Athenians changed the form of money by adding copper and tried to turn it from limited into unlimited property. This is the first time that Greece faced with hyperinflation. The Romans also repeated this. First, they produced the gold coin called "dinarus." Since gold was a limited resource, money produced from gold was also limited but is solid money. The dinarus, which was brought into an unlimited form by adding different metals into it, eventually caused hyperinflation and played a major role in the collapse of the Western Roman Empire. Emperor Constantine, who founded Istanbul, likewise produced pure gold coin called "solidus" (Tandy 2004).

Money (Fiat Money) has seven basic properties. It is interchange-able, divisible, acceptable, durable, unit of account, portable, and limited (Krugman and Wells 2005). We can say that the unlimitedly produced (Fiat) money does not have some of these features anymore that we use in place of money. For example, the durability property of money means that it retains its value over a long period of time, but the money in your accounts and in your pocket will over time lose its value for some reasons, such as inflation and demonetization. We can no longer talk about the last and most important feature, the limited circulation feature. The money that central banks issue unlimitedly, especially during periods of recession and crisis, loses this most important feature and causes the loss of system sustainability.

This is the main subject of our study. Thus, money can essentially be studied in two forms, limited form and unlimited form. Limited money can-not be produced in the desired amount by the states, and this limited amount expresses an intrinsic value of precious metals such as gold, silver, and platinum. Recently, digital currencies have been added to these. The limited feature adds strength to the money.

Unlimited money, on the other hand, was issued by the Chinese in eleventh century A.C. as first paper money of the world. The name of this money is jiaozi. This money was originally based on limited assets such as spices and silver. Later, in the 1260s, the Mongolian-origin Yuhan Dynasty, Kublai Khan, abolished this money from being based on limited assets.

Thus, he initiated the transition to unlimited money called "fiat money." Naturally, hyperinflation started and it was decided to revert to limited money (Barnett 2015). Another unlimited money experiment was the Continental paper currency, which was issued on May 10, 1775, in the American War of Independence. The first four emissions included one-dollar bill until May 6, 1776. There were no one-dollar bills in the next six issues. This money has been called "currency" and, like other unlimited money experiments, it has been an experiment that caused inflation (Wolfeboro 1991, Newman July-August 1952). Finally, the United States completely abolished the convertibility of U.S. dollar to gold in 1971. The world population experienced the unlimited money experiment globally for the first time in history.

GOLD STANDARD

One of the reasons for the global financial crisis we are now in, and are just at the beginning, is that we do not know the difference between the exchange tool called fiat money (originally called currency) which we use as cash and is issued unlimitedly and money based on commodity which is limited and has its own intrinsic value. Fiat money, as we mentioned before when defining money, has features such as being a medium of exchange, being a unit of value calculation, being portable, being divisible. Money, on the other hand, has an intrinsic value like gold and silver, apart from the above. Therefore, whoever owns gold makes the rules.

About 5,000 years ago, Egyptians began using gold and silver as cash. The gold and silver coins paid to the workers when the Egyptian pyramids were built are still in circulation today. Therefore, gold is the only item in history that has not been thrown into the rubbish bin. One of the reasons why gold is preferred compared to any other metal is that it can be processed easily.

The gold standard is a monetary system in which paper money can be freely converted to a fixed amount of gold. The paper money mentioned here is referred to as a gold certificate. In other words, gold supports the value of paper money in such a monetary system. In countries where the gold standard is applied, banknotes are issued by central banks on the basis of gold. The amount of paper money in circulation depends on the amount of gold stock in central banks and, if requested, this paper money is paid as the amount of gold it represents (Bordo 2003).

Increased production and trade with the Industrial Revolution ramped up with great gold discoveries. Thus, the gold standard preserved its value for the next century (Elwell 2011). United Germany passed the gold standard in 1871. The United Kingdom, which was the dominant state economically and politically at the time, also played an important role in the adoption of the gold standard by other countries, with the effect of using this standard and the fact that the heart of the financial system is in London as it is today.

By 1900, all countries except China and some Central American countries followed the Gold Standard. This continued until it was disrupted by World War I. Gold was a reliable value commonly accepted in trade, causing the states to be motivated to stock this metal as a solid money. States still have these stocks today, and the country's central banks have started to attach great importance to gold production and purchase, especially after the 2008 crisis.

FIAT MONEY (FIDUCIARY/DEPOSIT MONEY, CURRENCY) SYSTEM, DOLLARS AS RESERVE MONEY

Toda's money system has two pillars: fiat money (fiduciary money, fiat money), which is issued without any reference, and a fractional reserve banking system, which is being explained in the rest of the study, consisting of digital credits created by banks by keeping some of the money they receive as deposits in their reserves based on leverage in the banking system. We will refer to assets in banknote and coin form, which are issued/printed unlimitedly as "fiat money," which is also known as fiduciary or nominal money, which is deformed and has no commodity equivalent. As mentioned, with Nixon's disconnection of the dollar from gold in 1971, the world began a complete Fiat monetary system experiment that was not supported by anything and could be issued without limit. Thereafter occurred a basic difference between previous monetary system and the monetary system we are living with since 1971. While the previous monetary system was based on gold, the present fiat monetary system is not based on anything and completely unbacked.

Since this currency is no longer commodity-backed, central banks can create as many currencies as they want (Tyler and Lukas 2015). Fiat money is produced in two forms. Coins and paper money. The metal form is around 1 percent in the money base in the market. The treasury of the state through central banks mints coins and sells them for nominal value. In other words, this nominal total amount is entered into the treasury's safe by the central bank. Treasury makes investments, covers expenditures, and makes payments with this money. In short, this coin form of money is the portion that makes up approximately 1 percent of the total monetary base and is truly the state's money. For the creation of paper money, the central bank buys bonds and government debt securities, and issues money equivalent to these securities.

The important point here is that the state is indebted for this money. That is, state pays a certain interest on government bonds and bills when they are due. The state pays this debt from the revenue item in its budget. Most of the state's revenues are taxes collected from the public. Therefore, this is the debt of the people.

KEY INDICATORS OF THE GLOBAL MONETARY CRISIS

When examining crises within the historical cycle, it is noteworthy that crises have a repetitive cycle. Generally, we can say that the main indicators of major crises are the bubbles seen in the important markets of the relevant period. Crises followed the recurrence of these bubbles. Nowadays, as we will mention in the rest of this study, significant bubbles that make the crisis felt are mainly from the stock market, bond, and real estate markets. On the other hand, the first known financial bubble in history was the "Tulip Bubble" or "Tulipmania," which took place in the Dutch stock market in the seventeenth century (Garber 2000).

Unlimited issue of money has caused various crises over time. The main reason being that price increases in the stock markets due to the fact that money can be issued in the desired quantity and the value increases that do not result from real production. These increases bubbles in various markets. Bubbles in the markets often occur when investors buy assets in anticipation of short-term gains due to rapidly rising prices. These speculative increases in prices continue until another speculative situation occurs. Crises, which can also be defined as the explosion of bubble markets, cause a sharp decrease in demand and asset prices in most cases. Such crises increased after 1971. For example, the first global financial crisis occurred in the autumn of 1987, on October 19, known as "Black Monday." This crisis caused the Dow Jones index to lose 22.6 percent of its value, and it also marked the sharpest market decline in the United States since the Great Depression. Federal Reserve Bank (Fed) encouraged the banks to lend normally the security firms in trouble; that is to say, it encouraged them to feed the system with credit. These loans to protect the system provided liquidity, and the crisis was temporarily halted (Bernanke 1990, Carlson 2006). In 2008, the real estate bubble burst in the United States and the world financial system collapsed.

It is possible to examine the main indicators of the monetary crisis that started the collapse of the financial system we are in under three headings:

the bond market and the stock market, the real estate market, and the partial reserve money system.

BOND AND STOCK MARKET

The period in which the international bond market entered a rapid expansion was the early 1980s. The international bond market, a market for foreign currency bonds that are issued and traded beyond the national borders, has played an important role in the internationalization of capital markets since 1980. After the Bretton Woods system collapsed in 1971, the dollar started to be issued unlimitedly and floating exchange rates were adopted and the Euro-bond market entered a new period. The majority of euro-bonds issued in the 1970s were based on dollar. In those years, the bond market formed one-third of the financial system (Benzie 1992).

One of the most important indicators that show the bubble in the stock market is the "Shiller P/E Ratio," that is, the price/earnings (also known as the CAPE ratio) used in the stock markets developed by Yale University professor Robert Shiller, who won the Nobel Prize in Economics in 2013. Shiller emphasized that there was a bubble with the excessive increase in the U.S. stock market in the late 1990s, and this was an important warning for the crisis. The P/E ratio is calculated as follows: Annual earnings per share (EPS) of a stock index such as S&P 500 in the last 10 years are taken as basis, and these earnings are realized according to the CPI. The 10-year average of the newly acquired values is taken and the current level of the S&P 500 is divided by this 10-year average. In fact, here we are calculating the ratio between the company's stock market value and the actual earning amount of the stock (Campbell and Shiller 1987). The Shiller P/E ratio also gives an idea of how many years the company can pay you back when you deposit money with a company on the exchange. For example, if this ratio is between 10 and 15, the company can pay your deposit back in 10–15 years. This rate went up to 30 in the crisis that broke out in the U.S. New York Stock Exchange on October 29, 1929, called the "Great Depression." The year 2000, when this rate was exceeded, is the year when the technology (dot.com) bubble burst in the United States . This ratio is around 30 by 2020.

Another important indicator is the "Buffet Indicator" developed by Warren Buffet, the famous U.S. investor. This indicates that the Stock Exchange is in bubble and the crisis is approaching. In this indicator, we see the ratio of the value of the stock market to the annual production value of the United States on a yearly basis. If this ratio started to exceed 100, we can understand that there is a danger and it is necessary to exit the stock market. This indicator has its highest value with 136.9 in the technology bubble in 2000. The last measured value of the indicator is 138 as of 2020 (Buffet Indicator). In addition to this indicator, another of the most important indicator of the global crisis is the "margin debt" developed by the U.S. investor Mike Maloney (Maloney 2008). This indicator is calculated as follows: When you trade on the stock exchange, the investment company lends you and you play with this loan. For example, if you have 10 TL, they will pay you 10 TL and you play with 20 TL. The problem here is the risky 10 TL credit you get. If you win, you will win with 20 TL, but if you lose you will lose 20 TL, not 10 TL. Mike Maloney also blended this indicator with the Buffet indicator and created the "market fragility index." Buffet indicates when the market is overvalued. The market fragility index gives information about how close it is to collapse, that is, market fragility. These two important and explanatory indicators are combined into a single index, allowing us to see the size and weakness of the stock market bubble (Maloney and Clark 2018). The Market Fragility Index has been evaluated in a six-category table. The categories start from the lowest level, no threat, normal, time to worry, unstable, super fragile, and threat to the global financial system. The first peak in the table was in 1998, when a huge "Hedge Fund" with assets of 126 billion dollars called "Long-Term Capital Management" collapsed. This incident affected the entire world economy adversely. We have now passed the peak of 2008. The index has also exceeded the threat dimension and indicates a systemic collapse (https://goldsilver.com/blog/introducing-the-market-fragility-index -what-its-saying-now).

REAL ESTATE MARKET

Another important indicator of the global crisis is the bubble caused by excessive pricing in the real estate market. If summarized briefly, there are certain situations that indicate problems in the real estate market, and most of them are the risk factors of market collapse if they happen and knowing them is necessary to understand the market. Data can be summarized showing the current situation of the market in five main items. The realization of these phenomena is the sign for the beginning of a very critical period for the market.

The first is that the bubble of assets bursts. Crisis usually occurs when the wealth bubble bursts. The sign of the bubble that caused the crisis is the rapidly rising house prices. Prices started to rise rapidly before the crisis that started with the burst of the real estate bubble in 2008. Prices, which started to decrease with the crisis, created a deflationary environment. The national average house price in the United States reached a record high at $ 212,433 in January 2020. This was 15 percent higher than the record price high of

$ 184,613 in July 2006, according to the Case Shiller House Price Index. The S&P Homebuilders Select Industry Index increased 250 percent from 1,372.60 in October 2011 to 4,867 on February 12, 2020 (BIS 2020).

The second is the increase in the number of mortgage brokers who are not regulated and cannot be controlled. The second is the increase in the number of mortgage brokers who are out of regulations and cannot be controlled. Why this poses a risk? Because these institutions are out of control and regulation and cannot survive when the crisis begins. Fed interest rates followed a downward course until 2006, after the crisis experienced in 2000 with the explosion of the technology bubble (dot.com bubble). The crisis has caused investors to seek safer ports, and eyes turned to the real estate market. Demand for real estate has begun to increase when asset returns have fallen. Thus, house prices nearly doubled between 2000 and 2008, when the crisis broke out, (McKibbin 2006).

Another important indicator to be considered while evaluating the real estate market is the "capitalization rate" or shortly the "CAP" rate. Capitalization rate, or cap rate, is the ratio of net operating income (NOI) to the real estate asset value. For example, if a property was recently sold for $ 100,000 and NIG value is $10,000, the upper rate will be $10,000/$100,000 or 10 percent CAP rate = NIG/Real Estate Sale Value (cost). The opposite of the CAP ratio is the price/earnings ratio. The trend of CAP rates in the real estate market over the past few years is an important indicator for the market direction. For example, if CAP rates are falling, it indicates that property prices are rising and the market is starting to warm. So, if the CAP rate is increasing, it means that the earnings are increasing more than the cost; therefore, investors change the direction toward the real estate market. Here, at what level this ratio may pose a risk is another matter of consideration. If we examine the CAP rate and house price indices during crisis periods, we see that the rapidly increasing house prices between 2000 and 2008 decrease the CAP rate (Advisors).

Another indicator that evaluates the real estate market is the inverted yield curve. A warning sign for the real estate market is the inverted yield curve in the U.S. treasury. We can explain the situation of inverted yield curve as follows: When the short-term treasury bills interest rates are higher than the long-term treasury bills yields, the yield curve is reversed. Normally, short-term bond returns are lower because the risk is also low. In contrast, this shows that investors think that short-term Treasury bills are more risky than long-term ones. This harms the real estate market as well and often indicates a recession.

The yield curve is one of the best economic indicators that most investors and economists neglect. Since 2012, the curve has entered an overall downward trend and slightly upward in 2020, this movement increases the crisis expectation in 2021. So far, we have mentioned about the unlimited money issue experienced globally, as a natural result of this, excessive pricing and bubbles are formed in the markets. The aim is to understand, perhaps, the reasons for the biggest financial crisis in history we are entering into and to discuss the possible results, as will be mentioned in the rest of the study.

PARTIAL RESERVE MONEY SYSTEM

One of the main indicators of the great global monetary crisis that is about to begin at the present time is the partial reserve monetary system itself. In the partial reserve system, we can explain how the deposits that come to the bank create loans as follows: A certain percentage of the deposits coming to the bank, like 10 percent, are kept in cash in the bank's safe and the rest, that is, 90 percent, is given as loans. An obligatory proportion of the reserve money held in the bank is kept in the bank's account at the central bank. If the bank wishes, it can keep more than this rate (reserve requirement ratio) set by the central bank in its own safe. For example, if the bank received a deposit of 100 TL, the bank keeps 10 percent of it in cash in the central bank account as a required reserve (reserve). The remaining 90 TL is given as credit. 90 TL taken as a loan enters another bank as a deposit, that bank keeps 10 percent of 90 TL, that is 9 TL, as required reserve and gives the rest 81 TL as loan, these loans continue until they are reset, and as a result, 1000 TL is created, 100 TL of which is required as reserve and 900 TL as credit. These credits, which are created digitally on the screens of the commercial bank's computers and are only 100 TL in return, are actually debts. Besides, if we remember that even 100 TL is fiat (fiat) money, which is issued unlimitedly without being based on any commodity, as mentioned before, we understand that the system creates an illusion of money. Therefore, we can say that in our financial system the cash (fiat) money issued by the central banks is converted into loans in multiple manner in digital environment by commercial banks. If customers request their credits or deposits in cash by going to the bank, it is inevitable for the banks to go bankrupt because such money is not existence in reality (Çetin 2019). As understood here, contrary to popular belief, most of the money (such as 90 percent, 95 percent, 99 percent, in short, as loans created at varying rates based on the required reserve ratios deposited in the central banks of the country) is not produced by the state and its affiliated institutions but rather by private organizations aiming profit. Moreover, the amount of dollars printed as metal coins or issued as banknotes all over the world is approximately 66 trillion dollars, where the required reserve ratio is average 5 percent, with the partial reserve banking system, depending on this amount, digitally generated fiat money is approximately twenty times more than this.

In its current form, the system has been turned into an ideal environment for crises to burst, as mentioned at the beginning. In the old system, when a bank or company goes bankrupt, the state cannot issue extra (unbacked) money to save these banks/companies, as the state issues money based on gold. In this case, banks and corporates have to be extra careful about taking risky steps. Also, they have to save for the rainy days. In the new system, banks, companies, and individuals do not feel the need to save, because in a crisis, they are saved by the unlimited money that is printed by the state without any basis.

CONCLUDING REMARKS

As summarized above, the markets analyzed are mainly stock market, bond, and real estate markets. The resulting financial bubble has reached a global level of 1 quadrillion dollars. Its real asset equivalent in production is approximately one-third. Therefore, the debt created by the loan is not in a position to be paid with current values, and this can be compared to a time bomb. The only difference is that although the exact time cannot be known, it can be predicted by means of analyzing the current situation. While nation-states are in the midst of such an out-of-control danger, it is useful to examine their economic and financial situation.

That is to say, the production systems, based on money, are approaching the end and the production systems, with the wind of rapidly developing technology, will be transformed into a new form based on knowledge. It is clear that this new form will be accelerated or be shaped by a crisis created by the current financial environment. The system will naturally reset itself, and the change will begin to enter its new form. It is inevitable that this new form will be based on knowledge. In a further study, this new situation in which production will transform simultaneously with the systemic collapse of money may be studied. Of course, this will not happen soon. However, the position that nation-states will assume at the beginning of such a transformation will be the answer to the question of what or who will be the determinant.

REFERENCES

Advisors, Green Street. https://www.greenstreet.com/.

Barnett, Vincent. 2015. *Routledge Handbook of the History of Global Economic Thought*. London: Routledge.

Benzie, R. 1992. The Development of the International Bond Market. *BIS Economic Papers, Bank for International Settlements* 32.

Bernanke, Ben. 1990. "Clearing and Settlement during the Crash." *Review of Financial Studies 3* 1: 133–151.

BIS. 2020. Bank for International Settlements, European Central Bank, Federal Reserve Bank of Dallas, Savills and National Sources. www.bis.org.

Bordo, M. D. 2003. "Gold as a Commitment Mechanism: Past, Present and Future," *Gold and the Modern world Economy,* Taylor and Francis, Routledge, London, p. 224.

Bordo, M. D., & Eichengreen, B. (1993). The Bretton Woods International Monetary System: A Historical Overview. *A Retrospective on the Bretton Woods System: Lessons for International Monetary Reform.* University of Chicago Press: Chicago.

Buffet Indicator, 2020. Buffet Indicator (Producer). Retrieved from http://www.currentmarketvaluation.com/models/buffett-indicator.php

Campbell, John Y., and Robert J. Shiller. 1987. "Stock Prices, Earnings, and Expected Dividends." *The Journal of Finance* 43(3): 664.

Carlson, Mark. 2006. A Brief History of the 1987 Stock Market Crash with a Discussion of the Federal Reserve Response. In *Finance and Economics Discussion Series* Washington, DC: Divisions of Research & Statistics and Monetary Affairs, Federal Reserve Board.

Çetin, E. (2019). *Nomisma, Bağımsız ve Milli Para Sistemi*: ALFA., İstanbul.

Elwell, C. K. 2011. *Brief History of the Gold Standard in the United States, Congressional Research Service.* R41887, 7–5700.

Garber, P. M. 2000. *Famous First Bubbles: The Fundamentals of Early Manias.* Cambridge: Cambridge, MA: MIT Press.

Historian, O. 2020. Nixon and the End of the Bretton Woods System, 1971–1973. *Office of the Historian.* https://history.state.gov/milestones/1969-1976/nixon-shock.

Krugman, P., & Wells, R. 2005. *Economics*: Worth Publishers., NewYork.

Maloney, Michael. 2008. *Guide to Investing in Gold and Silver.* New York: Hachette Book Group.

Maloney, Mike, and Jeff Clark. 2018. "Introducing Mike Maloney's Market Fragility Index: What It's Saying Now." *GoldSilver Blog.*

McKibbin, W. 2006. Bursting of the US Housing Bubble. *Bursting of the US Housing Bubble*, 14: 36.

Meltzer, Allan H. 1991. "U.S. Policy in the Bretton Woods Era." *Offsite link Federal Reserve Bank of St. Louis Review* 73(3): 54–83.

Newman, E. (July-August 1952). The 1776 Continental Currency Coinage. *The Coin Collector's Journal*, 1–9, pp.13–14.

Tandy, David. 2004. *Trade and Commerce in Archilochos, Sappho, and Alkaios, MELAMMU V.* Stuttgart: Franz Steiner Verlag.

Tyler, W., & Lukas, S. 2015. Current Evidence on the Resource Costs of Irredeemable Paper Money. *Cato Journal*, 35(2): 2–3.

Wilde, R. (Aug. 27, 2020). The Development of Banking in the Industrial Revolution. *ThoughtCo.,* https://www.thoughtco.com/development-of-banking-the-industrial-revolution-1221645.

Wolfeboro, N. 1991. *NH: Bowers and Merena*, 7–18., The E-Sylum: Volume 15, Number 41, September 30, 2012, Article 21

.

Chapter 7

Intermediary Institutions and COVID-19

A Comprehensive Financial Analysis

Lale Aslan

INTRODUCTION

Intermediary institutions form the foundation of capital markets and financial system functions through the intermediation of parties interested in investing in securities. Having been around for more than thirty years, intermediation is said to have a permanent history in Turkey. Therefore, capital markets are very much in tune with these institutions and any disruption means a hit for the capital markets. The functioning of financial institutions plays an important role in the functioning of capital markets.

The soundness of financial intermediaries has been a concern of governments and academia alike. Since the global crisis of 2008 showed how vulnerable these institutions can be in cases of uncertainty and risk, especially the capital structure of these institutions became a focal point. To secure the health of the financial system, many regulations were updated or enacted from scratch during the past decade in Turkey. Even though these regulations have acted to secure the healthiness of the sector, an unforeseen event has disrupted the world markets: COVID-19 pandemic.

Since financial markets have gained importance with the influence of globalization, advances in international banking and technology, a global crisis such as COVID-19 pandemic is considered to impact the financial markets as workforces are required to obey quarantine rules, and liquidity of real sector declined due to diminished social activities. Governments all over the world took several measures to revive the real sector and financial sector was greatly involved in these measures as well. Therefore, COVID-19-related matters have shown an effect on capital markets and institutions as a result.

In Turkey, the majority of intermediary institutions are subsidiaries of banks, and they are required to oblige with the aforementioned measures.

In this chapter, intermediary institutions in Turkey will be investigated and the effects of COVID-19 on the sector will be researched by analyzing the consolidated financial statements of all brokerage houses established in Turkey. Moreover, the financials of public brokerage houses will be examined separately and compared to the sector in order to present a comprehensive approach. Financial statements of Turkish brokerage houses will be analyzed by comparative financial statements analysis, vertical analysis, trend analysis, and ratio analysis. The diversity in analyses will be providing detailed insight to the sector and how the pandemic has affected the financial situation of capital market institutions.

The chapter consists of the following parts: first, the aim of the analysis is covered, followed by presenting of data and methodology. Finally, the results of the comprehensive financial analyses are presented.

AIM OF ANALYSIS

The financial situation of the sector has been neglected in the studies about the brokerage sector until today, and company-based analyses are not included at all. At the same time, no detailed analysis studies are representing the sector, including the financial structure and problems related to the sector. In this chapter, a detailed financial analysis study has been conducted in order to determine the financial structure and problems of the Turkish brokerage sector based on companies, aiming to evaluate the sector, in general.

This study aims to examine the current position of the sector following the major change in the Capital Market legislation of the brokerage house sector in 2013 and to reveal the financial effects of the COVID-19 outbreak on the brokerage houses that form the backbone of the capital market. For this purpose, a comparison has been made to bring into consideration the similarities and differences between the sector in general and the publicly held brokerage houses.

Developments regarding the financial status and operating results of the brokerage sector as of 2013–2020 have been examined in the analyses. Based on the financial information of enterprises operating at the micro-level, the entire sector has been financially evaluated using comparative financial statements analysis, vertical analysis, trend analysis, and ratio analysis.

DATA AND METHODOLOGY

In this chapter, a detailed financial analysis for Turkish intermediary institutions will be presented to show how COVID-19 pandemic affected these institutions. Comparative financial statements analysis, vertical analysis, ratio analysis, and trend analysis will be applied to consolidated financial statements of the sector for the period starting from Q2 2013 to Q2 2020. The analysis begins with Q2 2013 because all intermediary institutions were required to prepare and announce their financial statements according to International Financial Reporting Standards as of Q2 2013. Consolidated financial statements of the sector are announced to the public by Turkish Capital Markets Association every quarter and all data are inflation-adjusted by using the deflator of the Central Bank of Turkey.

Even though the pandemic started in mid-March, the author expects a limited effect on financial statements as of Q1 2020. Direct effects expected of the pandemic concern profitability, liquidity, credit quality, and workforce (Deloitte 2020). With these analyses, the author aims to present the overall state of the sector and the outlook for the future as the influence of the pandemic is expected to create mandatory changes for institutions.

In the analysis made in order to determine the general economic and financial trend and future situation of the sector, a trend analysis of twenty-eight periods covering the period of Q2 2013–Q2 2020 and ratio analysis for the relevant period were performed. In practice, two parallel studies were conducted based on two separate financial datasets. The first group of the study covers Q2 2013–Q2 2020 period, which consists of the public-made data of all publicly held brokerage firms quoted in Borsa Istanbul (BIST). Parallel analysis for group two, similarly covers the period of Q2 2013–Q2 2020 concerning all of the actively operating brokerage firms established in Turkey. The purpose of the study with two separate datasets is to determine the similarities and differences between the financial structure and trends of the public companies traded on the BIST with the general structure of the sector and to compare the effects of COVID-19 in terms of companies that are traded on the stock exchange and not traded. Thus, while obtaining sector-wide results, the basic financial characteristics of publicly held companies consisting of larger-scale companies were determined.

Financial statements for both groups are consolidated beforehand. In practice, ratio analysis including selected ratios and trend analysis, which investigates specific financial and economic trends and the relationships between them, were performed using the available data for both groups. While interpreting the data obtained as a result of both applications, it was expressed as "intermediation sector" or "brokerage sector" interchangeably.

The dataset of all companies included in the analysis consists of quarterly balance sheets and income statements for the period between Q2 2013 and Q2 2020. Data were obtained from the announced reports by Capital Market Association of Turkey. Consolidated financial statements were prepared for each period. In the preparation of the consolidated statements, the relationship of the companies with each other has not been taken into account.

In order to reduce the effects of Turkish Lira price changes on the consolidated balance sheets and to reflect the real situation, the prices were brought to Q2 2020 level by using the Central Bank of Turkey's deflator for each quarter during the implementation period. Q2 2013 was chosen as the base period for trend analysis. Relationships between selected financial statement items are investigated in ratio analysis. These include short term trade receivables - net sales, current assets - net sales, financial investments - net sales, current assets - short term liabilities, operating profit - net sales, total liabilities - equity.

FINDINGS

Before the analysis results are presented, information on the application framework and basic indicators will be provided in order to make a sound evaluation of the sector.

The number of brokerage houses traded in Borsa Istanbul between 2013 and 2020 corresponds to 8 percent of the sector. During this period, there was no change in the number of brokerage houses traded on the stock exchange. On the other hand, there has been a dramatic change in the total number of brokerage houses operating in the sector. While ninety-five companies were operating in the sector in 2013, this number decreased to sixty-one in 2020. At the end of 2012, the entry of the Capital Market Law No. 6263 and the increase of the minimum capital amount of the brokerage houses depending on the activities of the intermediary institutions within the framework of the provisions of this law and its related sub-regulations stands out as the reason for the dramatic change in the number of intermediary institutions.

The effect of the amendment made at the end of 2012 caused intermediary institutions to be merged or closed between 2014 and 2019, after the transition period granted by the Capital Markets Board (CMB). The 36 percent decrease in the total number of companies in the sector increased the rate of publicly traded companies in the sector to 8 percent.

Average asset size calculated using the Central Bank deflator represents the average firm size. Besides, the data have been converted into dollars from the June 30, 2020, exchange rate. Although the asset size of public brokerage houses is high, the asset size of the sector is much higher. The asset size of public companies constitutes 34 percent of the industry total. Furthermore, asset sizes were USD 1,268,418,394 in the publicly held brokerage firms for Q2 2013, the asset size of the sector was USD 3,761,820,750 in the same period. In Q2 2020, the asset size of publicly traded brokerage firms was

USD 1,196,863,308, while the sector asset size of the same period was USD 483,836,134. The increase and decrease of assets in both groups of companies follow a cyclical course. The average asset growth rate of public companies for the period of Q2 2013–Q2 2020 was 2 percent, while the average asset growth rate of the sector for the same period was 5 percent. The asset growth rate of the sector and publicly traded companies can express a cyclical contraction and expansion. While there was a contraction in 2015 and 2016, there was a growth in 2017, a contraction in 2019 and a growth again in 2020.

Sales revenues of public companies and sector companies move in an opposite cyclical direction when compared to the asset size. Moreover, sales revenues are also dependent on the trade volume of the sector. It is observed that sales revenues decreased in 2014, 2017, and 2020, when the total assets increased, and the sales revenues increased in 2015, 2016, and 2019, when the total assets decreased. This situation is thought to be closely related to the general macroeconomic situation and the liquidity status of the market. In the period when the liquidity is high in the market, the tendency of investors to the stock market increases and the sales revenue of intermediary institutions also increase. During periods of liquidity shortage in the market, interest in brokerage houses decreases and sales revenues decrease as a result. While the average sales growth rate of public brokerage houses in the 2013–2020 period was 17 percent, the growth rate of the average sales of the sector for the same period was 13 percent. Public firms seem to have a higher potential to increase their sales. Sales revenues decreased by 17 percent for the sector in 2014, decreased by 6 percent in 2015, increased by 8 percent in 2016, decreased by 39 percent in 2017, increased 11 percent in 2018, increased by 124 percent in 2019 and increased by 10 percent in 2020. Public brokerage houses, on the other hand, are affected more acutely by sales revenue changes. Especially in 2018 and 2020, public brokerage houses are negatively differentiated from the sector in general.

While the transaction volume for publicly traded companies decreased only in 2017 and 2018, it is seen that this picture was repeated for the sector in general. While the 2013–2020 average transaction volume growth rate of public brokerage houses was 13 percent, this rate was 17 percent for sector companies. While the peak period of the transaction volume in terms of the sector was in the second quarter of 2015, this level has not been achieved in the transaction volume despite the increases seen after this date. The trading volume of brokerage houses traded on the stock exchange corresponds to 16 percent of the sector's trading volume. This amount is significant but does not approach the majority of the transaction volume. When the relationship between transaction volume and sales revenue is analyzed, a parallel course is observed. Between the second quarter of 2017—when the transaction volume shrunk—and the second quarter of 2019, there is also a contraction in sales revenue. Sector-wide sales revenue declined in Q2 2017, recovered in Q2 2019, and even surpassed Q2 2013. However, the transaction volume level for public brokerage houses did not reach the Q2 2016 level, where it peaked until Q2 2020. Sales revenue, on the other hand, increased in Q2 2019 but fell again in Q2 2020.

The financial structure of the sector is also based on activity. Generally, the activity structure of brokerage houses requires very short-term loan usage such as two or three days. During Q2 2017, when the transaction volume decreased, the use of short-term loans increased for both publicly traded brokerage houses and the sector in general. Short-term debts decreased in the following periods; however, in Q2 2020, there is an increase in short-term debts again. It is believed that the low-interest loans reflected on the financial markets especially during the COVID-19 period. As of Q2 2020, the short-term debt amount of the sector is 3.5 billion USD. While the average growth rate of the sector's short-term debt was 6 percent, this rate was 1 percent for public brokerage houses. Although the amount of long-term debt in the sector remained quite low compared to short-term debt, a significant increase was achieved in this item during the analysis period. In Q2 2019, the long-term debt item, which was generally low, increased by 104 percent in public companies and 525 percent in the financial sector. In the following period, the long-term debt ratio, which increased in public companies, increased by 53 percent and decreased by 78 percent throughout the sector. As of Q2 2020, the long-term debt amount of the sector is approximately 47 million USD, while the total long-term debt of public companies is approximately 8.5 million USD.

One of the most important items related to the debt structure of brokerage houses is financial expenses. Financing expenses of public brokerage houses do not contain much fluctuation and are approximately constant. It is not possible to expect the same situation for the sector in general. Financing expenses of the sector, in general, are very volatile. While the average growth rate of financing expenses is 1 percent for public companies, it is 31 percent for the sector. For the sector, financing expenses in the period of Q2 2017–Q2 2019 increased considerably, then started to decrease as of Q2 2020. In Q2 2020, the financing expense of publicly traded brokerage houses was approximately 4.3 million USD, while it was 75 million USD for the sector.

Equity levels of brokerage houses are important as they guarantee the healthy functioning of these institutions. Brokerage houses are obliged to comply with the limits set by the Capital Markets Board of Turkey for this purpose. Nevertheless, it is striking that brokerage houses hold much more capital than the minimum capital requirement. In general, a slight increase trend is observed in equity amounts on a year-over-year basis. When compared with the short- and long-term debt structure, it is observed that brokerage houses hold a much higher share of equity than the regulation requires. For Q2 2020, the average equity amount of publicly traded brokerage houses is USD 36,188,820, while the industry average is USD 17,948,798. It is estimated that the reason for the higher equity level of public brokerage houses is the higher transaction volume and a higher number of customers.

Financial intermediation sector is one of the important sectors which is constantly increasing in terms of profitability. Especially in recent years, increased public interest in stock market investments, in turn, increased the income of these institutions. However, the gradual decrease in the number of institutions in the sector has been a major factor in increasing profitability for existing brokerage houses. The shrinkage experienced in the sector, especially after Q2 2013, caused a decrease in the profitability rates, and the sector recovered after two years. In the period when COVID-19 was dominant, the profitability of brokerage houses was not affected, on the contrary, profitability increased. In the analysis period of public brokerage houses, the average growth rate of net profit for the period was 33 percent, while the same rate for the sector was 29 percent. As of Q2 2020, the net profit of public brokerage houses is 65 million USD, and the net profit of the sector is 267 million USD.

Overall trend analysis indicates that total assets of the sector have stayed consistent over the years, although the last two quarters seem higher than usual. When the breakdown of assets according to their maturity is considered, it is possible to see that intermediary institutions have managed their fixed assets to cover for their lack of current assets with the beginning of 2019. The year 2019 was problematic with many uncertainties and 2020 just added more to it with the COVID-19 pandemic. Therefore, the liquidity shortage was covered by liquidizing the fixed assets. Intermediary institutions seem to manage their need for liquidity by using their long-term portfolio and turning it into cash over the last year. Likewise, short-term liabilities have stayed consistent through the years, just barely rising in 2017. However, long-term liabilities show a peak in the first quarter of 2016, the third quarter of 2016, between the fourth quarter of 2018, and the second quarter of 2019. This is an indicator of an economic shock and a reflection of the currency deficiency in the economy.

In general, the total assets of brokerage houses show a stable course, while their cash and cash equivalents show a stable outlook, except for a relatively small increase of 150 percent in the period 2016–2017. Short-term financial assets act in direct opposition to cash and cash equivalents. Between 2016 and 2017, when cash and cash equivalents increased, there was a decrease at approximately the same rate in short term financial assets. During the epidemic period, while cash and cash equivalents decreased, short-term financial assets increased by 150 percent. While there was a trend close to cash and cash equivalents in the receivable accounts until 2019, there was an increase in the trade receivables despite the decrease in cash and cash equivalents after this date. The reason for this may be that investors want to overcome the cash congestion caused by COVID-19 in the market by using loans.

Net revenue and cost of sales lines completely coincide, and a highly volatile course is observed. Net sales revenues and cost of sales peak at the end of the year. This situation reflects the profit management efforts of brokerage houses to melt their portfolios to show high revenues in their year-end balance sheets. Especially at the end of 2019, a considerably higher rate of sales revenue compared to other years can be seen. Despite the decrease in sales in 2017 and 2018 compared to previous years, a significant increase trend is observed in the rate of net profit. The net profit rate has increased by 400 percent in the last quarter of 2019. Even if there is a drop by half in the first quarter of 2020—there is a similar decrease seen at the beginning of each period—it has reached the end of 2019 again in the second quarter. In this profitability, as a result of the decrease in deposit interest rates in Turkish economy, the effects of investors' orientation to the stock market, gold, and foreign currency, and an increase in the incomes of brokerage houses and thus their net profits is felt.

When looking at the relationship between net sales revenues, EBIT, and total assets, although total assets generally display a stable outlook, EBIT ratios are highly volatile and similar to the net profit margin mentioned above, there are particularly peaks at the end of each the year and especially at the end of 2017, 2018, and 2019. On the other hand, although net sales decreased in 2017 and 2018, the EBIT rate has increased significantly in the last three years.

In the ratio analysis part, primarily the liquidity structure of the sector will be examined. Considering the development of the current ratio since Q2 2013, it is below the traditionally accepted ratio value of 2. While it is in the 1.2–1.4 band for the sector in general, the current ratio of public brokerage houses is in the range of 1.1–1.2. Interestingly, in the second quarter of 2020, the last period of the analysis, the current ratio of the sector decreased, while that of publicly traded companies increased. The quick ratio values are quite different from the table drawn by the current ratio. It is observed that the effect of receivables is quite a determinant for public brokerage houses. For this reason, the quick ratio value of public brokerage houses has moved around 1.8 for a long time. However, it has decreased especially since 2020 and has decreased to 1.5. For the sector, there is a fixed course at 1.2. In this case, it is seen that the receivable level of the sector is lower compared to public brokerage houses. Analysis of the cash ratio values of the sector shows that cash is kept at a higher level compared to public brokerage houses. Even if the cash levels of public brokerage houses are slightly lower than the sector average, the movement of the cash ratio develops in parallel with the sector.

A sharp decline has been observed for both groups since the last quarter of 2018. The sector, in general, declined from 0.9 to 0.58 and for the public brokerage houses decline started at 0.73 and ended in 0.34. This shows that the cash reduction available in the sector has become even more serious during the COVID-19 period.

Finally, when the net working capital levels for the two groups are analyzed, the net working capital of public brokerage houses generally hovers around TRY 800 million, but in 2020, it entered an increasing trend and reached TRY 1.3 million. Net working capital, which has a fluctuating course for the sector, also appears to be in an increasing trend in 2020. Among the previous findings, it was noted that the cash amount of the sector is gradually decreasing, and trade receivables are seen as the source of the increase in net working capital. This situation indicates that the sector is going through a loan-based expansion.

Next, the activity ratios of the sector and public brokerage houses are examined. From the current asset turnover ratio, it can be observed that the graph values of the sector and public brokerage houses almost coincide. Only in 2019, the current asset turnover rate of publicly traded brokerage houses doubled, and in 2020, it reached the level of the sector again. Current asset turnover rate shows how much revenue brokerage houses generate with current asset levels. In this case, 2019 stands out as a period in which much higher income is generated in terms of assets compared to 2020. The same graph with the current asset turnover ratio is also valid for the total asset turnover ratios. However, when the equity turnover ratio is analyzed, it is clear that the equity turnover ratio of the sector approaches half of the turnover rate of public brokerage houses. This situation shows that public brokerage houses have a higher return on equity than the sector in general. However, from 2016 to 2018, there was a 50 percent decrease in the equity turnover of publicly traded companies, this period was followed by a peak period in 2019 and a decline period with COVID-19 in 2020. Compared to this, although the equity turnover ratio is lower throughout the sector, a more stable course is observed. A very similar structure is also valid for working capital turnover ratio. The receivable turnover ratio, which is the last efficiency ratio examined, draws a very different picture between the sector and public brokerage houses. The receivable turnover ratio of the sector, which is very low, fluctuates according to the periods, it moves cyclically between 5 and 50. Although the receivables turnover ratio of public brokerage houses also moves cyclically, they reach quite high peak values at the end of the period. The highest value of this cycle was 352 in the last quarter of 2016 and the lowest value was 6 in the first quarter of 2018. Starting from the beginning of 2020, a new cycle begins for the sector and public brokerage houses.

When solvency ratios are considered, it is striking that the brokerage sector carries a high rate of debt. While the total debt ratio develops in the range of 70 percent and 75 percent for the sector as a whole, for public brokerage houses, this ratio varies between 80 percent and 90 percent. When the maturity structure of debts is examined, for both sector in general and public brokerage houses, the majority of this debt is short-term. Although this ratio decreased to 92 percent periodically for the sector in general, it increased to 99 percent again by 2020. While debt is carried about three times the equity in the sector, in public brokerage houses, this ratio increases to 9 at the end of 2018, then decreases to four times the equity by 2020. While the financial leverage ratio for the entire sector is generally around 4, the financial leverage ratio for public brokerage firms increased to 10 until half of 2018 and then decreased to 5.4 in 2020. Until 2016, the interest coverage rates of the sector and public brokerage houses did not remain very high. The sector's interest coverage ratio started to rise only after the end of 2019. For public brokerage houses, this ratio increased three times by the end of 2016 and reached 18 by peaking in 2020. This indicates that the profitability of publicly traded brokerage houses has increased significantly and borrowing costs have decreased with the increase in the profitability of the sector. In general, the preference for short-term borrowing in the sector stems from its activity structure.

Between Q2 2013 and Q4 2018, the gross profitability of the industry and public brokerage houses showed an upward trend; however, with the end of 2018, a sudden contraction occurred in gross profitability ratios. With the end of 2019, the industry has started to recover. However, operating profitability, which started to increase at the end of 2016, as in the gross profitability ratio, fell sharply at the end of 2018 and entered a recovery trend at the end of 2019. The pre-tax profit ratio and the net profit ratio of the sector and publicly traded brokerage houses fluctuated during the analysis period; however, they follow a trend similar to that of gross profit and operating profit. As of the second quarter of 2020, the net profit ratio of public brokerage houses and the sector was 6 per thousand. While the financial expenses/revenue ratio followed a stable course at very low levels for public brokerage houses, it followed a very volatile course for the sector in general, peaking at 1.2 percent in Q1 2019; however, as of 2020, it started to decline quite rapidly and approached public brokerage houses. The sector's return on equity shows a cyclical course. Return on equity peaks at the end of each year and declines sharply at the beginning of the following year. As of the second quarter of 2020, the sector's return on equity was 2 percent, while the return on equity of public brokerage houses was 3 percent. Considering that the equity amount of public brokerage houses has two times more equity than the sector average, the high profitability ratio indicates that these institutions perform more effective capital management. Return on assets of the sector is affected by cyclical fluctuations and still shows an increasing trend, albeit slowly. As of the second quarter of 2020, return on assets was 6 percent in the sector and 5.5 percent in public brokerage houses. Despite the decrease in the total value of the assets compared to 2017, the increase in the asset profitability is perceived as an indication of the more efficient use of assets.

Although the return on capital employed also includes cyclical fluctuations, it is realized at a much higher rate for public brokerage houses when compared to the whole sector. As of the second quarter of 2020, permanent return on total capital is approximately 22 percent for the sector and 32 percent for public brokerage houses. The reason for the fluctuations in the aforementioned periods is that the companies in the sector generally sell their short-term financial assets at the end of the year and show high profitability figures in the year-end income statement. In this way, brokerage houses and their managers can present a bright situation in terms of year-end financial statements, and they can gain higher annual premiums.

CONCLUSION

Brokerage sector is an important actor in capital markets, and sound capital markets can exist with strong intermediary institutions. In this chapter, the researcher investigated the financial statements of Turkish brokerage sector between Q2 2013 and Q2 2020 for trends and the effects of coronavirus. The following are the key takeaways from the analysis.

* The change brought in capital adequacy levels with the regulation update in 2013 has resulted in condensation in the number of institutions in the sector.

* Asset sizes are highly affected by cyclical fluctuations. There was an expansion between 2013 and 2015, contraction between 2015 and 2016, expansion in 2017, contraction in 2019 and expansion again in 2020. The expansion in 2020 has been an important factor in the profitability of the sector, with the increase of cash directed to the capital market with the effect of the loans given to the market within the scope of coronavirus measures.

* Brokerage houses are well-informed of the cyclical movements in the capital markets and the behavior of investors as they are successfully managing their assets to cover for contraction periods when income is scarce. Therefore, it has been possible for the sector to provide a constant profit margin for their shareholders.

* Due to the nature of the sector's activities, institutions prefer to borrow short term. This situation brings a significant amount of financial burden to the sector. Although the sector, in general, is good at meeting financing

expenses, public brokerage houses can meet their financing expenses more easily with their higher profitability.

* The capital adequacy of intermediary institutions is handled quite well. The sector's average equity amount is quite above the minimum level specified in CMB regulations. This situation shows that the sector has strengthened its financial structure within the framework of the measures taken after the 2008 credit crisis.

* The negative effects of the coronavirus on the industry include a decrease in equity turnover, low financial expenses/revenue ratio, low quick rate, and low debt levels. Profitability ratios are among the areas not affected by coronavirus pandemic. The decrease in current asset amounts suggests that the sector sold the short-term financial investments in order to maintain profitability levels.

REFERENCE

Deloitte. 2020. "How COVID-19 infects financial reporting and results presentations." Accessed October 10, 2020. https://www2.deloitte.com/ch/en/pages/audit/articles/financial-reporting-survey-q1-2020.html.

Chapter 8

Dream of Japanification

A Pandemic-Based Analysis

Cem Berk

INTRODUCTION

Chorofas (2011) defines Japanification as those events that faced Japanese economy in the last three decades. However, these events are also seen today in many developed economies. For a developed economy, consequences may reflect in the form of an interest rate below 0.5 percent, economic growth average of 1 percent, a drop in the performance of industrial businesses, an increase in unemployment and a drop in inflation (possibly deflation) particularly real estate prices.

One of the primary focuses of Japanification is that its effects have been more visible following the pandemics. Ando et al. (2020) investigate emergency budgets of Japanese government during COVID-19 crisis. The budget includes monetary aids for households, loan expansions, and subsidies.

A characteristic effect of Japanification is the negative interest rates. Khoury and Pal (2020) show the benefits of negative interest for various agents. Accordingly, governments can borrow to stabilize budget deficits. Banks can also implement regulatory compliances more easily.

As a result of Japanification, most of the world is experiencing deflation. Kichikawa et al. (2020) point out that deflation combined with low interest rates is a threat for the economy. Despite quantitative easing, it is often difficult to reach the target inflation. They found that inflation is correlated with the exchange rate and price of crude oil.

The Japanese currency, Yen, has been an important currency but is not a world currency to trade with. The 1985 Plaza Agreement is an important milestone in Japanification. Belke and Volz (2020) claim that the agreement a result of political pressure exerted by the United States. As a result, the U.S. companies gained competitive advantage due to the Yen appreciation.

Japan was also hit by several natural disasters. The 2011 Earthquake is most notable for Japanification. As Estrada et al. (2020) point out, the earthquake took place in northeast Japan. It is followed by a Tsunami and destruction of power plants. These have seriously damaged the economic performance of Japan.

Abenomics is one of the fundamental elements associated with Japanification. According to Grabrowiecki and Dabrovski (2017), Abenomics is based on the reforms proposed by Shinzo Abe in 2012. The practice includes public expenditures, weakening Yen, and favoring private industry by practices such as lowering corporate taxes and deregulation. They claim that these practices were insufficient due to the unfavorable population structure of Japan.

Shinzo Abe is an important figure for Japanification. Prezedicka et al. (2019) point out that Economic Partnership Agreement signed by Abe in 2018 with Europe is a significant agreement of European Union. This includes removal of customs duties and elimination of barriers between the participants. However, it can also be associated with the Euroification which occurred in most European countries.

This population disadvantage is elaborated in many different studies. As Nguyen (2020) points out, the average age in Japan is 48.4 by 2020. Moreover, there is an increasing trend in average age and decreasing trend in birth rate in the past five years. Only 23 percent of the population is between fifteen and sixty-four years of age. On the one hand, it is difficult to find the right resources for the right job, on the other hand, maintaining the advanced age population with social security costs the exchequer dearly. For businesses, this means decreased demand, forcing the companies to produce less or outsource. This also has a deflationary effect.

Bank of Japan (BoJ) is one of the most important economic actors among central banks. Shioji (2020) says that BoJ applied Quantitative and Qualitative Easing (QQE). Despite eight times increase in central bank reserves, loans given by banks did not increase much. This shows that overall the actions of BoJ are ineffective.

The risk-taking behavior of Japan's businesses has been quite conservative. This is also an important factor contributing to Japanification. Mutoh et al. (2020) studied the overseas contractors in Japan. They found paradoxical behavior while operating overseas. Companies prefer to go overseas only when they try to rescue their business from financial distress.

The aim of this chapter is to analyze the effects of Japanification based on capital markets. The markets analyzed in this research are Nikkei (Japan), Standard & Poor's (US), Financial Times Stock Exchange (UK), Hang Seng Index (Hong Kong), and Borsa Istanbul (Turkey).

The remainder of the chapter is organized as follows. The next section is a review of important works in literature. Data and methodology section covers the details of the data and methodology used in the research. Solutions and recommendations section include elaboration of research findings. Finally, the conclusion section includes the final remarks.

LITERATURE REVIEW

Credit default swap (CDS) is a financial instrument by which payment is made to investors when the issuer of a security defaults. It is also commonly used as an indicator of sovereign risk. Guo et al. (2020) proved that there are co-movements in CDS prices in Asia. This is true for both emerging and developed economies. The research period is 2011–2014. The data include CDS prices of ten Asian countries including Japan. The research methodology includes a Granger causality analysis and news diffusion model. Accordingly, CDS spreads in Kazakhstan predict other Asian economies. Information diffusion can explain this relationship. Kazakhstan's spreads also have out-of-sample predictive power for other countries. The possible reasons for these findings are Kazakhstan's rating, cultural linkages with Europe, and the issuer of the bond which is an energy company.

There are also spillovers from Asia to Europe, the United States, and the rest of the world. Fukuda and Tanaka (2020) explore the spillovers from Asia to the developed economies. They develop GVAR models and then analyze variance decomposition. They find that spillovers from Asia to advanced economies are smaller than those from advanced economies to Asia. Among industries, manufacturing industry spillovers are larger than banking sector. Stock market spillovers are also experienced.

Citing some studies focused on Japan: Wang et al. (2020) analyzed the link between treasury spreads and economic policy uncertainty (EPU) in Japan. The data obtained is between 1990 and 2019. They develop non-linear autoregressive distributed lags model (NARDL). The results show that a long-term relationship exists between treasury spreads and EPU. Due to the economic environment since 1990 (low interest and low economic growth), financial markets are more sensitive to negative shocks. Unconventional monetary policy plays an important role in bond and stock markets.

Some studies focus on the capital flows between countries. Özyesil (2020) studies portfolio investments, Uncovered Equity parity, in particular. For this, capital flows, stock index, and exchange rate data are used. The countries in the study are Japan, South Korea, and Turkey. The long-term results show that first stage and third stage of UEP is valid for Japan and Turkey, whereas second stage of UEP is valid for South Korea.

Academic works focusing on Japanification is very limited. Koeda and Sekine (2020) made a Nelson Siegel yield curve analysis for bond markets. The results show that the decay factor has been reduced, which is a downward pressure for the entire yield curve. The long-term premium is reduced by negative decay factor shocks. Possible explanations are BoJ's long-term bond purchases and factors contributing to economic growth.

DATA AND METHODOLOGY

The data used in this research are major indices of stock markets of different countries. The capital market of Japan is a dependent variable while that of the United States, the United Kingdom, Hong Kong, and Turkey are independent variables. More specifically, the indices used in the research are Nikkei 225(N225), Standard and Poor's 500 (SP500), Financial Times Stock Exchange 100(FTSE100), Hang Seng Index (HSI), Borsa Istanbul Industrial (XSIST).

The growth of the variables is used instead of raw data. The growth values are calculated with the following formulas:

$$gN225 = \log\left(N225_t \,/\, N225_{t-1}\right) * 100$$

$$gSP500 = \log\left(SP500_t \,/\, SP500_{t-1}\right) * 100$$

$$gFTSE100 = \log\left(FTSE100_t \,/\, FTSE100_{t-1}\right) * 100$$

$$gHSI = \log\left(HSI_t \,/\, HSI_{t-1}\right) * 100$$

$$gXSIST = \log\left(XSIST_t \,/\, XSIST_{t-1}\right) * 100$$

RESULTS

The first analysis of the research is constants and trends. When terms of constant and trend are examined, it is found that the XSIST variable has a trend.

The next analysis is to check whether any structural break exists. It was found that no structural breaks exist.

The stationarity of the variables should be tested before proceeding with model estimation. For this purpose, the stationarities of variables are analyzed by Augmented Dickey Fuller (ADF) and Philips Perron (PP) tests. Upon analysis, it is determined that all variables are stationary at level. All variables in the study are found as I (0). This is enough to build a VAR model.

Before constructing vector autoregression model (VAR), lag length selection criteria are analyzed. In order to determine the lag length, LR test was conducted to determine 4 lag length, whereas Final Prediction Error, Akaike and Hannan-Quinn test statistics determine 2 lag length as the most appropriate lag length, while Schwarz test statistics determines 0 lag length. When all the test results are evaluated together, model is built with 2 lag lengths because all three tests jointly give the same lag lengths.

Vector autoregression model with substituted coefficients is given below. VAR (2) model is developed.

$$GN\,225 = -0.034 * GN\,255_{(-1)} + 0.042 * GN\,225_{(-2)}$$

$$-0.017 * GSP500_{(-1)} - 0.002 * GSP500_{(-2)} - 0.016 * GFTSE100_{(-1)}$$

$$+0.018 * GFTSE100_{(-2)} + 0.030 * GHSI_{(-1)} + 0.034 * GHSI_{(-2)}$$

$$+0.018 * GXSIST_{(-1)} - 0.009 * GXSIST_{(-2)} - 0.017$$

$$GSP500 = -0001 * GN\,225_{(-1)} + 0.020 * GN\,225_{(-2)}$$

$$-0.144 * GSP500_{(-1)} + 0.055 * GSP500_{(-2)}$$

$$+0.010 * GFTSE100_{(-1)} + 0.107 * GFTSE100_{(-2)}$$

$$-0.019 * GHSI_{(-1)} + 0.015 * GHSI_{(-2)} + 0.039 * GXSIST_{(-1)}$$

$$+0.014 * GXSIST_{(-2)} - 0.024$$

$$GFTSE100 = 0.001 * GN\,225_{(-1)} - 0.003 * GN\,225_{(-2)}$$

$$-0.024 * GSP500_{(-1)} - 0.016 * GSP500_{(-2)}$$

$$+0.0002 * GFTSE100_{(-1)} - 0.017 * GFTSE_{(-2)}$$

$$\text{—} | | | | | \backslash \, | | . \text{rl} \, | | \, _{(=1)} \text{—} | | | | | \, | \, \text{ll} \, . \text{rl} \, | | \, _{(=2)}$$

$$+0.046 * GXSIST_{(-1)} - 0.012 * GXSIST_{(-2)} - 0.008$$

$$GHSI = 0.006 * GN225_{(-1)} - 0.042 * GN225_{(-2)} + 0.002 * GSP500_{(-1)}$$

$$+0.073 * GSP500_{(-2)} - 0.007 * GFTSE100_{(-1)}$$

$$+0.083 * GFTSE100_{(-2)} + 0.014 * GHSI_{(-1)}$$

$$+0.005 * GHSI_{(-2)} - 0.008 * GXSIST_{(-1)}$$

$$+0.001 * GXSIST_{(-2)} - 0.007$$

$$GXSIST = -0.004 * GN225_{(-1)} - 0.009 * GN225_{(-2)} + 0.168 * GSP500_{(-1)}$$

$$+0.164 * GSP500_{(-2)} + 0.077 * GFTSE100_{(-1)}$$

$$-0.014 * GFTSE100_{(-2)} + 0.038 * GHSI_{(-1)} + 0.003 GHSI_{(-2)}$$

$$-0.008 * GXSIST_{(-1)} + 0.036 * GXSIST_{(-2)} - 0.016$$

The inverse AR roots obtained from the VAR (2) model created in the study are within the unit circle, therefore it can be said that the model created is stable. In the analysis, all inverse roots of AR are also checked.

Cointegration analysis is made based on VAR model. Accordingly, there are five cointegrating vectors which mean long-run relationship between variables.

Vector error correction model (VECM) is developed for short-run analysis. The model with substituted coefficients is given below.

$$D(GN225)$$

$$=-0.004 * \left(\begin{array}{l} GN225_{(1)} - 11.495 * GSP500_{(-1)} + 1.818 * GFTSE100_{(-1)} \\ +1.297 * GHSI_{(-1)} + 6.711 * GXSIST_{(-1)} - 0.068 \end{array} \right)$$

$$-0.533 * D(GN225_{(-1)}) - 0.0315 * D(GSP500_{(-1)})$$

$$-0.018 * D(GFTSE100_{(-1)}) + 0.007 * D(GHSI_{(-1)})$$

$$+0.032 * D(GXSIST_{(-1)}) - 0.0003$$

$$D\left(GSP500\right)$$

$$= 0.064 * \begin{pmatrix} GN\,225_{(-1)} - 11.495 * GSP500_{(-1)} + 1.818 * GFTSE100_{(-1)} \\ + 1.297 * GHSI_{(-1)} + 6.710 * GXSIST_{(-1)} - 0.068 \end{pmatrix}$$

$$-0.044 * D\left(GN\,225_{(-1)}\right) - 0.222 * D\left(GSP500_{(-1)}\right)$$

$$-0.105 * D\left(GFTSE100_{(-1)}\right) - 0.056 * D\left(GHSI_{(-1)}\right)$$

$$-0.209 * D\left(GXSIST_{(-1)}\right) - 0.0004$$

$$\left(GFTSE100\right)$$

$$= -0.004 * \begin{pmatrix} GN\,225_{(-1)} - 11.495 * GSP500_{(-1)} + 1.818 * GFTSE100_{(-1)} \\ + 1.297 * GHSI_{(-1)} + 6.710 * GXSIST_{(-1)} - 0.068 \end{pmatrix}$$

$$+0.006 * D\left(GN\,225_{(-1)}\right) - 0.030 * D\left(GSP500_{(-1)}\right)$$

$$-0.488 * D\left(GFTSE100_{(-1)}\right) + 0.003 * D\left(GHSI_{(-1)}\right)$$

$$+0.033 * D(GXSIST_{(-1)}) + 1.615e--05$$

$$D\left(GHSI\right)$$

$$= -0.016 * \begin{pmatrix} GN\,225_{(-1)} - 11.495 * GSP500_{(-1)} + 1.818 * GFTSE100_{(-1)} \\ + 1.297 * GHSI_{(-1)} + 6.711 * GXSIST_{(-1)} - 0.068 \end{pmatrix}$$

$$+0.029 * D\left(GN\,225_{(-1)}\right) - 0.068) + 0.029 * D(GN\,225_{(-1)})$$

$$-0.124 * D(GSP500_{(-1)}) - 0.033 * D(GFTSE100_{(-1)})$$

$$0.105 * D(GHSI_{(-1)}) + 0.010 * D(GXSIST_{(-1)}) \quad 0.0001$$

Table 8.1   Granger Causality Result

Dependent/Independent	gN225	gSP500	gFTSE100	gHSI	gXSIST
gN225	–	0,2140	0,3741	0,6602	0,0975
gSP500	0,0001	–	0	0	0
gFTSE100	0,6328	0,1259	–	0,8204	0,0280
gHSI	0,0446	0	0,0833	–	0,0254
gXSIST	0,0134	0	0	0	–

Source: Calculated by author.

$$D\left(GXSIST\right)$$

$$= -0.064 * \begin{pmatrix} GN\,225_{(-1)} - 11.495*GSP500_{(-1)} + 1.818*GFTSE100_{(-1)} \\ +1.297*GHSI_{(-1)} + 6.711*GXSIST_{(-1)} - 0.068 \end{pmatrix}$$

$$+0.033 * D(GN\,225_{(-1)}) - 0.356 * D(GSP500_{(-1)})$$

$$+0.108 * D(GFTSE100_{(-1)}) + 0.06 * D(GHSI_{(-1)})$$

$$-0.310 * D(GXSIST_{(-1)}) - 0.0004$$

Finally, Granger causality analysis is made to check the short-run relationships. The results are given in table 8.1. Accordingly, no variables Granger causes gN255. All variables Granger cause gSP500. Only gXSIST Granger causes gFTSE100. All variables except gSP500 Granger cause gHSI. All variables Granger cause gXSIST.

CONCLUSION

Japan followed a Keynesian approach in the economy. According to Chapman and Kulkarni (2020), a decline in interest rates may trigger growth. However, due to limited domestic demand, this is difficult to achieve. A liquidity trap occurs when the interest rates approach zero. Keynesian theory suggests the only way to get out of this situation is fiscal easing.

An important aspect for countries facing Japanification is to focus on exports. Zufarovich et al. (2020) reveal that Japan's international trade is mostly based on Asia Pacific Region. There are also interactions with China, the United States, and Republic of Korea. Japan might expand its markets if it chooses to focus on trades with Russia.

Grimes (2020) explains in the review of the book *Japan's New Regional Reality: Geoeconomic Strategy* by Saori Katada that Japan is no longer the neomercalist economy but a liberal one. The major reason for this transformation is globalization and the growth of China. The process however was not easy. Altura et al. (2021) explain how Airbnb and Uber entered Japan. Prime Minister Abe had to face resistance to deregulation.

Japan however does not gain the most from globalization. As Manhas (2020) points out how following a liberalization program, India grew 9.7 percent in 2008. This makes India, the third largest economic power in the world, ahead of Japan.

Japan also does not have the best labor market. According to Lozano (2020), there is more demand in labor market than supply due to the aged population in Japan. This makes the economy not realize its potential. One of the direct ways to deal with this is to accept immigrants in Japan.

One of the common problems with countries facing Japanification is income inequality. Chakraborty et al. (2020) argue that Japan also has regional inequality in addition to income equality. However, there is an opportunity hidden in this problem. The economic performance of Japan can be increased by investments that help to generate equality in the economy.

Another issue with Japan is that it does not have the best competitive power based on entrepreneurship and digital innovations. Aujirapongpan et al. (2020) argue that the way to increase competitive power in Japan is to invest in e-commerce and e-payment fields.

The COVID-19 experience showed that the economies lacked necessary precautions for the periods of crises. Hutchinson (2020) emphasizes that economies with better fiscal discipline can act more effectively in crises.

The experience of Japan is very important for the rest of the world since Japanification takes place in most developed economies. Most of the solutions indicated above for Japan can also be applied for countries facing Japanification.

An empirical analysis is available in the research. Accordingly, the capital market of Japan affects the capital markets of the United States, Hong Kong, and Turkey. That is to say, Japanification occurs in these countries. But there is no statistically significant Japanification effect seen in the capital market of the United Kingdom according to the data.

The research is limited to few academic studies on Japanification. The results show evidence on Japanification in three of the four countries analyzed. The future research in this field might include other macroeconomic variables and markets.

REFERENCES

Altura T.G., Hashimoto Y., Jacoby S.M., Kanai K., and Saguchi K., 2021. "Japan Meets the Sharing Economy: Contending Frames," *Social Science Japan Journal*, 24(1), 137–161.

Ando M., Chishio F., Nakata D., and Sumiya K., 2020. "Fiscal Responses to the COVID-19 Crisis in Japan: The First Six Months," *National Tax Journal*, 73(3) 901–926.

Aujirapongpan S., Songkajorn Y., Ritkaew S., and Sirichai D., 2020. "Japan's Digital Advance Policy Towards Performance in Multilateral Asean's Innovation Business," *Entrepreneurship and Sustainability Issues*, 8(1), 1081–1094.

Belke A., and Volz U., 2020. "The Yen Exchange Rate and the Hollowing Out of the Japanese Industry," *Open Economies Review*, 31(2), 371–406.

Chakraborty A., Inoue H., and Fujiwara Y., 2020. "Economic complexity of prefectures in Japan," *PLos One*, 15(8), e0238017.

Chapman G.O., and Kulkarni K.G., 2020. "Comparison of Monetary Policy Actions: UK, Japan, and USA During the Financial Crisis of 2008," *SCMS Journal of Indian Management*, January-March, 17(1), 5–15.

Choforas D.N., 2011. "Sovereign Debt Crisis: The New Normal and the Newly Poor," *Palgrave Macmillan*.

Ruiz Estrada, M. A., & Park, D. (2011). "The Natural Disaster Vulnerability Evaluation Model (NDVE-Model): An Application to the Northeast Japan Earthquake and Tsunami of March 2011," Available at SSRN 1906936.

Fukuda S., and Tanaka M., 2020. "Financial Spillovers in Asian Emerging Economies, Asian Development Review," 37(1), 93–118.

Grabowiecki J., and Dabrovski M., 2017. "Abenomics and Its Impact on the Economy of Japan," *Optimum. Studia Economiczne.* 5(89), 23–35.

Grimes W.W., 2020. "How Neomercantilist Japan Became a Leading Defender of Economic Openness," *Asia Policy*, 27(4), 146–149.

Guo B., Han Q., Liang J., Ryu D., and Yu J., 2020. "Sovereign Credit Spread Spillovers in Asia," *Sustainability*, 12(4), 1472.

Hutchinson M.M., 2020. "The Global Pandemic, Policy Space and Fiscal Rules to Achieve Stronger Stabilization Policies," *Seoul Journal of Economics*, 33(3), 307–331.

Khoury S.J., and Pal P.C., 2020. "Negative Interest Rates," *Journal of Risk and Financial Management*, 13(90), 1–12.

Kichikawa Y., Iyetomi H., Aoyama H., Fujiwara Y., and Yoshikawa H. 2020. "Interindustry linkages of prices—Analysis of Japan's deflation," *PLos One*, 15(2), e0228026.

Koeda J., and Sekine A., 2020. Nelson-Siegel Decay Factor and Term Premia in a Low Interest Rate Environment. Available at SSRN 3538961.

Lozano, D.A.C., 2020. "How Immigration Can Boost the Japanese Economy by Mitigating the Effects of Population Aging," *Revista Mundo Asia Pacifico*, 9(16), 105–117.

Manhas N.S. 2020, "Globalization and Its Impact on Indian Economy," International *Journal of Social Impact*, 5(2), 170–175.

Mutoh T., Kotani K., and Kakikanaka M., 2020. "An Overseas Business Paradox: Are Japanese General Contractors Risk Takers?" *PLos One*, 15(9), e0238570.

Nguyen D.T.T., 2020. "The Effects and Solutions of Population Aging on the Japanese Economy and the Society," *International Journal of Mechanical and Production Engineering Research and Development*, 10(3), 16255–16260.

Ozyesil M., 2020. "Testing the Validity of Uncovered Equity Parity Theory among Foreign Capital Flows, The Stock Market Indices and Exchange Rates: An Econometric Analysis for Japan, South Korea and Turkey," *İstanbul Ticaret Üniversitesi Sosyal Bilimler Dergisi*, 19, Special Issue: Prof.Sabri Orman

Prezdziecka E., Gorska R., Kurznar A., and Menkes J., 2020. "The Effects of EU–Japan Economic Partnership Agreement for Poland's Economy," *Ekonomista*, 6, 701–733.

Shioji E., 2020. "Response of Bank Loans to the Bank of Japan's Quantitative and Qualitative Easing Policy: A Panel Data Analysis," *Seoul Journal of Economics*, 33(3), 355–394.

Wang M.C., Kuo P.L., Chen C.S., Chiu C.L., and Chang T., 2020. "Yield Spread and Economic Policy Uncertainty: Evidence from Japan," *Sustainability*, 12, 4302, 1–14.

Zufarovich G.M., Rustamovna N. A, Gabdelhamitovna M.N., Talifovich N.I., Sergeevna V.J., and Fargatovna G.F., 2019. Economic Relations of Japan with the Developing Economies Within Asia Pacific. In "New Silk Road: Business Cooperation and Prospective of Economic Development"(NSRBCPED 2019) 991–996. Atlantis Press.

Chapter 9

Monetary Policy Response to Pandemic in Developing Countries

Tuba Gülcemal

INTRODUCTION

Emerging markets and developing countries (EMDEs) are particularly vulnerable to economic shocks such as that posed by COVID-19, not least because of their often weaker monetary policy frameworks. Emerging markets and developing economies have long suffered from procyclical macroeconomic policies. Expansionary policies during boom times have often led to unmanageable credit expansions and a significant build-up of vulnerabilities. Conversely, contractionary policies in bad times have turned busts into major recessions—the "when it rains, it pours" phenomenon (Kaminsky et al. 2004).

The pandemic has affected all major economies including the G7 countries, which jointly share 60 percent of world supply and demand (GDP), 65 percent of world manufacturing, and 41 percent of world manufacturing exports; therefore, as these economies are now severely affected, the rest of the world will follow suit. di Mauro (2020) terms such outcomes as "macroeconomic flu"—a temporary negative supply and demand shock—causing output to fall temporarily, followed by a quick recovery and possibly a full catch-up on the shortfall. But that happens when it is a normal flu or a macroeconomic sneeze —not a pandemic like COVID-19 which is seemingly producing large-scale, global, and possibly persistent economic disruption (di Mauro, 2020).

Baldwin and di Mauro (2020) suggest that the COVID-19 pandemic is both a demand shock and a supply shock that is likely to slow down aggregate trade flows significantly and that a manufacturing distress and supply-side contagion is imminent through international supply chain distortions. The effect of finance and banking risks created by the pandemic would depend on three factors: the extent of the pandemic's economic effects globally, the fiscal and monetary policy reactions to the shocks, and regulatory reactions addressing possible bank fragility.

Based on the experiences of modeling the economic effects of influenza pandemic, COVID-19 estimated reduction in economic growth, coming as a result of reduced labor supply, higher production cost, higher temporary inflation, and reduced social consumption. Baldwin and di Mauro (eds.2020) use a macroeconomic model and showed that the spread of the COVID-19 outbreak might cause a demand-driven slump, give rise to a supply-demand doom loop, and open the door to stagnation traps induced by pessimistic animal spirits. Assuming that the supply disruption will be severe and persistent, the pandemic might induce a demand-driven recession through its negative impact on agents' expectations of future productivity growth (Barua, 2020). Such impacts have spread across industries including automotive, pharmaceuticals, medical supplies, and high-tech manufacturing. The shock becomes structural when credit mobilization is disrupted, capital stock does not grow, recovery is slow, workers leave the workforce, skills are lost, and productivity falls. Countries such as the United States, Britain, China, Australia, Canada, and Malaysia have already cut benchmark interest rates to stimulate the economy.

Monetary policy expresses the whole set of decisions to affect the availability and cost of money in order to achieve goals, such as economic growth, employment growth, and price stability. Central banks are the organizations responsible for implementing monetary policy. In Turkey, the main purpose of the central bank is to ensure price stability, which is governed by the CBRT Law. The central bank is responsible for storing the reserves of gold and foreign currency in Turkey and managing them in the interests of the country. Achieving the inflation target is very important in the management of monetary policy. The central bank therefore tries to influence total demand and inflation expectations through policy interest rates and other monetary policy instruments. Central Bank's inflation forecasts are explained by inflation report published four times a year (Eğilmez, 2020).

Multilateral financial institutions have promised to do whatever it takes to let emerging markets and developing countries to fill a $2.5 trillion financing gap to combat COVID-19 and subsequent economic crises. Stubbs, Kring, Laskaridis, Kentikelenis, and Gallagher (2020) present new datasets to track the extent to which multilateral financial institutions are meeting these goals and conduct a preliminary assessment of progress to date.

They find that the International Monetary Fund and the principal regional financial arrangements have made relatively trivial amounts of new financing available and have been slow to disburse the financing at their disposal. As of July 31, 2020, these institutions had committed $89.56 billion in loans and $550 million in currency swaps, totaling $90.11 billion—just 12.6 percent of their current capacity (Stubbs, Kring, Laskaridis, Kentikelenis, and Gallagher, 2020). It is the duty of the global financial security network to provide such support to countries. The global financial security network is a network of "financial resources and institutional regulations that provide a rebound during the financial or economic crisis." This includes, in particular, the bilateral swap lines of central banks and foreign reserves of countries. Bilateral swap lines are also only available in a few countries. The other has been declining since the beginning of the pandemic, with governments attempting to protect their currencies in light of capital outflows. As a result, countries have no choice but to look for support from multilateral financial institutions. These include only multilateral liquidity financing of the IMF and regional financial regulations (RFAs) and do not cover long-term development financing, such as those provided by the World Bank and regional development banks, because these issues are available elsewhere.

G20 declared its commitment to do whatever it takes and to use all available policy tools to minimize the economic and social damage from the pandemic, restore global growth, maintain market stability, and strengthen resilience. The cost of a one-year lockdown in a less developed country is probably higher. G20 countries' debt transparency and debt delays to become more permanent may prevent the recurrence of the debt and poverty seen in the 1980s, especially in Latin American countries (https://www.bloomberght .com).

Macroeconomic policies such as monetary, fiscal, and exchange rate management can play an important role in managing the financial stability risks of financial globalization. As financially integrated economies are suffering from a brutal sudden stop in capital flows and extreme exchange rate volatility, access to foreign currency liquidity is again essential to prevent the health crisis from developing into an economic depression. Amid escalating concerns about the real implications of the COVID pandemic (Baldwin and Weder di Mauro 2020), emerging markets (EMs) are, once again, in the line of fire. While developed countries can—and should—fund massive fiscal stimuli by issuing debt at interest rates close to zero, EMs are at the short end of the flight to quality: they face a sudden stop, widening of credit spreads and mounting exchange rate pressure; in addition to the generalized decline in global demand and in most cases, terms of trade (Yeyati, 2020).

Salisu, Sikiru, and Vo (2020) have examined the response of emerging stock markets due to the uncertainty of pandemics and epidemics, including the COVID-19. They demonstrate this by evaluating the stock return predictability of twenty-four emerging market stocks and for comparison, similar data on twenty-one developed stock markets using the new datasets on uncertainty due to pandemics as well as the global fear index for the COVID-19 pandemic. They partition the data sample into periods before and after the announcement of the COVID-19 and employ panel data techniques that account for salient features of both the series and predictive model and found that emerging stock markets are more vulnerable to uncertainty of pandemics or epidemics than developed market stocks. That is, developed stock markets provide a better hedge against pandemics than emerging stock markets. Furthermore, it has been found that including the uncertainty due to pandemics and epidemics (UPE) indicator in the stock valuation, particularly during pandemics, is crucial for investment decisions. The results suggest that government policies have no significant influence on the effect of UPE on the stock returns of EMs.

The chapter will then discuss the IMF, World Bank's practices, regional arrangements, and monetary policies, especially in developing countries, throughout COVID-19.

THE INTERNATIONAL MONETARY FUND

As a broker between central banks and emerging economies, the IMF has a unique opportunity to complete the international financial architecture and fill the lender of last resort role that has long eluded it. Dollar shortages and the real consequences of the COVID pandemic may lead to the next wave of emerging market debt crises. During this period, the IMF is trying to support countries through policy proposals, financial support, capacity building, and debt easing of the poorest countries. In monitoring economic developments and the effects of the pandemic at the global, regional, and country level, the IMF recommends the policies necessary to overcome the crisis, protect the most vulnerable, and prepare the ground for economic recovery.

IMF has offered to mobilize its $1 trillion emergency lending capacity through its flexible and rapid-disbursing emergency response facilities. These are again limited to only a few economies that are doing well with the IMF and are confident that they will benefit from aid but leave out the countries that may need most. The IMF works as an independent broker that manages existing central bank swap agreements in a single large network of foreign currency liquidity. Since the joint statement in March, the IMF has approved financing requests for eighty-four countries totaling $88.1bn, of which $36.2bn has been disbursed ($4.2bn under programs approved prior to the pandemic). RFAs have committed just eight loans totaling $1.48bn, activated one currency swap for $150mil, and formalized an additional swap arrangement for $400mil (Stubbs, Kring, Laskaridis, Kentikelenis, and Gallagher, 2020).

Prior to the pandemic, the Poverty Reduction and Growth Trust had an annual access limit of 100 percent and cumulative limit of 300 percent of the quota, while the annual limit to the Rapid Credit Facility was 50 percent of quota. The Catastrophe Containment and Relief Trust provides debt-flow relief on debt service owed to the IMF to countries impacted by health or environmental emergencies for up to two years (IMF, 2020). Initially financed with amounts left over from the Multilateral Debt Relief Initiative, it was used to assist Ebola-afflicted countries with $100 mil in 2015, leaving $200mil remaining in the trust (IMF, 2020). The Trust for Special Poverty and Growth Operations for the Heavily Indebted Poor Countries provides loans or grants with the ostensible aim of reducing debt levels under the Heavily Indebted Poor Country Initiative. It is financed through donors' grant contributions, borrowings, or from transfers from other IMF accounts and currently contains $339 mil (IMF, 2019).

The fund's activities are mainly as follows: the IMF has responded to an unprecedented number of emergency funding requests from more than 100 countries. The fund temporarily doubled access to emergency fast loans (RCF) and the rapid Financing Tool (RFI) to meet the financial assistance requests of member-states during the crisis. The total number of countries in which the IMF also approved financial support under other loan arrangements increased from seventy-six to eighty-one during crisis. The IMF helps the poorest and most vulnerable countries to reduce their debt obligations to the IMF for the period April 2020–April 2021, helping these countries divert most of their scarce financial resources to emergency medical and other aid efforts, while support-ing these member-countries to combat the impact of the COVID-19 pandemic. An alternative option to increase access to central bank swaps would be to use the IMF as a bridge between the Fed and other central banks as a money bro-ker, credit risk assessor, and risk holder. The role of the fund is similar to the role played by the treasures of developed countries, but in a more functional format in the unraveling of liquidity crises: fast, quantitatively multi- and front-loading, that is, the IMF will act as a lender of last resort (LLR).

The IMF and the World Bank have urged bilateral creditors to suspend debt collections from the poorest countries until the end of June 2021. IMF approves establishment of Short-Term Liquidity Line (SLL) to further strengthen global financial security. In response to the pandemic, the IMF has provided real-time policy proposals and capacity building to more than 160 countries to address pressing issues such as cash management, financial supervision, cybersecurity, and economic governance. Peculiarly, the fund works with tax administrations and budget offices in many countries to help them ease operations and strengthen support for businesses and individuals without compromising on the security measures and accountability

IMF financing consists of the following sources (https://www.imf.org):

General Resources Account (GRA), which consists of the IMF's quota and borrowed resources and is available to all IMF members.

Poverty Reduction and Growth Trust (PRGT), which borrows from IMF members and on-lends these borrowed resources to low-income countries on concessional terms. The PRGT's annual lending envelope, which can be supported on a self-sustaining basis, is SDR 1.25 billion and is separate from the accounts of the IMF. To meet the higher demand from low-income countries in response to the COVID-19 pandemic, the IMF is approaching bilateral lenders and donors to augment the PRGT's resources.

WORLD BANK

The Bank has partnered with the IMF on the Debt Service Suspension Initiative (DSSI), helping the poorest countries raise resources, setting the stage for gains in debt transparency and preparing the path to deep debt relief. As of April 2020, the IMF and the World Bank have jointly committed $1.160 billion to help emerging economies cope with COVID-19. This is an astonishing number, accounting for 4 percent of the total GDP of low and middle-income countries. However, assuming taxes in emerging economies are proportional to income; this benefit is lower than the expected loss of tax revenue due to the recession (Hevia and Neumeyer, 2020). And also, in emerging countries, a large share of the labor force is employed in very small firms and these workers have a relatively low level of education. These features of developing countries increase the direct cost of social distancing because the share of jobs that can be done at home is much smaller.

The Bank has worked to provide a quick and comprehensive response in terms of its essence and provision of financial support. According to the 2020 annual report of the World Bank published on its website, the World Bank Group expects distribution up to $160 billion by June 2021 for private financing for health, economic, and social shocks faced by countries due to the COVID-19 pandemic; the bank already provided support to more than 100 countries (https://www.worldbank.org). That support will be guided by the framework, which can be adapted to local country contexts. The assistance provided by the bank is as follows: save lives, protect the poor and most vulnerable, ensure sustainable business growth and job creation, strengthen policies, institutions, and investments for rebuilding better.

The Bank Group also helping countries access critically needed medical supplies by reaching out to suppliers on behalf of governments. In addition to the current health support, it specifically highlights social protection through cash transfers, poverty reduction, and policy-based funding. The World Bank is also working to restructure, redeploy, and reallocate existing resources in projects it finances. International Finance Corporation is providing $8 billion in fast-track financial support to existing clients to help sustain economies and preserve jobs during this global crisis, which will likely hit the poorest and most vulnerable countries the hardest (https://www.worldbank.org).

REGIONAL FINANCIAL ARRANGEMENTS

Regional Financing Arrangements (RFAs) are mechanisms or agreements through which groups of countries mutually pledge financial support to countries experiencing financial difficulties in their regions. The European Stability Mechanism (ESM) is the Regional Financing Arrangement for the euro area, while a few other world regions have their own RFA. Together they are the regional line of defense in the Global Financial Safety Net. The GFSN has a triple objective vis-à-vis sovereign governments: to provide precautionary insurance against a crisis; to supply liquidity when crises hit; and to incentivize sound macroeconomic policies. The other major RFAs are the Arab Monetary Fund, the BRICS Contingent Reserve Arrangement, the Chiang-Mai Initiative Multilateralization, the Eurasian Fund for Stabilization and Development, the EU Balance of Payments Facility, the European Financial Stabilization Mechanism, the Latin American Reserve Fund (FLAR), and the North American Financial Agreement (https://www.esm.europa.eu).

A well-structured cooperation between the IMF and RFAs will generate synergies for resource allocation and surveillance. It will also trigger a mutual learning process for institutions to improve their own policy frameworks. Coordination failure with respect to conditionality could lead to "program shopping" and associated moral hazard.

RFAs have committed just eight loans totaling $1.48bn, activated one currency swap for $150mil, and formalized an additional swap arrangement for $400mil. However, RFAs have recently grown to become a major component of the Global Financial Safety Net, boasting a combined lending capacity that rivals the IMF's—at roughly $1tn. RFAs provide member-countries with either loans from paid-in capital or currency swaps, the majority of which are multilateralized. The IMF and RFAs have formally engaged on an annual multilateral basis since 2016, presenting an opportunity to enhance the global response to the pandemic. On April 21, 2020, several RFAs and IMF Managing Director Georgieva issued a joint statement on cooperation efforts to mitigate the economic impact of COVID-19 (Stubbs et al. 2021:3).

MONETARY POLICY EFFECTS

Monetary policy is key in determining the economy's vulnerability to boom–bust cycles, its long-run evolution, and hence also that of the (equilibrium) real interest rate. For the central bank, this creates path dependency, that is, future policy depends on constraints determined by current policy. This gives rise to an intertemporal policy trade-off: easier policy today boosts output in the short run but at the expense of a build-up of financial imbalances and large output losses down the road, which then in turn constrain the central bank's room for policy maneuver. Emerging market economies of central banks have generally focused their monetary policy operations on lowering funding rates for governments and financial institutions. Banks' elastic supply of financing allows aggregate demand and supply to be matched *at any interest rate level;* there is no single real interest rate—the natural rate—that balances real saving and investment, thereby ensuring goods market equilibrium. It is up to the central bank to anchor the level of the interest rate, and hence the levels of bank financing and output. In competing for market share, banks inadvertently take on excessive risk when interest rates are low. Ensuing losses then deplete bank capital to a point where the risk of bankruptcy is so high that banks revert to a conservative strategy, charging higher rates and rebuilding capital. The loan market is thus subject to multiple equilibria—exhibiting phases of excessive risk-taking (booms) followed by periods of risk aversion (busts).

Interest rates influence risk-taking, the nature of these fluctuations depends on the central bank's reaction function, as monetary policy sets banks' funding costs and can thereby mitigate lending frictions. The monetary regime is an integral part of the economy's equilibrium, as some empirical evidence appears to indicate (Borio et al. 2018). The interaction between monetary policy and the financial cycle has a long-term impact on the economy and gives rise to an intertemporal trade-off. A higher policy rate today counteracts risk-taking and restrains the boom at the cost of more subdued growth in the short run. But this "leaning" strategy promotes a more robust and better capitalized banking sector, which not only reduces the risk of a bust but also the economic damage, should one occur.

Central banks in EMs lowered their policy rates substantially between March and July in 2020 to ease financial conditions and support economic growth. As a result of the reductions in policy rates, as well as expectations that rates will remain low for some time, local currency government bond yields have declined to historic lows in many EMs economies, thereby reducing borrowing costs more broadly. In contrast, a few emerging economies, such as South Africa and Turkey, continue to face borrowing costs that are substantially higher than at the start of the year, reflecting elevated concerns about their economic outlooks and the capacity of policy makers in those economies to respond to any further significant shocks. While a depreciation typically supports the economy through net exports, it can also lead to large and persistent increases in inflation when inflation is not well-anchored.

Higher inflation can reverse some or all of the benefits of a nominal deprecia-tion for the price competitiveness of domestically produced goods by markets of emerging economies. Moreover, for economies with substantial foreign currency borrowing, a depreciation in the exchange rate can increase the cost of servicing and repaying debt that is unhedged. Similarly, a decline in interest rates and depreciation of the exchange rate can encourage large-scale portfolio outflows, making it difficult to roll over external funding.

Negative nominal interest rates are a new and unexplored area and raise questions about the impact on the real economy, banking system, and finan-cial stability (Eggertsson et al. 2019, Andersson and Jonung, 2020). One of the most important problems is the extent to which lowering monetary policy interest rates into negative territory is reviving the economy. Negative deposit rates can basically affect the perception of firms for the future. For example, negative deposit rates send a very direct signal to affected firms about general supportive monetary conditions that stimulate the economy and encourage the firm's customers to increase demand.

Denmark, for example, is the first country in the world where the basic monetary policy interest rate has been negative for several years. As a result, many Danish non-financial firms have faced negative interest rates on bank deposits for several years. Denmark has high-quality micro-data in administrative and statistical records and offers extensive opportunities to link detailed information from various records at the firm level. This makes Denmark an interesting case to consider when it comes to tracing the effects of negative interest rates on the real economy (Abildgren and Kuchler, 2020).

In their study, Altavilla et al. (2020) previously found that firms with large cash assets exposed to negative rates on deposits tend to reduce their short-term assets and increase their fixed investments. Negative deposit rates can also serve as a strong signal, interpreted by the firm as an increase in the likelihood that interest rates will be "low for a long time," thus during which they can provide the firm with low financing costs in the coming years. These direct signals can cause a firm facing negative deposit rates to invest more than other firms and hire more employees.

Negative deposit rates could also serve as a strong signal which is inter-preted by the firm as an increase in the probability that interest rates would be "low for long" and thus provide the firm with low financing costs over many years to come. These direct signals may induce a firm faced with negative deposit rates to invest more and hire more employees than other firms. There is an additional channel of monetary transfer when nominal interest rates pass zero and negative (Abildgren and Kuchler, 2020: 25).

As policy rates have approached zero or become negative, some central banks have also resorted to non-traditional monetary policy tools such as forward guidance and quantitative expansion through large-scale bond purchases to lower the risk premium at the long end of the yield curve (Bernanke, 2020; Boungou, 2020). Furthermore, the move toward negative interest rates has been quite permanent. This ignited a broader, more general debate about whether and to what extent negative interest rates stimulated the economy (Rogoff, 2017; Eggertsson et al., 2019).

Turkey has experienced a large depreciation of the exchange rate and high inflation, and the central bank has responded recently by increasing policy interest rates (https://www.rba.gov.au). Argentina has also experienced continued high inflation and exchange rate depreciation. In India, recent high inflation is expected to be temporary, but the central bank has indicated it is an obstacle to the provision of further monetary stimulus. EME central banks intervened extensively in the foreign exchange market during the most acute phase of the COVID-19 crisis to support their currencies. These interventions dampened financial stability risks that can arise from sudden increases in the value of foreign currency obligations.

The outcome is critically dependent on how long the central bank's policy lasts. When the central bank is less forward-looking (it has a lower discount factor β), the economy is more vulnerable to booms and busts, and output is more volatile. More importantly, real interest rates are *lower on average* in such a case—they are lower during the boom as the central bank leans little, and low for longer during the bust as the financial cycle is more virulent. Starting in a boom, policy first leans against the financial upswing and then eases to support the economy once a bust ensues. As the economy recovers and enters a boom again, the central bank starts to tighten, but this time inertia keeps the interest rate lower than what is necessary to rein in the boom. As a result, the next bust occurs sooner, which forces another round of rate cuts. This ratcheting process continues to push the interest rate down over successive cycles, with busts becoming more frequent and booms shorter-lived. The central bank in effect falls into a kind of "low interest rate trap"—an increasingly potent financial cycle and a downward trend in the interest rate reinforce each other. In this sense, low rates beget lower rates (Rungcharoenkitkul, Borio and Disyatat, 2020).

Central banks in Turkey and Hungary raised interest rates in late September, the only banks among the twenty-five to tighten policy for 2020 and the first sign that the loosening cycle may be about to reverse. Hungary left its main policy rate unchanged but raised its influential one-week deposit rate for the second time after its currency depreciated steeply (https://www.ft.com). Normally central banks often raise interest rates to avoid inflation, which can be triggered by the weakening of the currency. However, the collapse in economic activity since the outbreak began means that suppression of demand will probably keep pressure on prices to a minimum. These days, central banks worry about exchange rates for other reasons also. A devalued currency means lenders will demand higher returns on government bonds, making borrowing of course more expensive at a time when many national budgets are under considerable pressure. The currency of many emerging countries, including Brazil, South Africa, and Russia, have sharply devalued during the crisis. Many have also benefited from emergency lending from the IMF and World Bank, while others have been able to draw on relatively deep domestic financial systems, where banks, pension funds, and others can be relied on to buy government bonds. But it is their historically low policy rates that have underpinned the borrowing spree. Policy rates are at or below 1 percent in seven of the twenty-five countries surveyed—even though, adjusted for inflation, they have not fallen by as much as rates in advanced economies in the decade since the global financial crisis.

If interest rates remain low and economies recover quickly, countries will repay their tightening policies. But if interest rates rise and economies cannot restore healthy ground, this can lead to serious problems. Falling currencies in EMs raise the fear of further devaluation and add risk premia to all kinds of credit spreads. Recent declines in nominal interest rates should not obscure the fact that real interest is relatively high in developing countries compared to developed countries and that cheap government debt and low real interest rates are unsustainable (https://www.ft.com). The negative real interest rates that may well be necessary to equilibrate the system, as real growth slows in the face of a reversal of globalization and falling working populations, will happen. Even if central banks feel uncomfortable with such higher inflation, they will be aware that the continuing high levels of debt make our economies still very fragile. And if they try to raise interest rates in such a context, they will face political ire to a point that might threaten their "independence." Only when indebtedness has been restored to viable levels can an assault on inflation be mounted (Goodhart and Pradhan, 2020).

In some cases, the exchange rate and interest rate move in the same direction, but in other cases, the exchange rate and interest rate move in opposite directions. This is not surprising because monetary policy is only one of many factors that affect exchange rates. That is, the relation between monetary policy and the exchange rate can be obscured by other factors that can affect the exchange rate and monetary policy. Kim, Kim, and Park (2020) empirically have investigated the effects of monetary policy shocks on exchange rates in Asian countries. These results show that an interest rate increase (or fall) in response to a U.S. interest rate increase (or decrease) may not protect the currency of India, Indonesia, the Philippines, and Thailand from devaluation (or devaluation) pressures.

CONCLUSION

Monetary policy affects firms' investment behavior through interest rate and balance sheet channels. Through the interest rate channel, monetary policy can affect firms' demand for capital as an input into the production process. This is because interest rates affect decisions on saving or investing and can boost aggregate demand. Through the balance sheet channel, monetary policy can make it less expensive for firms to borrow externally and reduce the firm-specific user cost of capital, allowing them to invest more. In many emerging economies, it is not possible to borrow from other countries to alleviate the COVID-19 shock. This is largely because they find it more difficult to reliably transfer future tax revenues to pay for today's fiscal expansion. The negative correlation between per capita income and the ability to tax may explain why poor countries have less access to financial markets.

The firms exposed to negative deposit rates to a higher degree than other firms increase their fixed investments and employment after due control for changes in the level of interest rates. They also tend to rebalance their portfolio of liquid assets away from bank deposits and reduce their degree of leverage. These findings are suggestive of an additional monetary transmission channel that operates as nominal interest rates cross zero and become negative. The transmission channel might imply that firms become more aware of their portfolio composition and alternative opportunities when deposit rates cross zero and become negative. Policymakers in less developed countries face a very difficult dilemma. They have to protect their communities from the pandemic with a poor health infrastructure. Long-term policies of social distancing in economies already affected by major negative global shocks can be devastating, and moreover, they will have difficulty funding social insurance policies that alleviate the cost of social distancing.

COVID-19 especially will hit certain segments of the population, especially those exposed to lockups. Many advanced economies will be able to mitigate their impact by redistributing resources from safe workers to those who will be most affected. However, such policies are unlikely to be implemented in emerging economies, making for policymakers the compromise between health and well-being even more pronounced. There are challenges of the reallocation of real resources in the economy and the difficulty of relying on fiscal and monetary incentives. The need for structural reforms is greater than ever.

REFERENCES

Abildgren, K. and Kuchler, A. 2020. "Do firms behave differently when nominal interest rates are below zero?" *Danmarks Nationalbank Working Paper*, 164. https://www.nationalbanken.dk/da/publikationer/Documents/2020/11/DNWP164.pdf

Altavilla, Carlo, Lorenzo Burlon, Mariassunta Giannetti and Sarah Holton. 2020. "Is there a zero lower bound? The effects of negative policy rates on banks and firms." *CEPR Discussion Paper,* No. 14050.

Andersson, Fredrik N. G. and Lars Jonung. 2020. "Don't do it again! The Swedish experience with negative central bank rates in 2015–2019." https://voxeu.org/ar ticle/swedish-experience-negative-central-bank-rates.

di Mauro, B.W. 2020. "Macroeconomics of the flu." In Baldwin, R. and di Mauro, B.W. (eds). 2020. *Economics in the Time of COVID-19.* A CEPR PressVoxEU.org eBook, Centre for Economic Policy Research, London. https://voxeu.org/system/ files/epublication/covid-19.pdf.

Bernanke, Ben S. 2020. "The New Tools of Monetary Policy." *American Economic Review*, Vol. 110(4), pp. 943–983.

Baldwin, R. and B. Weder di Mauro. 2020. *Mitigating the COVID Economic Crisis: Act Fast and Do Whatever It Takes*, a VoxEU.org eBook, CEPR Press.

Barua, Suborna. 2020. "Understanding Coronanomics: The economic implications of the coronavirus (COVID-19) pandemic." *Munich Personal RePEc Archive*, 1–45, https://mpra.ub.uni-muenchen.de/99693/.

Borio, C., P. Disyatat, M. Juselius and P. Rungcharoenkitkul. 2018. "The 'real' illu- sion: how monetary factors matter in low-for-long rates." VoxEU.org, October 18.

Boungou, Whelsy. 2020. "Negative interest rates policy and banks' risk-taking: Empirical evidence." *Economics Letters*, Vol. 186, pp. 1–3.

Brunnermeier, Markus K. and Yann Koby. 2018. "The Reversal Interest Rate." *NBER Working Paper*, No. 25406.

Eggertsson, G. B., Ragnar E. J., Lawrence H. S. and Ella, G. W. 2019. "Negative Nominal Interest Rates and the Bank Lending Channel." *NBER Working Paper*, No. 25416.

Eğilmez, Mahfi. 2020. *Türkiye Ekonomisi.* İstanbul: Remzi Kitabevi.

Fernández Arias, E. and E. Levy Yeyati. 2012. "Global Financial Safety Nets: Where Do We Go from Here?" *International Finance,* 15(1): 37–68.

Goodhart, C. and Pradhan, M. March 2020. "Future imperfect after coronavirus." https://voxeu.org/article/future-imperfect-after-coronavirus.

Hevia, C. and Neumeyer, P.B. 2020. "A perfect storm: COVID-19 in emerging econ- omies." https://voxeu.org/article/perfect-storm-COVID-19-emerging-economies

https://www.rba.gov.au/publications/smp/2020/nov/box-b-the-policy-response-of- central-banks-in-emerging-market-economies-to-covid-19.html.

https://www.bloomberght.com/dunya-bankasi-g20-yi-borclar-konusunda-uyardi-2 269152.

https://www.imf.org/en/About/FAQ/imf-response-to-covid-19#Q1.

https://voxeu.org/article/covid-fed-swaps-and-imf-lender-last-resort.

https://www.ft.com/content/99603ed2-0580-455f-823a-d138685e2b4f.

https://www.worldbank.org/en/news/factsheet/2020/02/11/how-the-world-bank- group-is-helping-countries-with-covid-19-coronavirus.

https://www.worldbank.org/en/about/annual-report#anchor-annual

https://www.esm.europa.eu/about-us/how-we-work/regional-financing-arrangements-rfa

Kaminsky, G. L., C. M. Reinhart and C. A. Vegh. 2004. "When it Rains, it Pours: Procyclical Capital Flows and Macroeconomic Policies," NBER Working Paper 10780.

Kim, J., Kim, S. and Park, D. 2020. "Monetary Policy Shocks and Exchange Rates in Asian Countries." *Japan and the World Economy*, Vol. 56, 1–19. https://doi.org/10 .1016/j.japwor.2020.101041.

Rogoff, K. 2017. "Dealing with Monetary Paralysis at the Zero Bound." *Journal of Economic Perspectives,* Vol. 31(3), pp. 47–66.

Rungcharoenkitkul, P., Claudio Borio, and Piti Disyatat. 2020. "The long shadow of monetary policy." https://voxeu.org/article/long-shadow-monetary-policy.

Salisu, A. A., Sikiru, A. A. and Vo, X. V. 2020. Pandemics and the emerging stock markets. *Borsa Istanbul Review*, https://doi.org/10.1016/ j.bir.2020.11.004.

Stubbs, T., Kring, W., Laskaridis, C., Kentikelenis, A., and Gallagher, K. 2021. "Whatever it takes? The global financial safety net, COVID-19, and developing countries." *World Development*, Vol. 137, p. 105171. https://doi.org/10.1016/j .worlddev.2020.105171.

Wheatley, J., and Romei, V. 2020. "Emerging economies face rising interest rates as capital flows ebb." https://www.ft.com/content/99603ed2-0580-455f-823a-d138 685e2b4f.

Yeyati, E. L. 2020. "COVID, Fed swaps and the IMF as lender of last resort." https:/ /voxeu.org/article/covid-fed-swaps-and-imf-lender-last-resort.

Chapter 10

Central Bank Response in Emerging Economies during COVID-19

Ünay Tamgaç Tezcan

INTRODUCTION

The COVID-19, which is short for coronavirus disease, was first identified in December 2019 in Wuhan, China. On January 30, 2020, the director general of the World Health Organization (WHO 2021) declared the outbreak as a public emergency of international concern, and a *pandemic* in March 2021.[1]

On March 26, U.S. death toll reached 1,000. Nearly a third of the world's population was already living under coronavirus-related restrictions. The outbreak of the virus quickly reached a global scale. By April 4, 2020, there were over 1 million cases worldwide confirmed by the WHO. On January 30, 2021, one year after the WHO alarm, globally the cumulative numbers of reported cases since the start of the pandemic was over 98.2 million with over 2.1 million deaths (daily reported new cases globally is 1 million) (WHO, 2021)

As a rarely occurring global health crisis, the COVID-19 pandemic continues to have major implications on countries worldwide. Besides its detrimental health effects, many lost lives, and the immense pressure on the healthcare system, the virus continues to cause many adverse effects on world economy.

Similar to how the nature of the virus was unknown by medical experts, the nature of the coming economic crisis was unknown to many economists. What makes the crisis unique is that it is a demand shock and supply shock occurring simultaneously. Moreover, traditional policy measures to boost demand would fail to operate due to lockdown measures needed to contain the spread. Hence quickly after its outbreak, the global health crisis initiated a global economic crisis. Economists and policy makers were challenged to find the right set of tools in reviving their markets amid so much uncertainty.

The initial economic impact was felt in the financial markets. Heightened uncertainty and the liquidity crunch caused a sharp downturn in global equity

123

and bond markets. In March 2020, there was a large-scale sell-off, and stock prices declined steeply. The sell-off in U.S. treasury market caused spikes in long-term yields (Schrimpf, Shin, and Sushko 2020). Similar pressure was felt in the Euro Area and Japanese markets. Also, equity markets plummeted, volatility rose, and emerging markets also came under pressure.

The Federal reserve (FED) and other major banks acted swiftly to contain the initial impact and stop the liquidity crisis. Drawing on the experience from the Global Financial Crisis (GFC), the measures were prompt and forceful (Cavallino and De Fiore 2020). The initial repose came when FED cut its benchmark interest rate by half percent on March 3. The Bank of England and the Bank of Canada followed with rate cuts.

The FED, the ECB, and the Bank of Japan opened swap lines. The five major central banks all offered new lending operations and either extended or inaugurated asset purchase programmers. On March 23, the FED put in place a package of several measures. With near-zero interest rates, central banks have been injecting liquidity (*Quantitative Easing*) into the financial sector, among others, through an asset purchase program from the market, including government bonds, private bonds, and credit securities. For the first time, the FED and the Bank of Canada announced corporate bond purchase programs. Between March and April, many crisis management policies were put in place by monetary authorities. Besides monetary easing and other liquidity enhancing measures, fiscal policy was also implemented to the fullest. On March 25, the U.S. Senate unanimously passed a $2 trillion stimulus plan, which is signed by President Trump on March 27 after passing the house.

These programs were successful to take the pressure off the market. Besides supporting flow of credit, the measures restored confidence that monetary policy would be supportive during the COVID crisis. They were also supportive for emerging market economies who were hit hard during the initial capital flight.

In this chapter, we discuss the monetary policy action of emerging economies, specifically their monetary policy response since the onset of the pandemic. We focus on four emerging economies—Brazil, India, Indonesia, and South Africa. These countries have similar inherent economic structures, similar vulnerabilities to external shocks like the COVID crisis and similar limitation on their use of monetary policy.

Compared to the advanced economies, emerging economies are more constrained in their use of policy tools to contain the crisis. This is mainly through exchange rate effects. By cutting interest rates, countries risk currency depreciation. Depreciation can also cause inflationary pressure, especially if expectations are not anchored. The countries we study have all adopted inflation targeting (IT) policies and were operating under favorable inflation outlook. However, reliance on external financing and currency mismatch are factors that limit their policy response. Also weaker institutional settings, shallower markets, informality, tax collection are some other shared factors that can constrain their scale of interventions.

We focus on the central bank response through the pandemic in each of these four countries. We study how monetary policy has been used to fight the economic adversities caused by COVID-19 crisis. First, we analyze how the traditional tools, the interest rates, and reserve requirements have been implemented. Then we analyze other set of policies adopted by central banks to ease the functioning of the financial system and ensure the flow of credit.

BRAZIL

In Brazil, Banco Central do Brasil (BCB) and the National Monetary Council (CMN) (created on December 31, 1964) are the highest macroeconomic and financial regulatory authorities.[2] CMN is in charge of formulating monetary and credit policies, to preserve monetary stability and to promote economic and social development.[3] The Monetary Policy Committee (Copom) of the BCB is responsible for setting the target for the policy interest rate (Banco Central do Brasil. 2020.a). On June 21, 1999, Brazil adopted IT as monetary policy. Under the IT regime, monetary policy decisions are made by Copom to achieve the inflation targets (a midpoint and its tolerance interval) set by the CMN.

The yearly increase in the broad national consumer price index (IPCA) is considered as the reference for the inflation target. The primary instrument of monetary policy is the selic rate which is the interest rate that balances the market for bank reserves. It is the average overnight interest rate charged on the daily loans (i.e., with a maturity of one day) backed by government securities registered and traded at the Special System for Settlement and Custody (Selic), that is, it is the Brazilian federal funds rate. Copom sets the target for the selic rate.

Starting with an inflation rate of 8.94 percent in 1999 the IT framework was successful in curbing down inflation with an inflation target of 4.5 since 2005 (figure 10.1). Despite the spike of 10.67 percent in 2015, inflation has been on a downward trend hitting an all-time low 2.95 percent in 2017. Inflation targets set for the years 2019 through 2022 are 4.25 percent, 4.00 percent, 3.75 percent, and 3.50 percent, respectively with a +/-1.5 percent tolerance band (Banco Central do Brasil 2020.b).

After a rate hike of 25 basis points (bps) to 14.25 amid inflationary pressures, the highest in nine years, on July 29, 2015, the BCB kept the rate unchanged for a long period. The selic rate was cut first time on October 19, 2016, after four years during a severe contraction and slowing inflation. As

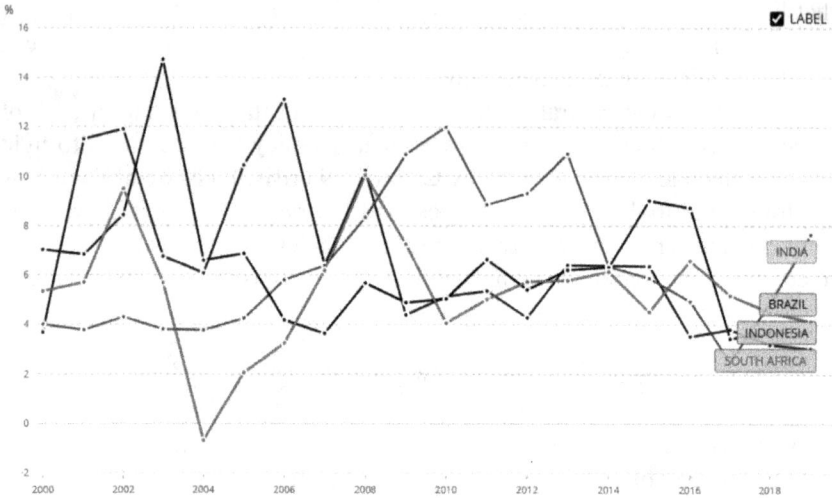

Figure 10.1   Year-to-Year CPI Inflation Rates (%). *Source*: IMF, World Development Indicators. https://datacatalog.worldbank.org/dataset/world-development-indicators

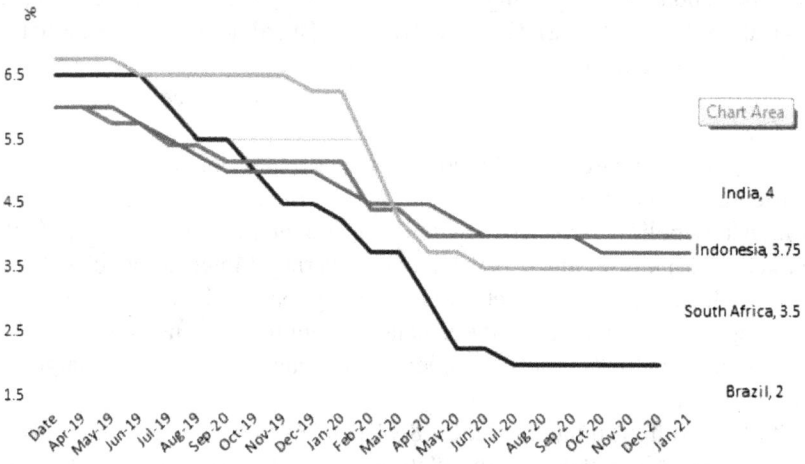

Figure 10.2   Policy Rates (%). Data retrieved on May 17, 2021, from Refinitiv Eikon Data

inflation converged to target, the BCB was on a downward trajectory of the policy rate. After eleven interest rate cuts, between 25 and 100 bps, and a final cut of 25 bps on March 21, 2018, the selic rate came down to 6.50 percent (figure 10.2). In its fight with inflation the CB managed to bring borrowing costs to the lowest in its history with below-target inflation and a gradually improving economy.

In the first quarter of 2019, the Brazilian economy shrank by 0.2 percent, compared to a 0.1 percent growth in the previous period. With indications of weaker growth and lower inflation, the bank cut the selic rate by 50 bps on July 31, 2019, to a record low of 6 percent. With indications for weaker economic activity; a decelerating global economy and slower domestic inflation with three more rate cuts of 50 bps followed in 2019. In its first meeting in 2020 on February 5, considering the global outlook, low inflation expectations and high level of economic slack, Copom decided for a further 25 bps cut. Hence when the pandemic hit the world, at the end of February 2020, the selic rate was at a historically low 4.25 percent and inflation target for 2020 was 4 percent (Banco Central do Brasil 2020.c.).

Brazil had its first COVID case reported on February 26, 2020. On March 18, the Copom unanimously decided to cut the selic rate by 50 bps to 3.75 percent, stressing that full range of monetary, exchange rate, and financial stability policies would be used to fight the crisis. On May 6, Copom lowered the selic rate further by 75 bps to 3 percent, stating that the economic contraction would be significantly deeper than forecasted in the previous meeting however space for further easing were very limited and by another 75 bps on June 17. By the middle of the year, monetary policy was mostly in wait and see mode, with some fine-tuning but no big changes. There was a further 25 bps cut on August 5. Hence through a total of four rate cuts in 2020, since the onset of the pandemic in mid-February, the policy rate was lowered by 225 bps, to the historical low of 2 percent.

On August 11, the BCB adopted *forward guidance* as a new strategy assuring markets that interest rates will not be raised for months or even years. This policy was adopted due to concern that further cuts in the interest rate could put financial stability and asset markets under pressure despite the need for further stimulus.[4]

As economic recovery gained pace toward the end of 2020, higher than expected inflation raised inflation expectations and expectations for a rate hike. (The headline inflation was on an upward trend in the last 7 months, that is, 3.9 percent in October, 4.3 percent in November, and 4.5 percent in December). However, in all following meetings in 2020 (September 16, October 28, and December 9), Copom kept the policy rate unchanged at 2 percent. On its December 9 meeting, BCB stated that forward guidance for keeping the rates low could no longer apply because of worsening inflation expectations.

On January 21, 2021 with inflation expectations converging toward target, the MPC announced that they dropped the forward guidance. They also warned that the removal did not imply automatic interest rates hikes since growth uncertainties still prescribed an extraordinarily strong monetary stimulus. The selic was again kept untouched for the fifth consecutive policy meeting despite several inflation measures above compatible range with the inflation target.

In support of the COVID-hit economy, and to preserve the smooth functioning of the financial system, several measures were put in place. As a first step, the BCB has injected liquidity through purchases of bank loan portfolios, central bank foreign exchange intervention, and repurchases of dollar-denominated sovereign bonds. (Reuters 2020).

Starting on March 18, BCB established criteria for conducting repurchase operations in foreign currency with external federal public debt securities as collateral are (Global Bonds), and a haircut of 10 percent over bonds' market value.[5] BCB would act as a donor of funds through repurchase operations backed by, with up to one-year term federal government securities. BCB also opened a facility to provide loans to financial institutions backed by private corporate bonds as collateral. Through the Special Temporary Liquidity Facility (LTEL-LFG) BCB would grant loans to financial institutions backed by financial letters collateralized by credit operations or securities. These operations were also guaranteed by reserves that financial institutions hold at BCB.

On March 23, a central bank program equivalent to 16.7 percent of GDP *"the biggest liquidity* and capital injection plan ever made" as referred to by President Roberto Campos Neto (Franklin 2020). These policies mostly aimed to provide liquidity to the financial system and provide better conditions to banks—regarding liquidity and capital availability—to strengthen the flow of credit to households and businesses (Neto 2020). In that regard, several capital relief and more flexible regulations allowing banks to offer firms and households increased loans were put in place:

- Local banks were no longer required to deduct the tax effects of over hedge transactions in foreign equity investments from their capital.
- The spread of liquidity leveling operations for the end-of-day punitive interest rate charges of the financial institutions is reduced from 65 bps to 10 bps.
- New Term Deposit with Special Guarantees (NDPGE) an alternative funding mechanism for financial institutions allowing them to increase their funding while being guaranteed by the Credit Guarantee Fund (FGC) is introduced. Later financial institutions are allowed to purchase the DPGE issued by institutions associated with FGC.
- Capital requirements for small financial institutions was temporarily reduced.
- More flexibility on the Agribusiness Credit Bills' (LCA) regulation is introduced to facilitate agribusiness credit and strengthen the liquidity of banks.

- The ceiling for bank security repurchases was raised from 5 percent to 20 percent. This way the biggest banks were allowed to repurchase a larger volume of their own financial bills.
- Lenders were allowed to combine their credit portfolios into long-term deposits which can be purchased by the central bank.
- Working Capital for Business Continuity (CGPE) program that aims to provide incentives for credit provision to micro, small, and medium-sized companies to preserve business continuity was introduced.
- The use of the same real estate as collateral in more than one credit operations was allowed.

BCB was already authorized to purchase private securities in the secondary market.[6] On May 7, Brazil amended its constitution temporarily to allow direct purchase of government debt by the BCB during the COVID-19 crisis and on June 23 BCB announced its private sector bond-buying program on the secondary market. Assets non-convertible into shares, with a credit rating equivalent to "BB-" or higher by at least one of the three major rating agencies, and with a maturity of at least twelve months, were eligible for purchase. These changes allowed BCB to purchase a variety of private and public assets, including both government and corporate bonds through the end of 2020.[7]

Some measures were targeting the external sector of the economy. On April 24, changes in regulation for foreign exchange operations related to exports and imports were introduced. Specifically, advance payment of imports was extended from 180 to 360 days. For exporters, a single maximum period of 1,500 days to settle the FX operation and to freely ship the goods or render the services within that period is established.

The reserve requirement has also been used in fight during the pandemic. On March 5, reserve requirement ratio on time deposits was reduced to 25 percent from 31 percent, effective March 16.[8] BCB also increased the share of reserve requirements to be taken into account in the liquidity coverage ratio (LCR) set by the Basel Committee. These measures would correspond to 8.5 bps reduction for each new time deposit that must comply with those requirements. On March 26, on top of this 6 bps reduction, a further reduction from 25 percent to 17 percent effective March 30 was announced. On October, the BCB extended the reduction, initially planned to be effective till December 14, for four months till April 2021. After that date, the requirement ratio would be increased to 20 percent instead of the previously set 25 percent. Moreover, the remuneration on reserve requirements on savings accounts was lowered to encourage lending.

In addition, in March, a Swap line with the Fed was arranged to provide up to $60 billion to the central bank up to September 30, 2021.

INDIA

After a period of persistent inflation following the GFC during 2008–2013, India entered a disinflation period after 2014. With tighter monetary policy supported by falling commodity prices, especially crude oil, and a more stable exchange rate CPI-based inflation was brought down to 6 percent by January 2015 (Adrian, Laxton, and Obstfeld, 2018).[9]

India adopted an IT regime in June 2016. The government of India, in consultation with the Reserve Bank of India (RBI), set a CPI-based inflation target of 4 percent with a +/- 2 percent tolerance band for the five-year period from August 5, 2016, to March 31, 2021.

The primary objective of monetary policy is to maintain price stability while keeping in mind the objective of growth. The overnight call money market rate measured by the weighted average call money rate (the interest rate at which banks lend overnight money to each other) (WACR) is the operating target for the monetary policy. The main monetary policy instrument is the *repo rate,* the rate at which RBI lends money to banks when banks face shortage of funds (BIS n.d.). The policy rate required to achieve the target is set by a MPC of six members (three external, three internal) through a majority decision rule.

The reverse repo rate is the rate at which banks lend money to the RBI. The Liquidity Adjustment Facility (LAF), also known as the liquidity corridor, indicates the difference between the repo and the reverse repo rates around the policy repo rate. Reverse repo rate and Marginal Standing Facility (MSA) or the Bank Rate) constitutes the lower (floor) and the upper bound (ceiling) of the LAF corridor, respectively. When the MPC changes the repo rate, the reverse repo and the MSF rate are recalibrated based on the LAF corridor. The LAF was initially set at +/-100 bps. On April 2016, the corridor was narrowed to +/-50 bps and further down to +/-25 bps in April 2017.

Although IT experience has been short in India, inflation has been brought down from 9 percent (reaching 12.9% in 2009) within the target range around 4 percent. Inflation expectations had already been anchored down in the pre-pandemic period and gave room for accommodative monetary policy. While there has been an upward trajectory since December 2019, primarily due to higher food prices, headline inflation had been kept within the target range. The average inflation rate between October 2016 and March 2020 was 3.93 percent, reaching 5.84 percent in March 2020. In the last two meetings before the COVID-19 crisis (December 2019 and February 2020), the MPC kept the policy rate unchanged at 5.15 percent. Hence, the reverse repo rate and MSF were set at 4.9 percent and 5.40 percent, respectively, forming the 50-bps corridor.

After the first COVID-19 case on January 30, the first death was reported in India on March 13. Ten days later, on March 24, India announced a nation-wide lockdown that lasted about two months. As a first response to the pandemic on March 24–27, 1 week earlier than scheduled, the RBI announced measures to inject liquidity into the system. RBI cut the policy repo rate by 75 bps to 4.4 percent higher than market expectation of 50 bps. The reverse repo rate was cut by 90 bps 4.00 percent from 4.90 percent, the MSF was reduced by 25 bps to 4.65 percent from 5.40 percent.

By this policy, the LAF corridor widened by 65 bps. Moreover, it turned asymmetrical with a 40 bps difference between the repo and the reverse repo rate, and a 25 bps difference between the repo rate and the MSF. "The larger cut in the reverse repo rate was to discourage the banks to lend their money to the RBI and stimulate credit creation" (Dev and Sengupta 2020).

The immediate response was felt through a drop in the ninety-one-day Treasury bill rate to 4.31 percent from 5.09 percent on March 26 which measures the de facto stance of monetary policy. However, despite excess liquidity, banks found it risky to lend to business. Rather they were parking the excess liquidity with the RBI using the reverse repo window (Governor's Statement, April 17).

In response, on April 17, the MPC further widened the LAF corridor to 90 bps. The reverse repo rate was reduced by 25 bps to 3.75 percent, while the repo and the MSF rate were kept unchanged. A third rate cut followed after an emergency on meeting May 20-22, earlier than scheduled on June 3–5. The policy rate was reduced by 40 bps to 4.0 percent, while the LAF corridor was unchanged. Accordingly, the reverse repo rate was reduced to 3.35 percent, the MSF were reduced to 4.25 percent.

Since the onset of the pandemic in three consecutive meetings, the repo rate has been cut by a total of 115 bps from pre-pandemic level of 5.15 percent to 4.00 percent. The reverse repo rate has been cut by 155 bps from 4.9 percent to 3.35 percent, and the LAF corridor has widened to 90 bps from its initial level of 50 bps. During this period, the reverse repo rate has been changed, more frequently than the repo rate, and has in a way become the new effective policy rate (Dev and Sengupta 2020).

While the market was expecting a further cut of 25 bps, the MPC did not make any changes on its August 4–6 meeting. Rather the MPC kept the accommodative stance to mitigate the economic impact of COVID-19. There has not been a rate change in the October 7–9, December 2–4 meetings, and also on the first meeting in 2021 on February 3–5. While the decision not to change the policy rate caused some worry about inflation, MPC stated that they remain committed to achieving the medium-term target for CPI inflation of 4 percent within a band of +/- percent while supporting growth.

One point to note is that for three consecutive meetings since COVID outbreak, the RBI did not publish growth and inflation forecasts. One reason was that the headline inflation data was not released for April and May by the Central Statistical Office. This was due to the unavailability of prices with limited transactions and the inability to collect price quotations because of the lockdowns. Instead an imputed CPI data was released from April to May which is considered a break in the CPI series (Patnaik and Pandey 2020, 21).

Besides rate cuts, India adopted different measures to enhance liquidity and contain the negative economic impact of the pandemic on firms and the banking sector (Reserve Bank of India 2020.a). The measures under liquidity management, mostly implemented after RBI's March 26 meeting, are as follows:

- Open market operations by the RBI (including simultaneous purchases and sales of government securities), resulting in cumulative liquidity injections of 5.9 percent of GDP through September (IMF 2021)
- Targeted long-term repo operations (TLRO and 2.0) (March 27, April 17)
- Long-term repo operations (LTROs) (February 15, March 16)
- Enhanced borrowing under the MSF window to 3 percent of the Statutory Liquidity Ratio (SLR) (mandatory holding of government bonds) which was 2 percent (further extended to September 30, 2021)
- Cash reserve ratio (CRR) of all banks was cut by 100 bps to 3 percent of net demand and time liabilities (NDTL) beginning March 28
- The requirement of minimum daily CRR balance maintenance has been reduced from 90 percent to 80 percent until March 26.

Moreover, regulatory changes have been implemented to provide relief to borrowers and to mitigate the burden of debt servicing, some of which are as follows:

- Easing of working capital financing that allows lending institutions to declare a three-month moratorium on all term loans
- Deferment of interest payment on all working-capital facilities for three months, recalculation of drawing power by reducing margins, and/or by reassessing the working capital cycle for the borrowers
- Deferment of some requirements on the banking sector as per Basel standards (such as the net stable funding ratio and the capital conservation buffer) sector (Reserve Bank of India 2020.b).

As a measure to restore stability of the exchange rate, banks were permitted to deal in offshore non-deliverable rupee derivative markets. This would reduce arbitrage between onshore and offshore markets, hence improve depth and price discovery in the forex market segments.

INDONESIA

Indonesia is a country with a history of hyperinflation with two-digit inflation rates in the 1960s, reaching 1000 percent in mid-1966 mainly due to deficit financing through money printing. Following a strict balanced budget policy, inflation was reduced down to around 15 percent by 1969. After reaching over 50 percent during the Asian crisis, Indonesia entered an IMF stabilization program with inflation target of 3–5 percent after which inflation was brought around 13 percent in 2001.

Since 1999, Bank of Indonesia (BI) has been an independent central bank mandated with maintaining exchange rate stability which encompasses two dimensions: the price stability of goods and services, which is reflected by inflation, and rupiah exchange rate stability against other currencies.[10] On July 1, 2005, BI adopted IT as its monetary policy framework replacing base money as the target of monetary policy. When sole focus on price stability proved not enough during the 2008 GFC, the BI adopted a flexible IT framework. This framework integrates macroeconomic and financial sector stability with price stability through a policy mix of monetary, macroprudential, exchange rate, capital flow instruments, as well as strengthening the institutional arrangements.

The inflation target is set by the government in coordination with BI for the following three years through a Minister of Finance Regulation (PMK). IT is implemented using a policy rate as a signal of monetary policy and the interbank rate as the operational target. Previously, BI Rate equivalent to a twelve-month interest rate in the term structure of monetary operations was used as the policy rate. Since August 19, 2016, BI is using the BI 7-day repo rate as the monetary policy rate. The two other main rates being, the deposit facility (DF) and lending facility (LF) rates. The inflation target set for the period 2019, 2020, 2021 is 3.5 percent, 3 percent, and 3 percent within a +/-1 percent corridor for the years 2019, 2020, and 2021, respectively.

Even before the COVID-19 crisis, Indonesia's economy was already under pressure. In 2018, with concerns over the increasing current account deficit (reaching to 3% of GDP in the second quarter, biggest deficit since Q2-2014) interest rates were raised by 175 bps. In 2019, with trade tensions between China and the United States, global economic slowdown and a two-year low growth, BI cut its benchmark rate by a total of 100 bps through four consecutive cuts in July through October 2019.[11]

The first COVID case was reported on March 2, and social distancing measures (Large-Scale Social Restrictions, or PSBB I) were imposed on April 9 through June 4. Starting June 5, as the cases seemed to be stabilized, restrictions were eased, with shifting to a back-to-normal phase (PSBB Transition I) in mid-July and further easing in mid-September. With new insurgence of the cases on October 12, the government imposed new restriction (PSBB Transition II) (Habir and Wardana 2020, 4). In hindsight, the government is criticized to underestimate the pandemic and failed to provide immediate response as there were already 20 COVID-19 patients in January (Umam and Jazuli 2020, 4; Allard, Tom and Kate Lamb 2021).

When the COVID crisis hit the economy, immediate impact was felt in March. To restore liquidity in the initial sell-off in financial markets, and later on to fight the downturn in demand and restore business confidence, authorities implemented a wide range of policies. The low inflation around 3 percent was supportive for expansionary measures. Through four separate 25 bps policy rate cuts in February, March, June, and July, the BI lowered the BI-7-day reverse repo rate by 100 bps to 4.00 percent. The LF and DF rate were also reduced by 100 bps from their January 2000 values down to 4.75 percent and 3.25 percent respectively.

While with low inflation and declining deficit, there was room for easing, with the pressure on the exchange rate, BI did not make any rate changes in three consecutive meetings. With concern over currency stability and global uncertainty, other measures, that is, fiscal and macro prudential policies, took precedence to support economic growth. When October inflation was below the bank's 3–5 percent target range, with moderate inflation outlook and substantial appreciation of the rupiah/stable currency eased currency BI decided for a rate cut of 25 bps, to an all-time low of 3.75 percent in its November 18–19 MPC meeting. The DF and LF rates were cut to 3.00 percent and 4.50 percent, respectively. While there was no policy change on the December 6–17, and January 20–21 meetings, on the February 17–18 meeting, BI further cut the seven-day reverse repo rate by 25 bps to a new all-time low of 3.50 percent. The DF and LF rates were reduced to 2.75 percent and 4.25 percent, respectively.

Besides interest rates, monetary authorities implemented several measures to contain the economic impact of the pandemic.

On March 22, BI regulations concerning Rupiah and Foreign Currency Reserve Requirement were amended.[12] On April 14, the rupiah reserve requirement was lowered by 200 bps from 5.5 percent to 3.5 percent for business financing, especially for export-import operators and micro, small, and medium enterprises (MSMEs) (while the policy rate was held constant at 4.50% due to currency concerns).

The Ministry of Finance (MoF) implemented the national economic recovery program to contain the economic impact of the pandemic stimulus packages that were announced on February 25, March 13, and March18.[13] On

March 27, the cap on the state budget's deficit, which was set at 3 percent of GDP after the Asian financial crisis, was lifted temporarily to 5 percent.

The deficit is normally funded by debt issuance in the form of rupiah-denominated bonds. While these are popular for foreign investors in normal times, due to global outlook, there was not enough demand.[14] Hence, as part of its QE program BI, acting as a lender of last resort, was allowed to purchase government bonds directly from the MoF with the so-called burden-sharing scheme. BI supported the national economic recovery program through the purchase of government securities (Surat Berhaga Negara,or SBN) from the primary market (Joint Decree by the Minister of Finance and Governor of Bank Indonesia, April 16, 2020) and direct purchase (Joint Decree by the Minister of Finance and Governor of Bank Indonesia, July 7, 2020). This way, BI injected large amounts of liquidity into banks to support the national economic recovery program. BI has implemented QE of around 4.4 percent of GDP, the largest monetary stimulus among emerging economy central banks.

Central bank's active participation in buying government bonds in the primary market alarmed market participants about the central bank's independence in controlling inflation. With a history of hyperinflation, concern was that the program could be prolonged beyond its end 2020 deadline and impact the country's sovereign credit ratings. However, there is a capital clause that limits how much the BI can buy and the authorities reassured the market that it would be a one-time exercise.

Non-performing loans (NPLs) were on a rising trend, from 2.5 percent at end of 2019, to 2.8 percent in March 2020, and 3.1 percent in June 2020. To prevent the deterioration of the banking balance sheet, through NPLs other measures were put in place such as relaxation of microprudential regulations and credit restructuring for MSMEs to boost credit and financing for the economy.

- The Macro Prudential Intermediation Ratio (MIR) and Loan to Value (LTV) ratios were reduced to encourage businesses financing.
- Financial Services Authority (OJK) eased the bank's restructuring requirements. Borrowers hurt by the pandemic were allowed to defer their principal repayment schedule till March 2021. Also restructuring banks were allowed to delay installments of principal and interest of credit.
- To support credit demand, BI relaxed the rules on lending to the automotive and property sectors.[15]
- To attract foreign investment and to ease global supply chain disruptions caused by the virus, a new bill, the omnibus law, that simplifies the existing investment laws was passed on October 8, 2020. The bill attracted many protests as it also lifts several restrictions on imports and exports.

- BI also reaffirmed that global investors can use global and domestic custodian banks to conduct investment transactions in Indonesia.
- To ease the payment constraints, more non-cash transactions, such as using electronic money and internet banking, were encouraged (Herman 2020).

Maintaining exchange rate stability has also been a major concern, especially during the onset of the pandemic when rupiah depreciated by 17.6 percent against the U.S. dollar between January 31 and March 24. Large built-up of foreign exchange reserves was used as a support for the stabilization policies. BI intervened in the spot, domestic non-deliverable forward (NDF) markets. BI also established bilateral swap and repo line cooperation with several central banks in other countries, including the United States and China.

To stop the initial capital flight and restore market confidence, a repurchase agreement or repo-line is arranged under the Federal Reserves' Foreign and International Monetary Authorities (FIMA) repo facility in early April worth $60 billion, which will be in place until September 2021. BI also has a $30 billion bilateral swap agreement with China, $22.7 billion with Japan, around $7 billion with Singapore, and an undisclosed amount with Australia and other central banks. Furthermore, the central bank has also sealed a $2.5 billion repo line agreement with the Bank of International Settlements and another $3 billion with the Monetary Authority of Singapore.

Indonesia also increased the range of transactions foreign investors could use to hedge their holdings of rupiah. Hence, Indonesia's support was a combination of interest rate cuts, quantitative easing, foreign currency swaps, and a reduction in the rupiah reserve requirement.

SOUTH AFRICA

South Africa is the most industrialized country in Africa. However, South Africa has one of the world's highest rates of HIV infection. The primary purpose of the South African Reserve Bank (SARB) is to achieve and maintain price stability in the interest of balanced and sustainable economic growth in South Africa. Since February 2000, South Africa has adopted an IT framework with an inflation target range of 3–6 percent to achieve inflation close to the 4.5 percent (South African Reserve Bank 2021.a).

The overnight interest rate, the repo rate, is the policy tool which is set by the MPC that consists of up to seven members, including the governor of the SARB, the three deputy governors, and senior officials appointed by the governor. The constitution gives the SARB the mandate to protect the value of the rand to ensure financial stability. Hence, monetary policy is conducted within a flexible IT framework (South African Reserve Bank 2021.b).

Before 2008, inflation rate has risen to double digits with rising food and fuel prices and amid strong credit growth. In response, the MPC had raised the repo rate up to 12.0 percent in July 2008. This made the total increase of 500 bps in just 26 months. These have put inflation on track. Since 2010, monthly inflation readings have been within the target of 78 percent of the time compared to 40 percent in the previous decade.

South Africa, with unemployment hovering around 29 percent, was already in a recession before COVID-19. Hence, the country entered the COVID-19 crisis on the back of a technical recession combined with fiscal stress, growing public sector debt, and a downgrade to junk status in March 2020. The country has a large dependence on external financing due to its structural current account deficit. However, compared to the GFC, the inflation rates were stable, and also below or within target levels of inflation rate. This gave room for monetary easing. Following a one-time rate cut of 25 bps in June 2019, the repo rate stood at 6.25 percent after a 25 bps rate cut in January 2021.

The first COVID-19 case was reported on March 5, and the government imposed a restriction on March 15. Measures included social distancing, travel bans on visitors from high-risk countries, quarantine for residents coming back from abroad, close of schools, screening home visits, tracking and contact tracing using mobile technology. After the first coronavirus death was reported, starting March 27, the country entered into a three-week lockdown. Only critical workers, transport services, banking, essential food and medicine production, and retail was kept operational.

On May 1, a phased lifting of the lockdown began with broader relaxation effective from June 1. Most economic activities were allowed with strict safety measures in place. With decreasing cases, almost all restrictions including international travel were lifted on October 1. Number of high travel risk countries were decreased to twenty-two from sixty on October 20. The cases increased in December and new restrictions were introduced (December 3) and on December 9 second wave was officially announced. Lockdown and restrictions proved to be affective, and restrictions were eased on February 1, 2021. With compulsory mask and ban on alcohol during shortened curfew hours, most economic activity resumed on March 1, 2021.

South Africa entered the COVID crisis with stable and low inflation rates and moderate inflation expectations which provided room for *significant* interest rate cuts. The SARB reduced the policy rate systematically during the pandemic: by 100 bps on March 19, and on April 14; 50 bps on May 21 and 25 bps on July 23. Hence between March and July, the MPC lowered the repo rate by a total of 275 bps down to 3.5 percent, This was a much faster response than most other emerging countries.

South Africa has a large dependence on external financing due to its structural current account deficit that ranges within an average of –2.5percent to –3percent of GDP. Following a long history of deficit, South Africa had recorded a surplus of 1.4 percent in the first quarter in 2020, first time since 2003. However, in the second quarter, current account deteriorated to -3.1 percent of GDP in the second quarter. Concerns over external financing prevented South Africa to make any further cuts. With constrain on demand and business activity, South Africa recorded current account surplus of 5.9 percent and 3.7 percent of GDP in the third and fourth quarter of 2020, respectively. However, with concerns over exchange rate stability, there has not been any rate changes since the final cut in July.

The output gap in South Africa remained negative during the pandemic. With low medium-term inflation expectations, economic slack, and under-valued real effective exchange rate, inflation was not a problem and allowed SARB to keep interest rates relatively low. However, at the onset of the pandemic to prevent inflationary pressure due to supply shortages, on March 19 and 27, the Department of Trade and Industry took measures against price gouging and export control measures on essential goods (IMF 2020). These included specifications of the health essentials and setting maximum prices for the personal protective equipment.

As a main response to the pandemic, liquidity operations were performed to make sure that monetary policy transmission mechanism was not compro-mised. The SARB tried to ensure that the financial sector remained stable with banks having an ample and stable source of refinancing. The SARB injected liquidity in money markets with frequent and high volume repo operations. The regulatory capital requirements for banks were also relaxed temporarily. To guarantee smooth functioning of the bond market, SARB also purchased government bonds in the secondary market.[16]

As a first step to increase market liquidity, SARB announced the following measures on March 20:

- The number of repo auctions were increased to two. This provided intraday liquidity support to clearing banks at the policy rate.[17]
- The upper and lower bounds of the Standing Facilities (SF) to lend at the repo rate and borrow at were reduced. Specifically, the SF borrowing rate (the rate at which the SARB absorbs liquidity, that is, reverse repo rate) was reduced to the repo rate less 200 bps, from the current repo rate less 100 bps. The SF lending rate (the rate at which commercial banks borrow from SARB) was reduced to the repo rate, from the repo rate plus 100 bps. This policy is maintained until August 19 when the SARB returned to standard SF borrowing rates at +/- 100 bps the repo rate (South African Reserve Bank 2021.c).[18]
- The size of the main weekly refinancing operations would increase if required, to provide the average daily liquidity demand over a week.

As more firms and people were affected by the economic stress to providing debt relief to bank customers was also important. In that regard, a unified approach for bank support to borrowers was announced on March 23 with guidelines released on March 26. A program with further measures to ease liquidity strains in funding markets were declared on March 25. The program included purchase government securities in the secondary market across the entire yield curve. Also, the main refinancing instrument maturities were prolonged from three to twelve months.

Capital and liquidity requirements for banks were relaxed. A temporary relaxation of bank minimum capital requirements was announced on March 28, 2020. On April 6, the LCR was reduced from 100 percent to 80 percent capital relief the duration of the crisis on restructured loans that were in good standing before the crisis was announced. On the same day, SARB issued a guidance note on dividend and cash bonuses distribution to ensure bank capital preservation.[19]

SARB also provided guidance for businesses to mitigate the impact on the COVID-19. On May 12, guidance on prudential matters, supervisory activities, and governance and operational issues was announced by SARB for cooperative financial institutions.[20]

At the end of April, National Treasury enacted the Loan Guarantee Scheme, aimed at lending support to qualifying businesses. The scheme, which has been updated in July for more favorable conditions, provide funds in more favorable terms to cover businesses' operational expenses, such as salaries, rent and lease agreements, and contracts with suppliers. Commercial banks and the National Treasury share the risks of these loans, and SARB would provide the finances for the banks. However, after almost one year, the demand for the scheme remains significantly below the original expectations (Businesstech 2020).

While the SARB took many measures to contain the pandemic and provide liquidity into the market, it has maintained its long-standing practice of not intervening in the foreign exchange market.

CONCLUSION

The central banks around the world have announced a series of policy measures since the onset of the pandemic. The bulk of the response came in March 2020 when many countries announced containment measures and the panic caused a financial market liquidity crisis. FED and major advanced economy central banks stepped in swiftly providing ample liquidity into the system, and the initial sell-off was contained. With confidence that advanced economy's central banks would provide liquidity, emerging market's central banks followed through.

In this chapter, we have reviewed the monetary policy response of the four emerging economies, Brazil, India, Indonesia, and South Africa. Contrast to advanced economies, emerging economies had room for monetary easing as they were not constrained by the zero lower bound. However, they were limited in their use of monetary policy due to concerns over currency stability and capital flight.

The four emerging economies have a history of high inflation. However, starting with Brazil in 1999 and latest India in 2015, they all adopted IT policies and managed to bring down inflation expectations. As expectations were anchored down, with the economy operating with negative gap, they all reacted by cutting interest rates.

The countries have also used reserve requirements actively. Besides the monetary easing, they also implemented measures to relax credit conditions for businesses and banks to extend credit. The debt burden of the fiscal support was shared by the central banks though at a varying degree. Some countries have adopted policies targeting the external sector. Providing debt relief, favorable negation terms to financially stressed firms have also been used extensively. While most countries intervened, only the SARB did not intervene in the foreign exchange market and kept its longstanding nonintervention policy.

Low interest rates and loose liquidity were the main tools in fight of the economic downturns and will be maintained until there are signs of increasing inflationary pressure. The economic outlook is very contingent on the course of the pandemic, and there are continuing uncertainties like vaccine deployment. However, as economic activity resumes, inflation is expected to be on an upward trajectory, and we can expect the loose policies to be lifted up gradually parallel to economic recovery.

NOTES

1. "At that time there were 98 cases and no deaths in 18 countries outside China. Four countries had evidence (8 cases) of human-to-human transmission outside China (Germany, Japan, the US, and Vietnam" (www.who.int/emergencies/diseases/novel-coronavirus-2019/interactive-timeline#!).

2. Banking Law No. 4595.

3. As of 1995, the CMN had three members: The Minister of Economy (chairman), the Ministry of Economy's Special Secretary of Finance, the Governor of the BCB (Law 9069 of June 29, 1995, Chapter II).

4. Forward guidance had been used earlier in Brazil in late 2012 to early 2013 when interest rates were at a then-low 7.25 percent.

5. Banco Central Do Brasil Circular No. 3990, March 18, 2020.

6. Constitutional Amendment No. 106/2020.

7. Initially, however, BCB was reluctant for asset purchases, and BCB Chief Campos Neto had indicated that bond buying would be exercised only after conventional tools have been exhausted.

8. The rate was cut down by BCB to 31 percent on June 2019 from its previous 33 percent to improve market efficiency.

9. Inflation varied between 5 percent and 16 percent during 1990–2010, and between 8 percent and 13 percent during 2010–2015.

10. Bank Indonesia Act No. 23 of May 17, 1999.

11. During 2014–2019 economic growth averaged 5 percent. In year 2019 growth was 5.02 percent, slower than 2018 growth rate of 5.17 percent and slower than the government's promise of 7 to 8 percent.-

12. Bank Indonesia Regulation (PBI) No. 22/3/PBI/2020, as an amendment to PBI No. 20/3/PBI/2018 concerning Statutory Reserve Requirements in Rupiah and a Foreign Currency.

13. The program includes fiscal measures, such as tax breaks, subsidies for companies and individuals, and non-fiscal regulatory measures to stimulate exports and imports focused on trade liberalization.

14. Pre-covid, foreigners held nearly 40 percent of local currency bonds, but early in the crisis, capital flows reversed, as foreigners reduced their bond holdings to just over 30 percent. A significant amount of recently issued debt in Indonesia was denominated in rupiah rather than dollars.

15. Down payments for green motor vehicle loans were also reduced.

16. The purchasing of government bonds in the primary market is prohibited by section 13 of the SARB Act 90 of 1989, as amended. The bond purchases will be held by the SARB in the Monetary Policy Portfolio (MPP), a liquidity management tool of the SARB, and can be used for both injecting and draining liquidity.

17. Implementation of Intraday Overnight Supplementary Repurchase Operations (IOSROs). This policy was kept until May 11, when the number of repo auctions was reduced to once a day. On February 3, 2021 SARB decided to revert to discretionary end-of-day supplementary repurchase operations at the repo rate.

18. South African Reserve Bank Media Statement, March 20, 2020, "Changes to the money market liquidity management strategy of the South African Reserve Bank."

19. Another note was released on February 18, 2021.

20. On August 3, the macroprudential policy relaxation was extended until further notice.

REFERENCES

Adrian, Tobias, Douglas Laxton, and Maurice Obstfeld. 2018. "Chapter 11. India: Stabilizing Inflation." In *Advancing the Frontiers of Monetary Policy*. USA: International Monetary Fund. doi: https://doi.org/10.5089/9781484325940.071.

Allard, Tom, and Kate Lamb. 2021. "Endless first wave: How Indonesia failed to control coronavirus" Las modified August 20, 2020. www.reuters.com/article/us-health-coronavirus-indonesia-insight-idUSKCN25G02J.

Banco Central do Brasil. 2020.a "Monetary Policy Committee (Copom)" https://ww
w.bcb.gov.br/en/monetarypolicy/committee

Banco Central do Brasil. 2020.b. "Minutes of the 228th Meeting of the Monetary
Policy Committee (Copom)" February 4–5, 2020.

Banco Central do Brasil. 2020.c. "Preserving the regular operation of the financial
system and the Brazilian economy." *Measures to Face the COVID-19 Crisis.*

BIS. n.d. "India, Institutional Framework" Accessed May 4, 2020. www.bis.org/mc/
currency_areas/in.htm.

Businesstech. 2020. "South Africa's R200 billion COVID-19 loan scheme seems
to have failed—here's what happened." Last Modified February 3, 2021. https
://businesstech.co.za/news/banking/465242/south-africas-r200-billion-COVID-19
-loan-scheme-seems-to-have-failed-heres-what-happened.

Cavallino, Paolo and Fiorella De Fiore. 2020. "Central banks' response to COVID-19
in advanced economies" *BIS Bulletin* No 21.

Dev, Mahendra and Rajeswari Sengupta, 2020. "COVID-19: Impact on the Indian
economy." *Indira Gandhi Institute of Development Research, Mumbai Working
Papers* 2020-013, Indira Gandhi Institute of Development Research, Mumbai,
India.

Franklin, Margaret. 2020. "Roberto Campos Neto, CFA, on COVID-19, ESG, and
an Inclusive Recovery," CFA. Posted in Coronavirus, Economics, History &
Geopolitics, Investment Topics. https://blogs.cfainstitute.org/investor/2020/10/19/
roberto-campos-neto-cfa-on-COVID-19 -esg-and-an-inclusive-recovery.

Habir, Manggi Taruna, and Wisnu Wardana. 2020. "COVID-19 's Impact On
Indonesia's Economy and Financial Markets" *ISEAS- Yusof Ishak Institute
Perspective*, Issue: 2020 No: 142. http://hdl.handle.net/11540/12952.

Herman. 2020. "Bank Indonesia Reveals Six Monetary Policies to Keep Financial
System Stable." Last updated May 11, 2020. https:///jakartaglobe.id/business/bank
-indonesia-reveals-six-monetary-policies-to-keep-financial-system-stable.

IMF. 2021. "Policy responses to COVID-19, Policy Tracker." Accessed May
15, 2021. https://www.imf.org/en/Topics/imf-and-covid19/Policy-Responses-to
-COVID-19 #S.

Neto, Campos Roberto. 2020 "Dealing with the effects of the COVID-19 Crisis."

Patnaik, Ila and Rajeswari Sengupta. 2020. "Impact of COVID-19 on the Indian
Economy: An Analysis of Fiscal Scenarios." Working Papers 20/319, National
Institute of Public Finance and Policy.

Patnaik, Ila, and Radhika Pandey. 2020. "Four years of the inflation targeting
framework." *National Institute of Public Finance and Policy Working Paper* No.
20/325.

Reserve Bank of India. 2020.a. "Statement on Developmental and Regulatory
Policies." October 09, 2020

Reserve Bank of India. 2020.b. "Statement on Developmental and Regulatory
Policies." March 27, 2020

Reuters. 2020. "Update 2-Brazil's central bank to flood lenders with fresh liquidity"
Updated March 23, 2020. https://www.reuters.com/article/health-coronavirus-braz
il-banks-idUSL1N2BG0IX.

Schrimpf, Andreas, Hyun Song Shin and Vladyslav Sushko, 2020 Vlad Sushko. 2020. "Leverage and margin spirals in fixed income markets during the COVID-19 crisis." *BIS Bulletin* No. 2, April 2020.

South African Reserve Bank 2020.a. "The SARB fulfils its constitutional mandate to protect the value of the rand by keeping inflation low and steady." Accessed May 5, 2021. www.resbank.co.za/en/home/what-we-do/monetary-policy)

South African Reserve Bank. 2021.b. "Welcome to the South African Reserve Bank." Accessed May 1, 2021. https://www.resbank.co.za/en/home.

South African Reserve Bank. 2021.c. "Monetary Implementation Framework." Accessed May 7, 2021. https://www.resbank.co.za/en/home/what-we-do/financial-markets/monetary-policy-implementation-framework.

Umam Ahmad Khoirul, and Muhamad Rosyid Jazuli. 2020. "The Impact of the COVID-19 Pandemic on Indonesia's Political-Economic Order Asia's Path Forward." *Paramadina Public Policy Institute (PPPI) Center for International Private Enterprise (CIPE).*

WHO. 2021. "Weekly epidemiological update—January 27 2021."

Chapter 11

Investigation of Price Bubbles during COVID-19 Period in the Stock Exchange of Turkey and BRICS

İhsan Erdem Kayral

INTRODUCTION

The 2008 Global Financial Crisis affected many economies of developing country which are integrated into global markets including the economies of developed countries (Kayral 2019). After the 2008 crisis, the economies of only limited number of countries were affected, not the global economy, such as the EU was encountered with Debt Crisis (Kayral 2020). This relatively stable process has been corrupted by the virus called SARS-CoV-2 (widely used as COVID-19), instead of fluctuations in money and capital markets as in the past century. The People's Republic of China reported the first COVID-19 case to the World Health Organization (WHO) on December 31, 2019, and WHO declared COVID-19 as a worldwide pandemic on March 11, 2020 (Huang et al. 2020). By November 30, 2020, around 65 million cases were detected in the world, and approximately 1.5 million people died (Worldometer 2020).

The highest number of cases was seen in the United States, which is considered as the most important country in the global market, followed by India, Brazil, Russia, and France. The ranking in terms of number of deaths is in this order: the United States, Brazil, India, Mexico, and United Kingdom. As of November 30, 2020, the number of death cases in BRICS countries (Brazil, Russia, India, China, and Turkey) are as follows: 9 million cases in India, 6 million cases in Brazil, and more than 2 million cases in Russia.

These countries ranked second, third, and fourth after the United States which are among the top ten countries in the world in terms of death rates as of the same date. While South Africa and Turkey (top ten in terms of number of cases) are among the top twenty countries in terms of cases and death

145

numbers, China ranks last among countries with case numbers (71st) and death numbers (38th) due to the measures taken by the government to limit the cases in a short time.

A number of academicians started to focus on this issue. Especially after WHO announced the COVID-19 outbreak as a global pandemic, a rapid increase was observed in the number of academic studies. While some of these studies include estimates on the number of cases and deaths in countries with the pandemic (Cakir and Savas 2020; Fanelli and Piazza 2020; Hernandez-Matamoros et al. 2020), others focus on policies that can be followed during the pandemic period (Hale et al. 2020; Kayral and Buzrul 2020; Yan et al. 2020). While these studies focus on health sciences and health economics, studies associating the pandemic with the field of finance also increased rapidly.

Studies in finance generally focus on examining the effects of the COVID-19 pandemic on assets and stock markets in the money, commodity, and capital markets. Some of these studies have focused on the markets of a single country. Albulescu (2020) detected that official announcements about new infection and death rates of COVID-19 increased the volatility of the S&P index. Corbet et al. (2020) investigated the volatility relationships between major stock markets in China and assets, such as gold and cryptocurrencies for the pre-pandemic and post-pandemic period, and concluded that the COVID-19 pandemic affected the relationships between these assets. Kayral and Tandogan (2020) investigated the volatility contagion among BIST100, gold, and exchange rates for the period before and after COVID-19 and conclude that investors preferred gold due to the increase in volatility in the stock market index during the pandemic period. Baker et al. (2020) determined that the COVID-19 pandemic has created much more volatility in the S&P500 (USA) than previous pandemics. Moreover, it is also stated in the study that the current pandemic is one of the major shocks after the Great Depression (1929) and Black Monday (1987).

Some studies in the literature investigated how the countries are affected by the pandemic period are comparative studies. Sansa (2020) analyzed the effect of COVID-19 on stock markets in China and the United States using regression models and revealed that the pandemic has some effects on both stock markets. OECD (2020) has discussed the effect of coronavirus on development finance, and it has been found that private financing flows in developing countries exceeded the effect of the 2008 Global Financial Crisis. Ozili and Arun (2020) determined in their study that policies (shut-downs, travel bans, etc.) implemented against the pandemic have affected the prices of stock market indices on a global scale. Akhtaruzzaman et al. (2020) examined the spillover effect on firms and indices in G-7 before and after the COVID-19 pandemic period and concluded that financial spillover costs and hedge costs have increased during the pandemic period. McKibbin and Fernando (2020) examined different scenarios regarding the macroeconomic effects of the COVID-19 pandemic globally using the DSGE equilibrium model. This study showed that all countries will be negatively affected by the pandemic in the short term. At the same time, according to the results, this process will affect countries with low health investments and high population density.

It is seen that different econometric methods are applied in the studies, and comparison has been made between the pre-pandemic period and the pandemic period. Additionally, studies were also conducted investigating price bubbles in money, commodity, and capital markets in both developed and developing countries. Liu and Lee (2018) investigated the bubbles in spot prices in energy markets and found that the natural gas market has a more speculative structure when compared to other energy markets.

Koy (2018) used SADF derivative tests to determine the existence of price bubbles in the stock markets of many developing countries for the period 2001–2017 and determined that there were price bubbles in the stock markets of Brazil, Indonesia, India, South Korea, Qatar, Mexico, Russia, and Chile in the analysis period. Podhorsky (2019) investigated the price bubbles in bitcoin using SADF tests in the 2014–2019 period, and no price bubble can be found in the period in question. In our study, an empirical analysis investigating the price bubbles in the pre-pandemic and pandemic period will be carried out for the stock markets indices of BRICS countries, which are accepted as the major emerging economies, along with Turkey. Although there are different studies examining the price balloons, a contribution to the literature has been made by us to the price balloons during the pandemic period.

The second part of the study will include the data and the method applied, and in the third part, the findings of the study will be discussed.

DATA AND METHODOLOGY

An empirical study examines the price bubbles in the stock market indices of BRICS countries and also Turkey. In the study, the analysis period is between Jan 01, 2019 and Nov 30, 2020, covering the period between one year before (the period before December 31, 2019) and about one year after the first COVID-19 case was reported. The study aimed to examine whether there are price bubbles in the stock markets of major developing country during the COVID-19 period. The study considered the daily closing prices of the DV3P (Brazil), SSEC (China), SESN from India, MCX from Russia, JSE (S. Africa), and BIST100 (Turkey) indices. The data was obtained from the Data Stream database.

The price movements of the stock exchanges examined during the analysis period are shown in figure 11.1. In the pre-pandemic period (in 2019), although there were decreases in different periods on a stock market basis, it was observed that all indices except the JSE reached higher closing prices at the end of the year. While the JSE index showed a downward trend in 2019, the SSEC reached the highest closing value in 2019 in the first two quarters of the year. A stable increase was observed in the other stock markets such as BVSP, SESN, MCX, and BIST100 indices, and the highest closing prices of the year were observed in the last quarter.

As can be seen in figure 11.1, a rapid diminishing was experienced in the BVSP, SESN, MCX, and BIST100 indices at the end of the first quarter of

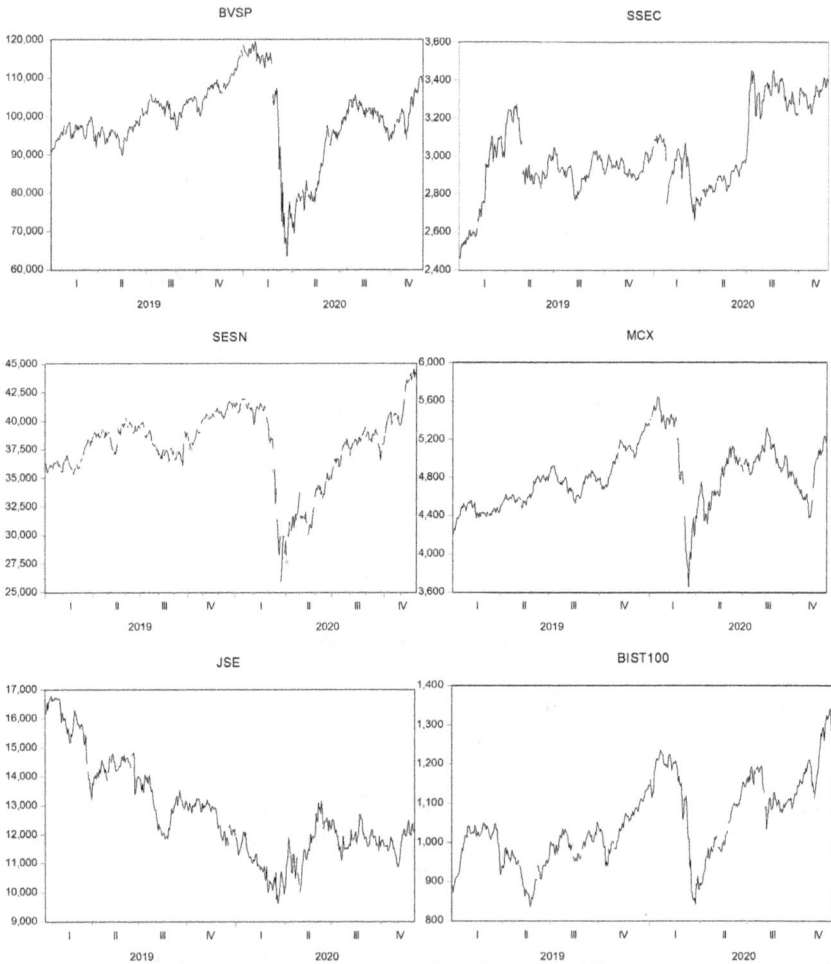

Figure 11.1   Stock Market Prices. *Source*: Author's Calculations (2020)

2020 under the influence of the pandemic especially after WHO declared COVID-19 as a pandemic. Although there was a decrease in SSEC and JSE indices in this period, the contraction in the index remained relatively limited compared to other stock markets. In addition, it was seen that the rapid fluctuations and contractions observed in the indices after the pandemic announcement were priced in the markets after a while and the indices have entered a recovery process.

METHODOLOGY

Philips et al. (2011) investigated the presence of price bubbles using the supremum ADF (SADF) test with the forward iterative test technique. The testing process begins with the least squares estimation of the standard autoregressive ADF regression. In the SADF test, despite the null hypothesis that there is no unit root ($H_0 : \varphi = 1$), the alternative hypothesis ($H_A : \varphi > 1$) with the right-tailed unit root is tested. SADF test statistics are calculated using the equation shown in $\sup\limits_{w \in [w_0, 1]} \int_0^w M dM \, / \left(\int_0^w M^2 \right)^{1/2}$; in the equation, M shows the standard Brown motion, and the test value obtained from the equation given in the equation is compared with the table values (critical values). If the calculated test value is higher than the critical value, the null hypothesis is rejected and it is concluded that there is a price bubble in the examined asset or stock markets.

In the context of our study, the SADF method presented by Philips et al. (2011) is used. In our study, the price bubbles observed in the stock markets in the pre-pandemic period and during the pandemic period will be examined using Monte Carlo Simulations of this method.

In the SADF method, the period when price bubbles are seen and whether these bubbles become concentrated in the COVID-19 process will also be presented within the scope of our study.

RESULTS

When the descriptive statistics of the exchange markets were evaluated within the scope of the study, while closing prices of SSEC (with the value of 5.7474 for Jarque–Bera test at 5 percent level) and MCX (with the value of 1.2014 for Jarque–Bera test at the same level with SSEC) indices have normal distribution, the other exchange markets do not have normal distribution. However, the skewness values of all the series are close to 0 and the kurtosis values vary between 2 and 4, and it is observed that they show a similar structure to financial time series.

The presence of price bubbles in the series is tested using the SADF test. In this test, the H_0 hypothesis stating that there are no price bubbles is tested. If the null hypothesis is rejected, then it is concluded that price bubbles are observed in the stock market index examined in terms of our study. The results of SADF tests applied to examine price bubbles before COVID-19 and during the COVID-19 period for six stock market indices are shown in table 11.1.

According to the SADF test results in table 11.1, statistically significant results are found at the 1 percent level in BVSP, SESN, MCX, at 5 percent level in the BIST100 Index, and at 10 percent level in the SSEC, and the null hypothesis stating that there are no price bubbles in the analysis period is rejected. According to these results, it is determined that there are price bubbles in all stock market indices except JSE (S. Africa) before COVID-19 and/or during the pandemic. According to the SADF test results, the periods of significant price bubbles for each stock market are shown in figure 11.2.

The curve at the top of figure 11.2 shows the price movements in the stock market. The presence of price bubbles is evaluated by comparing the values in the second curve, which follows a relatively stable path, and the third curve which is shown in thick lines. Accordingly, it can be stated that there are price bubbles at the points where the values of the third curve exceed the values of the second curve.

Accordingly, when the graphs of five stock exchanges, which are statistically determined to have a price bubble according to the SADF test statistics, were analyzed, it was found that all indices except the SSEC (China) had price bubbles in the COVID-19 pandemic. The bubbles seen in the SSEC in 2019 are detected in the pre-COVID-19 period. However, we found price bubbles in the SESN ans BIST indices both pre-COVID19 and the pandemic. The number and

Table 11.1   The SADF Test Applied to Stock Markets

Stock Market	SADF	SADF - Critical Values		
		90%	95%	99%
BVSP	2.9205***	0.3515	0.5855	1.0384
SSEC	0.3872*	0.3383	0.6005	1.0494
JSE	-0.8279	0.3370	0.5964	1.1546
SESN	3.5985***	0.3488	0.5551	0.9876
MCX	4.4220***	0.3370	0.5964	1.1546
BIST100	0.8987**	0.2965	0.5706	1.0889

Notes: Critical values of tests are obtained from Monte Carlo simulation with 1000 replications. *,**,*** denotes significance at the 10 percent, 5 percent, 1 percent level.
Source: Author's calculations (2020)

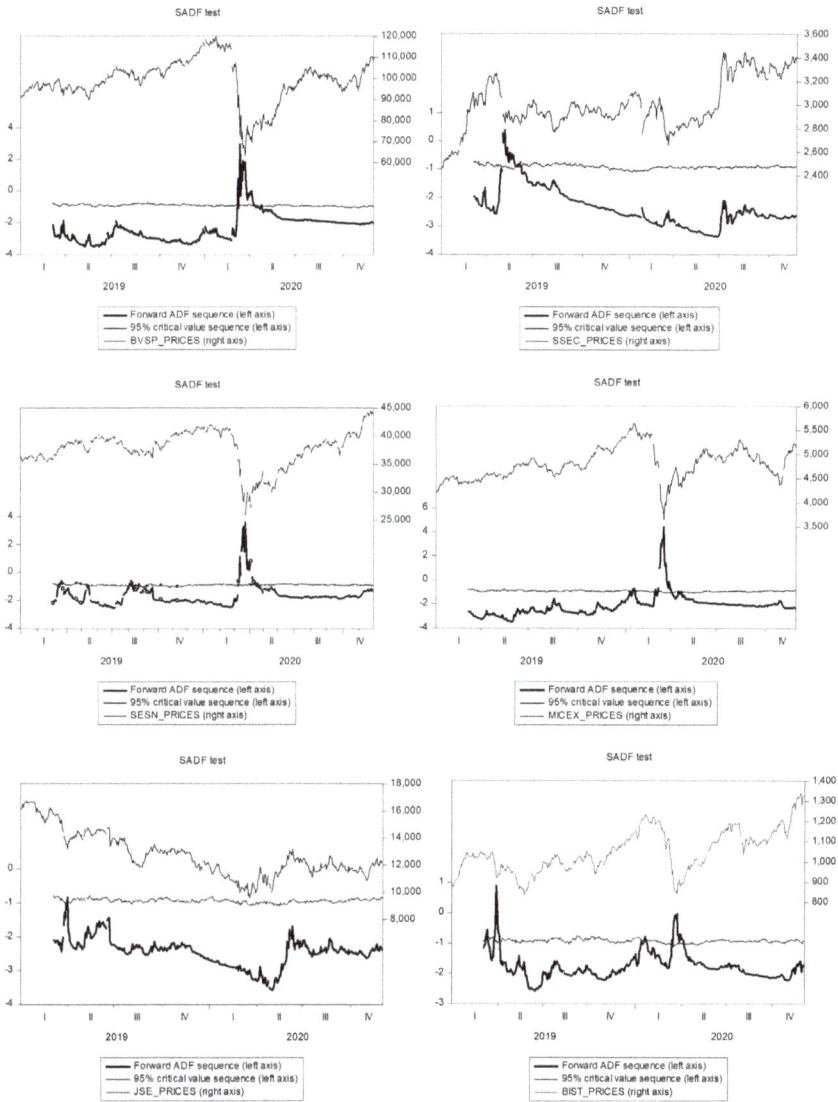

Figure 11.2 Date-Stamping Bubble Periods in the Stock Markets: The SADF Test.
Source: Author's Calculations (2020)

date range of price bubbles in the pre-COVID-19 period regarding the stock exchanges are also determined within the scope of the analysis.

Accordingly, it is determined that price bubbles are seen in SSEC, SESN, and BIST100 indices in the pre-COVID-19 period. These balloons are seen in the SSEC in the period May 06, 2019, to May 29, 2019, and June 04, 2019, to June 06, 2019; in the SESN in the period March 15, 2019, to March 20,

2019, May 13, 2019, to May 13, 2019, August 01, 2019, to August 09, 2019, during the date of August 13, 2019, and August 22, 2019 to August 23, 2019, respectively, and between March 07, 2019, to March 11, 2019, and March 26, 2019, to April 03, 2019, in the BIST100 Index.

Before December 31, 2019, when the first case was seen, the stock market with the highest number of price bubble is SESN (5 times), while the longest-lasting balloon is detected in SSEC (the first price bubble with eighteen trading days uninterrupted).

In the period of COVID-19, with significant SADF tests, price bubbles are detected in the stock exchanges of the countries except China (SSEC) where the pandemic started. Accordingly, price balloons are found in the BVSP during the date of March 10, 2020, March 12,2020 to April 07, 2020, during the date of April 09, 2020, during the date of April 16, 2020 and during the date of April 24, 2020. BVSP is the stock market index with the most bubbles in the COVID-19 period, with five different time periods.

This index is followed by MCX (January 17, 2020, to January 21, 2020; February 28, 2020, to March 02,2020; March 06, 2020, to April 01, 2020; April 15, 2020) and BIST100 (January 21, 2020 to January 22,2020; March 12, 2020; March 16, 2020, to March 25,2020; March 27,2020 to April 03,2020) with four balloons. The SESN index is the stock market with the least number of bubbles twice on March 09, 2020 to April 16, 2020 and April 21, 2020.

In the four indices other than SSEC, it is observed that the bubbles are intensified after the COVID-19 was declared as a pandemic by WHO on March 11, 2020, and the price bubbles disappeared as of May. This result shows as the stock market indices, which are considered to be one of the most important indicators of the capital markets, that is, they move together with the global markets, and as of May 2020, the pandemic conditions are priced in these stock markets.

During the period December 31, 2019, and November 30, 2020, the longest continuous balloon was detected in SESN with twenty-four trading days (between March 09, 2020, and April 16, 2020). Among the other stock markets with bubbles, the longest balloon in BVSP was realized as twenty trading days in the period March 12, 2020 to April 07, 2020, and eighteen trading days in MCX during the period between March 06, 2020, and April 01, 2020. The longest price bubbles in the BIST100 Index are observed as eight trading days between March 16, 2020, and March 25, 2020, and six trading days between March 27, 2020, and April 03, 2020. In addition, at least one-day bubbles were detected before and/or after these long-term bubbles seen in the stock markets. When the evaluation is made according to the trading days with price bubbles before COVID-19 and during the pandemic period, the number of trading days (forty-four days) with a price bubble in the pre-COVID-19 period is half of the pandemic (ninety days). The impact of the pandemic on the fluctuations in the stock markets of developing countries can be observed more clearly when the SSEC index, in which all price bubbles were seen during the pre-pandemic period, is removed. While more price bubbles were observed in the pandemic process in four stock markets other than SSEC, the highest trading day was reached in the SESN index (twenty-five days). While more price bubbles are observed in the pandemic process in four stock markets other than SSEC, the highest trading day is reached in the SESN (twenty-five days). While SESN is followed by BVSP (twenty-four days) and MCX (twenty-four days), the lowest number of days among the stock markets with a price bubble during the pandemic period is determined in the BIST100 (seventeen days) index. When the price bubbles seen in the indices during the entire analysis period are evaluated, SESN ranked first with thirty-eight trading days (fourteen days before the pandemic), while the BIST100 index ranked the second with twenty-seven trading days due to being one of the two stock markets in both sub-periods.

CONCLUSION

The COVID-19 outbreak, declared as a global pandemic by WHO as of March 11, 2020, has affected many developed and developing economies in a short time. Countries have taken different shut-down measures due to the rapid increase in the number of cases and the resulting deaths. Although the pandemic period continues on the global scale, the stock market indices, which are considered to be the most important indicators in the capital markets, have been affected at different levels in the eleven-month period after the first case was reported to WHO.

In this study, the existence of price bubbles has been examined in stock market indices of the BRICS countries including China and the major emerging economies consisting of Turkey in the pre-pandemic period (January 1, 2019, to December 30, 2019) and the pandemic period (December 31, 2019, to November 30, 2020).

In the empirical study using the SADF test, price bubbles are determined in all stock market indices except JSE (S. Africa). Price bubbles are found only during the pandemic period in BVSP (Brazil) and MCX (Russia), and before the pandemic in SSEC (China). Price bubbles are determined in SESN (India) and BIST100 (Turkey) stock market indices in both periods. The highest number of price bubbles in the pre-pandemic period is SSEC with twenty-one trading days, SESN (India), BIST100 (Turkey) stock market indices followed this index with, respectively, thirteen and ten trading days.

In the pandemic period, SESN is the index with the highest price bubble on a trading day basis (twenty-five), followed by MCX (twenty-four) and BVSP (twenty-four) and BIST100 (17). It is observed that a large part of the price bubbles observed during the pandemic intensified on March 11, 2020, when WHO announced that COVID-19 was a global epidemic. It has been that the price bubbles seen during the pandemic period disappeared in May 2020, in other words, the capital markets determine the price in pandemic conditions.

When all the analysis period is evaluated, the highest number of price bubble is detected in the SESN index with a total of thirty-eight days. Together with SESN, the BIST100 Index, one of the two stock markets in which price bubbles are detected both before the pandemic and during the pandemic period shows a price bubble in a total of twenty-seven trading days. The longest continuous price bubble (twenty-four) is observed in SESN.

It has been evaluated that studies investigating the effects of the pandemic on financial markets will increase in the upcoming period, and that studies examining price bubbles can be carried out both for the stock markets that are subject to our study and also for various developed and developing countries. Moreover, in addition to stock market indices, the determination of price bubbles for different money and capital market instruments will be an important issue in terms of evaluating the effects of the pandemic on these instruments.

REFERENCES

Akhtaruzzaman, M., Boubaker, S., and Sensoy, A. 2020. Financial contagion during COVID-19 crisis. *Finance Research Letters* (in press).

Albulescu, C. T. 2020. COVID-19 and the United States financial markets' volatility. *Finance Research Letters* (in press).

Baker, S. R., Bloom, N., Davis, S. J., Kost, K. J., Sammon, M. C., and Viratyosin, T. 2020. The Unprecedented Stock Market Impact of COVID-19. *NBER WORKING PAPER SERIES: Working Paper 26945*.

Cakir, Z., and Savas, H.B. 2020. A mathematical modelling for the COVID-19 pandemic in Iran. *Ortadogu Medical Journal* 12(2): 206–210. https://doi.org/10.2 1601/ortadogutipdergisi.715612.

Corbet, S., Larkin, C., and Lucey, B. 2020. *The contagion effects of the COVID-19 pandemic: Evidence from gold and cryptocurrencies.* https://ssrn.com/abstract =3564443.

Fanelli D., and Piazza F. 2020. Analysis and forecasting of COVID-19 spreading in China, Italy and France. *Chaos Solitons & Fractals* 134: 109761. https://doi.org/10 .1016/j.chaos.2020.109761.

Hale T., Angrist, N., Kira, B., Petherick, A., Phillips, T., and Webster, S. 2020. Variation in government responses to COVID-19, *BSG-WP-2020/032*, Version 6, pp. 1–23.

Hernandez-Matamoros, A., Fujita, H., Hayashi, T., Perez-Meana, H. 2020. Forecasting of COVID19 per regions using ARIMA models and polynomial functions. *Applied Soft Computing* 96: 106610.

Huang, C., Wang, Y., Li, X., Ren, L., Zhao, J., Hu, Y., and Cheng, Z. 2020. Clinical features of patients infected with 2019 novel coronavirus in Wuhan, China. *The Lancet* 395 (10223): 497–506.

Kayral İ.E., 2019. *2008 Küresel Finans Krizini Anlamak*, Gece Kitaplığı: Ankara, 1. Basım.

Kayral, İ.E., and Tandogan, N.Ş. 2020. Impact of COVID-19 Pandemic on Return and Volatilies of BIST100 Index, Exchange Rates and Gold (in Turkish). *Gaziantep University Journal of Social Sciences*, 19, COVID-19 Special Issue, 687–701. DOI: 10.21547/jss.786384

Kayral, İ.E., and Buzrul S. 2020. Forecasting of COVID-19 infections in E7 countries and proposing some policies based on the Stringency Index. *Journal of Population Therapeutics & Clinical Pharmacology* SI1: The Era of the Coronavirus (COVID-19) Pandemic: e76–e84. DOI: https://doi.org/10.15586/jptcp.v27iSP1.757.

Kayral, İ.E. 2020. "The Comparison of Ireland, Spain and Greece Stock Market Volatilities in the 10th Year of 2008 Global Financial Crisis," *Future of The European Union Integration: A Failure or A Success? Future Expectations*, 183–197, Peter Lang Publishing.

Koy, A. 2018. Multibubbles in Emerging Stock Markets. *Finans Politik ve Ekonomik Yorumlar* 55(637), 95–109.

Liu, T.Y., and Lee, C.C. 2018. Will the energy price bubble burst? *Energy* 150: 276–288.

McKibbin, W. J., and Fernando, R. 2020. The global macroeconomic impacts of COVID-19: Seven scenarios. *CAMA (Centre for Applied Macroeconomic Analysis)* Working Paper No. 19/2020. pp. 1–45.

OECD. 2020. *The impact of the coronavirus (COVID-19) crisis on development finance.* Access Date: 15 November 2020. https://read.oecd-ilibrary.org/view/?ref=134_134569-xn1go1i113&title=The-impact-of-the-coronavirus-(COVID-19)-crisis-on-development-finance.

Ozili, P., and Arun, T. 2020. Spillover of COVID-19: Impact on the global economy. *MPRA Paper 99317.*

Phillips, P.C.B., Shi, S., and Yu, J. 2011. Testing for multiple bubbles. No 09-2011, Working Paper, Singapore Management University, School of Economics. Access Date: 5 November 2020, https://econpapers.repec.org/paper/siuwpaper/09-2011.htm.

Phillips, P.C.B., Wu, Y, and Yu, J. 2011. Explosive behavior in the 1990s NASDAQ: when did exuberance escalate asset values? *International Monetary Review* 52(1). 1015–16.

Podhorsky, A. 2019. Bursting the Bitcoin Bubble: Assessing the Fundamental Value and Social Costs of Bitcoin. *ADBI Working Paper Series* No. 934, p. 1–57.

Sansa, N.A. 2020. The impact of the COVID-19 on the financial markets: evidence from China and USA. *Electronic Research Journal of Social Sciences and Humanities,* 2(2), 29–39.

Worldometer. 2020. Access Date: 10 December 2020. https://www.worldometers. info/coronavirus.

Yan, B., Zhang, X., Wu, L., Zhu, H., and Chen, B. 2020. Why do countries respond differently to COVID-19? A comparative study of Sweden, China, France, and Japan. *American Review of Public Administration* 50(6–7), 762–769 DOI: https:// doi.org/10.1177/0275074020942445.

Chapter 12

Dynamic Analysis of the Causality Relationships between COVID-19 Pandemic and Electricity Consumption

Case of Turkey

Pinar Koç and Ahmet Gülmez

INTRODUCTION

Having emerged in Wuhan, China, for the first time in February 2020, COVID-19 caused a high morbidity and mortality rate. The number of cases have globally reached 81 million since the date the virus emerged, and the number of people who died of this disease is about 2 million. Although progress has been made in the diagnosis and treatment of the disease compared to the early periods, the rate of spreading is still slow even in mid-2021 and vaccination is underway. Accordingly, the total number of deaths will probably reach millions. High mortality and morbidity rates have resulted in limitations on both national and international levels and have been deeply affecting the economic and social lives.

All economic and social costs undertaken due to a certain disease are assessed within the literature covering the economic costs that arise from diseases. These costs are basically divided into three as direct costs, indirect costs, and intangible costs, and the intangible costs that are not seen within the studies on economic impacts are not included (jo, 2014). All sorts of costs undertaken during the diagnosis and treatment periods reflect the direct costs; income and production losses arising from diseases through the channel of labor productivity reflect the indirect costs; and distortion that occurs in people's quality of life due to certain reasons such as pain, sorrow, stress, and so on, which emerge owing to diseases, are assessed under the category of intangible costs.

The macroeconomic and microeconomic effects of diseases in economic theory can be considered within the framework of the human capital theory developed by Becker (1964) and the capacity approach developed by Sen (1992). Rice (2000) divides the indirect costs caused by diseases into two as morbidity costs and mortality costs. Morbidity costs imply the loss of wages caused by the decrease in performance seen in sick individuals at full efficiency and the loss of productivity due to the inability to perform daily activities. Mortalite costs express the present value of future income losses caused by premature deaths resulting from disease.

Although education is accepted as the main determinant of human capital stock, health has an important place in determining the labor stock in terms of quantity and quality. Haacker (2002) emphasized that diseases will negatively affect the output level and thus the economic growth process by reducing the efficient supply of labor. Cuddington (1993) claimed that illnesses negatively affect not only the supply of labor but also the consumption and saving behavior of economic decision-makers. Costs undertaken by the society are higher in cases of diseases with high morbidity and mortality rates. Increases in the amounts of financial resources spared for the diagnosis and treatment of diseases cause adverse supply and demand shocks, resulting in losses in income. Diseases increase medical expenditures and reduce the consumption of non-medical goods and services (Jones, 2002; Bardhan, 1999; Mahal et al., 2010). Increases in medical expenditures reduce the amount of the resource spared for saving and investments, while causing losses in national income (Cuddington, 1993). Diseases adversely affect labor productivity and occupational continuation, while reducing labor supply. Decrease in labor supply adversely affects labor income and companies' output levels (Daly, 2000).

Apart from the human capital approach, it can also be evaluated within the framework of the capacity approach developed by Sen (1992). According to this approach, the main determinant of welfare is individual capacity, not the level of benefit obtained from the consumption of goods and services, and the concept of capacity is defined as the ability to accomplish valued functions. Illnesses create erosive effects on individual capacity by reducing the ability of individuals to work. In this context, the provision of health services within the scope of social opportunities in a way that will increase individual capacity will also accelerate the development process.

Diseases negatively affect economic development through three channels. The first channel that has a determining effect on economic development is the decrease in life expectancy. The second, increasing the amount of resources allocated for the treatment of the disease decreases the amount of resources allocated to children's education and the future qualified human capital stock decreases. The third, the returns of business and infrastructure investments go beyond individual labor productivity due to diseases.

High infectiousness rate compared to other diseases have caused losses in the productivity and income of both infected and healthy people. The greatest economic shrinkage since the Great Depression of 1929 has occurred during the COVID-19 pandemic period. Compared to the last quarter of 2019, the economic shrinkage that globally occurred in the first quarter of 2020 was 3.5 percent, rising to 4.9 percent in the second quarter. The shrinkage in the economies of the developed countries was 1.9 percent in the first quarter of 2020 compared to the previous quarter and the shrinkage in the second quarter was 12.2 percent. The shrinkage seen in the developing countries has been smaller compared to the developed countries. The loss of productivity in developing countries was 0.78 in the first quarter compared to the previous quarter, and the shrinkage seen in the second quarter was 11.7 percent (IMF, 2020). Statistics regarding labor productivity and labor costs indicate that labor costs have globally increased while labor productivity has decreased. Labor costs increased by 2.9 percent in EURO region in the first quarter of 2020 compared to the previous quarter. The increase seen in the labor costs in the second half of 2020 was 4.8 percent. The change in the labor costs within OECD countries is close to the one seen in EURO region. Labor costs increased by 2.1 percent and 4.8 percent in the first and second quarter of 2020 in OECD countries. Loss of productivity in EURO region was approximately three times higher than the loss seen in OECD countries. The decrease in the labor productivity in OECD countries was 1.5 percent in the first quarter of 2020 compared to the previous quarter, and it was 3.5 percent in the second quarter. The decrease in the labor productivity in EURO region was 3.5 percent in the first quarter of 2020, and it was 9.1 percent in the second quarter. Analysis of the data regarding the Turkish economy indicated that the rate of economic shrinkage seen in the first quarter of 2020 was 0.1 percent, which reached 10.6 percent in the second quarter. Expenses increased by 2.3 percent in Turkey in the first quarter of 2019. The first Corona virus diagnosis in Turkey was made on March 11, 2020; morbidity rate of the disease has been lower in Turkey compared to other countries. Therefore, the labor productivity increased in the first quarter of 2019 rather than decreasing. Labor cost and productivity statistics regarding Turkey in the second quarter of 2020 are yet explained (OECD, 2020). About 1.6 million informal workers lost 60 percent of their income. Global trade fell 3 percent in the first quarter of 2020 and commodity prices fell by a record 20 percent in March, driven by steep drops in oil prices. About 265 million people in low and middle-income countries were at risk of acute food insecurity by the end of 2020 (UN, 2020).

The losses in productivity and incomes are expected to adversely affect the energy sector. Instabilities in the energy markets largely depend on the economic conjuncture. In addition, shocks seen in energy markets affect the economic conjuncture through the energy prices. Accordingly, the aim of this study, which was conducted between March 12, 2020, and July 26, 2020, is to analyze how the pandemic affected the electricity consumption dynamics in Turkey. Initially, information regarding the literature of disease costs was provided, and the channels through which the pandemic affected the economy were explained. Then, the studies analyzing the impacts of pandemic on electricity consumption were mentioned. In the third section, the methods and dataset were introduced, and results of estimation were provided in the last section.

LITERATURE REVIEW

Many studies on the impacts of COVID-19 on energy markets have been added to the literature. COVID-19 has adversely affected energy markets. The studies analyzing the impacts of COVID-19 on energy consumption were mentioned in this section. The changes in the energy consumption that have occurred owing to the pandemic vary by countries. Electricity consumption in Italy decreased by 37 percent compared to the same period in 2019 (Ghiani, et al., 2020) additionally, electricity consumption decreased by 15 percent in Pakistan (Aslam et al., 2020), 17.6 percent in Kuwait (Alhajeri et al., 2020), 15 percent in Poland (Czosnyka, 2020), 6.5 percent in China (Norouzi et al., 2020), and 10 percent in the United States (Agdaş & Barooah, 2020) compared to the same period in 2019. The decrease in the demand for electricity in Latin America and Caribbean varied between 4 percent and 28 percent in the last week of March (Tolmasquim et al., 2020). A strong and negative correlation is present between the number of COVID-19 cases in the United States and electricity consumption (Ruan et al., 2020). Electricity consumption has significantly decreased in Southeastern Asia countries (Lowder et al., 2020). The shrinkage in the electricity demand of fifty-eight countries was 10 percent during the period between January and April (Buechlera et al., 2020). Electricity consumption in Turkey decreased by 5 percent in March, 20 percent in April, and 22 percent in May compared to the same months in 2019 (Bulut, 2020).

Restrictions brought due to COVID-19 have affected the sectoral and regional distribution of electricity consumption. The shrinkage in the electricity demand in the state of Ontario, Canada, was 14 percent in April (Aburayash & Dinçer, 2020), and the decrease in electricity demand was approximately 5 percent in Alberta, British Columbia, and New Brunswick (Leach et al., 2020). Electricity demand has decreased in all regions of Brazil. However, the region with the greatest decrease of electricity demand was the southeastern region (3.6 percent) (Carvalho, et al., 2020). The shrinkage in the electricity consumption of European Union (EU) and states of the United States has ranged between 4 percent and 13 percent (Prol and Sungmin, 2020).

Studies have noted that electricity consumption of households would increase owing to COVID-19 and that plans and organizations should be made to reduce the rapid increase in energy consumption (Quarnain et al., 2020) which has also been supported in empirical studies. The demand for electricity has decreased in the industry and service sectors in Europe and Nigeria, but the demands of households have increased in this regard (Bahmanyara, 2020; Edomah and Ndulue, 2020). Use of electricity has increased owing to remote working methods in the periods when restrictions have been gradually abolished (Burleyson et al., 2020).

METHODOLOGY AND DATASET

This study analyzed the dynamic relationships between the pandemic period and energy consumption of Turkey. Daily energy consumption statistics and number of COVID-19 cases were used in the study. Variables used in the model and data sources are presented in table 12.1.

This study analyzed the dynamic relationships between the pandemic period and energy consumption of Turkey. Daily energy consumption statistics and number of COVID-19 cases were used in the study. In the estimated models, the dependent variable is the electricity consumption (ELECTCONS), while the independent variable is the number of COVID-19 cases. Electricity consumption statistics were obtained from the database of the Turkish Ministry of Energy and Natural Resources, while numbers of COVID-19 cases were found from the database of WHO.

The causality relationship between the number of COVID-19 cases and electricity consumption was analyzed using the bootstrap causality test by Hacker & Hatemi J (2006) for the period reviewed in the study. Bootstrap causality in rolling window was used to test whether causality relationship changed in time; moreover, rolling window regression was used to test the change of slope parameter in time.

Table 12.1   Results of Fractional Fourier Unit Root Test

Variable	f	Min SSR	Lag	F	t	Critical Values* 1%	5%	10%	DECISION
ENGCONS	0.8	3.00	1	21.31	−7.45	−4.92	−4.33	−4.03	I(0)
COVID19	0.1	9.30	1	17.20	−4.79	−4.78	−4.26	−3.96	I(0)

*Critical values developed by Bozoklu et al. (2020) for the fixed and trend model were used.
**Critical F values were 14.62, 11.07 and 9.38 at the significance levels of 1 percent, 5 percent, and 10 percent, respectively. Critical F values were obtained from Omay (2015).
Source: Calculated by author

BOOTSTRAP CAUSALITY TEST

Developed by Hacker & Hatemi J (2006), bootstrap causality test is based on the causality test of Toda and Yamamoto (1995). The Toda and Yamamoto test estimated through the Vector Autoregressive (VAR) model in relation to the $(p+d_{max})$ rank can be reflected as the causality test equation.

$$y_t = \hat{v} + A_1 y_{t-1} + \ldots + A_p y_{t-p-d} + \varepsilon_t \qquad (1)$$

Model p. can be estimated by adding the maximum fixed rank to the VAR model. Whether there is a causality relationship between the variables is decided using the MWALD test statistics and the statistics fit the chi-square distribution. Hacker & Hatemi J (2006) noted that the effect of MWALD test statistics decreased in small samples and that bootstrap-based critical values should be used. The modified WALD test statistic was done to check whether there is a Granger causality between two variables formulated as follows:

$$\hat{\varepsilon}_{it}^m = \frac{\hat{\varepsilon}_{it}}{\sqrt{1 - h_{it}}} \qquad (2)$$

In cases where calculated MWALD statistical test values are greater than the critical values as absolute values, hypothesis of zero is rejected and a causality relationship is accepted to be present between the variables.

BOOTSTRAP CAUSALITY TEST IN ROLLING WINDOW

The period examined in the bootstrap causality test based on rolling windows approach is divided into sub-windows, and bootstrap causality test is implemented on each window. The number of sub-windows should be primarily determined in the analysis. The size of sub-sample is determined using the formula $S = T(0.01 + 1.8(1/\sqrt{T}))$ suggested by Caspi and Graham (2017). S represents the size of sub-sample while T indicates the total sample size in the formula. The sub-sample size was twenty-two in this study. The first window consists of the first twenty-two observation values. The second sub-window covers the range between the second observation to the 23rd observation value after the first observation value is extracted. The first observation value is extracted in every new test stage, and sub-windows are formed by adding an observation value to the latest observation. The process of forming sub-windows continues until the last observation value. Bootstrap causality test is implemented on every sub-window and modified MWALD test statistics are obtained. These statistical values are divided into critical values at 10 percent significance level, and the results are reflected in the graph. The areas over 1 indicate the presence of causality relationship between variables, while the areas under 1 indicate the absence of causality relationship between the variables. The dates when causality emerges can be found in the bootstrap causality test based on rolling window approach.

ESTIMATION RESULTS

Series should be fixed to perform causality tests. Therefore, whether series are fixed on the threshold should be determined first, and then the fixed ranks of the series that are not fixed on the threshold should be revealed later. For that purpose, fractional Fourier unit root test was used. This test was developed based on the flexible Fourier unit root test developed by Enders and Lee (2012). Fourier unit root tests yield stronger results than the traditional unit root tests as the former consider the structural fractions, and then the other tests considering the structural fractions as the number and shape of structural fractions do not affect the power of Fourier unit root test. Moreover, fractional Fourier unit root test provides information about whether the impacts of structural fractions are temporary and permanent. The fractional Fourier unit root test is conducted based on the Fourier equation below:

$$\Delta y_t = \rho y_{t-1} + c_1 + c_2 t + c_3 sin\left(\frac{2\pi kt}{T}\right) + c_4 cos\left(\frac{2\pi kt}{T}\right) + e_t \qquad (3)$$

In addition to the $\pi = 3.14$ value, k reflects the number of frequencies while t represents the trend and T means the number of observations. To select the appropriate value of frequency, the values between 0.1 and 5 are used in place of k to estimate the equation based on the study by Bozoklu et al. (2020), and the k value that minimizes the error sum of squares is selected as the appropriate frequency value. If the series are fixed, meanings of trigonometric terms should be examined. Statistical significance of the trigonometric terms in the equation indicates that structural fractions are effective. Null hypothesis indicates that series have unit roots while showing that alternative hypothesis series are fixed. In cases where statistical test values are greater than the critical values as absolute values, null hypothesis is rejected.

Table 12.1 presents the Fourier Unit Root test results. Results of the estimation indicate that statistical test values calculated for both series were greater than the critical values as absolute values. Therefore, both series were stable at the threshold values. The statistical F values used to test the significance of trigonometric terms were greater than the critical values; accordingly, trigonometric terms were statistically significant. Fixed threshold values of series suggest that the maximum fixed value to be used in bootstrap causality analyses should be zero. As noted before, bootstrap causality test is based on the VAR model in relation to the (p+ d_{max}). rank. The appropriate lag length was calculated for the VAR model using the formula developed by Schwert (1989), and the appropriate lag length value was found to be 2. Table 12.2 presents the results of bootstrap causality test. Calculated statistical test values greater than the critical values as absolute values suggest a causality relationship between the variables.

Table 12.2 indicates that the calculated test statistics were greater than the critical values at 10 percent significance level. Therefore, causality was present between the number of COVID-19 cases and electricity consumption at 10 percent significance level.

Figure 12.1 presents the results of bootstrap causality test in rolling window. Test statistics found in rolling window approach are reflected in the graph and the value 1 is accepted as the threshold. The periods when causality relationships emerged are determined by considering the number of sub-windows and the periods when the calculated test statistics are above the threshold value. The number of sub-windows is twenty-two in this study.

Results of estimation indicated that the causality relationship between COVID-19 and energy consumption emerged in the second sub-period. The sub-periods when causality relationship was seen were respectively as

Table 12.2   Bootstrap Causality Test

	Max lag	d_{max}	Test Stat	Critical Values*		
Direction of Causality	2	0	7.47	1%	5%	10%
Covid19⟶Êlectcons	12.51	8.28	6.46			

*Critical values were received from the study by Haacker and Hatemi J (2006).
Source: Calculated by author.

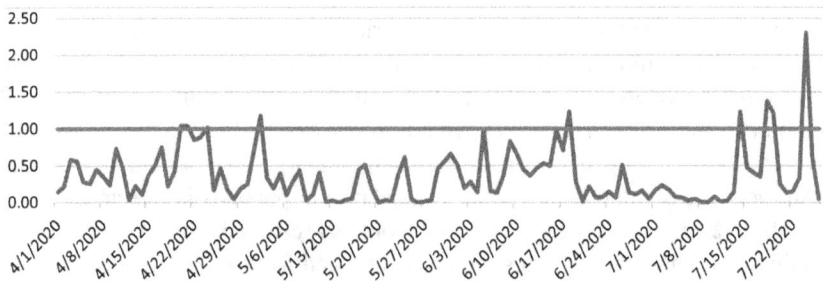

Figure 12.1   Bootstrap Causality Test in Rolling Windows. *Source*: Calculated by the author

follows: April 2, 2020 to April 23, 2020, April 10, 2020 to May 1, 2020, May 27, 2020 to June 18, 2020, and last days of July.

Rolling window regression approach was used to test how the energy consumption reacted to the change in the number of COVID-19 cases and how slope coefficient changed in time.

Figure 12.2 shows how the slope coefficient of energy consumption that reflects the sensitivity toward the changes in the number of COVID-19 cases has changed in time. The increase in COVID-19 cases decreased energy consumption until the last days of April. An increase in the number of cases reduced energy consumption by 0.1 unit in the second week of April, and by 0.28 and 0.24 units in the third and fourth weeks, respectively. Restrictions brought owing to the increase in the number of cases suggest that the initial shrinkage in demands grew in time. A positive relationship was present between energy consumption and number of cases in the first week of May. Although the slope coefficient was positive in May, lockdowns implemented in this period reduced the rate of increase in the energy consumption. With the new normalization periods in the early days of July, number of cases and electricity consumption increased. The increase in the demand for energy solely compensates the shrinkage of demands seen in the early days of April.

CONCLUSION

Having emerged in Wuhan, China, for the first time in February 2020, COVID-19 led to high morbidity and mortality rate. The number of cases has globally reached 31,425,029 within a year of the virus emerging. The daily number of cases was 246,165 on September 24, 2020, and the number of people who died of this disease is 967,164. Although progress has been made in the diagnosis and treatment of the disease compared to the early periods, the rate of spreading was not under control even after a year while vaccinating the population was still in progress. Accordingly, the total number of deaths will probably reach millions. High mortality and morbidity rates have resulted in limitations on both national and international levels and have been deeply affecting the economic and social lives. Diseases not only negatively affect effective labor productivity and labor supply but also individuals' consumption and savings preferences. As a matter of fact, as expected in Covid-19, it negatively affected economic decision-making units and significant income and output losses occurred.

The COVID 19 pandemic has been the period when the greatest loss of productivity occurred since the Great Depression of 1929. The global economy shrank by 3.5 percent in the first quarter of 2020 when compared to

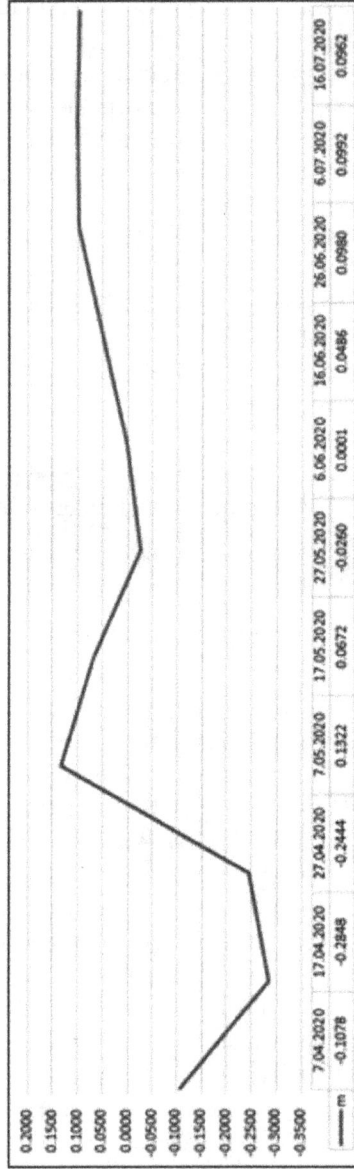

	7.04.2020	17.04.2020	27.04.2020	7.05.2020	17.05.2020	27.05.2020	6.06.2020	16.06.2020	26.06.2020	6.07.2020	16.07.2020
m	-0.1078	-0.2848	-0.2444	0.1322	0.0672	-0.0260	0.0001	0.0486	0.0980	0.0992	0.0962

Figure 12.2 **Rolling Window Regression (Change in Slope Coefficient in Time).** *Source:* Calculated by the author

the first quarter of 2019, and it shrank by 4.9 percent in the second quarter of 2020 compared to the same period of 2019. The shrinkage in the economies of the developed countries was 1.9 percent in the first quarter of 2020 compared to the previous quarter, and the shrinkage in the second quarter was 12.2 percent. The shrinkage seen in the developing countries has been smaller compared to the developed countries. The loss of productivity in developing countries was 0.78 in the first quarter compared to the previous quarter, and the shrinkage seen in the second quarter was 11.7 percent. High morbidity and mortality rates resulted in decreased labor productivity and increased labor costs. About 1.6 million informal workers lost 60 percent of their income. Global trade fell 3 percent in the first quarter of 2020 and commodity prices fell by a record low of 20 percent in March, driven by steep drops in oil prices. About 265 million people in low- and middle-income countries were at risk of acute food insecurity by the end of 2020.

Instabilities seen in real and financial markets during the pandemic are expected to distort the stability of the energy markets, which in turn is expected to trigger instabilities on macroeconomic level. Accordingly, energy market has a particular place in reducing the losses of productivity and income. Revealing the losses of productivity and income that are expected in the first wave is critical in terms of measuring the expenses that are likely to arise from the second wave and thereby minimizing the potential losses. This study conducted between March 12, 2020, and July 26, 2020, analyzed the dynamic relationships between COVID-19 pandemic and energy consumption and examined how causality relationships and slope coefficients changed in time. Results indicated a causality relationship between the number of COVID-19 cases and electricity consumption, and that causality relationships changed in time. The first sub-period when a causality relationship emerged between the number of cases and electricity consumption was between April 02, 2020, and April 23, 2020. This period covers two weeks after the emergence of the disease. Additionally, the periods between April 10, 2020, and May 01, 2020, May 27, 2020, and June 18, 2020, and last periods of July were the other sub-periods when causality relationships emerged. There was a negative relationship between the number of cases and energy consumption in the period between March 11 and early days of May; slope coefficient became negative when restrictions increased in May and positive when restrictions were partially abolished. The increase in the number of cases during the second week of April reduced energy consumption by 0.10 unit, and the shrinkage in the third and fourth weeks was 0.28 and 0.24 units, respectively. Slope coefficient was positive in the first two weeks of May and negative only in the third week. Change of the coefficient from being positive to negative may be explained with the lockdown implemented during the Eid al-Fitr. With the new process called new normal implemented as of July

1, number of cases of the virus and electricity consumption increased. The slope coefficient has been 0.09 unit as of the last days of July. Increase in the demand for electricity only meets the shrinkage in demands that occurred in the first days of April. Edomah & Ndulue (2020) explained the recent increase in the electricity consumption through distance learning and digital transformation period; businesses serving in the service sector started to operate once again in this period, which was effective in the change of slope coefficient from being negative to positive. However, increase in the demands for electricity still cannot compensate the shrinkage seen in the early periods. In addition, household electricity consumption at home has increased due to the restrictions imposed. However, the government decided to postpone the bill payments. In other words, electricity distribution companies continue their activities, but income expected to be generated in return for the services provided are deferred. Although the decision to postpone invoices has been presented as a brilliant idea in the short term, this decision will only increase the debt burden of households and damage electricity distribution companies. Reducing the economic losses can only occur by ensuring the continuity in production. For that purpose, protective medical precautions should be taken, and people's awareness should be raised. The studies conducted by WHO (2008; 2009; 2018, 2019; 2020) and Ouassou et al. (2020) indicated that the spread rate could be reduced by using good-quality masks and maintaining the physical distance. Mass media should be used to prepare public service announcements for raising people's awareness and more severe sanctions should be imposed against those who do not observe the precautions.

REFERENCES

Abu-Rayash, Azzam and Ibrahim Dinçer 2020. "Analysis of the electricity demand trends amidst the COVID-19 coronavirus pandemic." *Energy Research & Social Science*, 68, 101682.

Agdaş, Düzgün and Prabir Barooah, P. 2020. "Impact of the COVID-19 pandemic on the U.S. electricity demand and supply: an early view from data." *IEEE*, 8, 151523–151534.

Alhajeri, Hamad, Abdulrahman Soud, Almutairi, and Abdulrahman, Alenezi and Faisal Alshammari. 2020. "Energy demand in the state of Kuwait during the COVID-19 pandemic: technical, economic, and environmental perspectives," *Energies*, 13, 1–16.

Aslam, Hina, Nadeem, Sheikh and Ubaid Rehman. 2020. *Impact assessment of COVID-19 on Energy and Power Sector of Pakistan*. SDPI Policy Review. https://www.think-asia.org/bitstream/handle/11540/11904/impact-assessment-of-covid-19-on-energy-and-power-sector-of-pakistan.pdf?sequence=1.

Bahmanyara, Alireza, Abouzar, Estebsarib and Damien, Ernsta 2020. "The impact of different COVID-19 containment measures on electricity consumption in Europe," *Energy Research & Social Science*, 68, 101683.

Bardhan, Pranab, and Udry, Christopher. 1999. *Development Microeconomics*. Oxford UK: Oxford University Press.

Becker, Gary S. 1964. *Human Capital a Theoretical An Empirical Analysis with Special Reference to Education*. New York: NBER.

Bozoklu, Şeref, Yılancı, Veli and Görüş, Muhammed Şehid 2020. "Persistence in per capita energy consumption: a fractional integration approach with a Fourier function," *Energy Economics*, 104926.

Buechlera, Elizabeth, Siobhan, Powel, Tao, Sun, Chad M. Zanocco, Nicholas, Astier, Jose, Bolorinos, June, Flora, Hilary Boudet and Ram Rajagopal.2020. "Power and the pandemic: exploring global changes in electricity demand during COVID-19," *Physics and Society*, 1–33.

Bulut, Mehmet. 2020. "Effects of new normal life on electricity consumption in COVID-19 process," *Journal of Scientific, Technology and Engineering Research,* 1(1), 4–6.

Burleyson, Casey D., Aowabin, Rahman, A., Jennie, Rice, Amanda, D. Smith and Nathalie Voisin. 2020. "Changes in electricity load profiles under COVID-19: implications of the new normal for electricity demand," *Engrvix* https://doi.org/10 .31224/osf.io/trs57

Carvalho, Monica,Danielle Bandeira de Mello Delgado, Karollyne Marques de Lima, Marianna de Camargo Cancela, Camila Alves dos Squeira, Dyego Leandro Bezerra de Souza. 2020. "Effects of the COVID-19 pandemic on the Brazilian electricity consumption patterns," *International Journal of Energy Research,* e5877.

Caspi, Itamar and Meital Graham. 2017. *Testing for Bubbles in Stock Markets with Irregular Dividend Distribution. MPRA* https://mpra.ub.uni-muenchen.de/82261 /1/MPRA paper82 261.pdf.

Cuddington, John T. 1993. "Modeling the macroeconomic effects of aids, with an application to Tanzania," *World Bank Economic Review,* 7(2), 173–189.

Czosnyka, Michal, Wnukowska, Bogumila and Katarzyana Karbowa. 2020. Electrical energy consumption and the energy market in Poland during the COVID-19 pandemic.

Daly, Kieran. 2000. *The business response to HIV/AIDS: impact and lessons learned. Produced by The Joint United Nations Programme on HIV/AIDS*. The Prince of Wales Business Leaders Forum and The Global Business Council on HIV&AIDS, Geneva and London.

Edomah, Norbet and Ndulue, Gogo. 2020. "Energy transition in a lockdown: an analysis of the impact of COVID-19 on changes in electricity demand in Lagos Nigeria." *Global Transitions*, 2, 127–137.

Enders, Walter and Lee, Junsoo. 2012. "The flexible fourier form and the dickey-fuller type unit root tests," *Economics Letters*, 117, 196–199.

Chiaia, Dmiliu, Massi Ciali I Iviami williamim, and Alssmans Ivla. 2020. "Impact on electricity consumption and market pricing of energy and ancillary services during pandemic of COVID-19 in Italy," *Energies*, 13, 3357. https://doi.org/10.3390/en13133357

Haacker, Markus.2002. *The economic consequences of HIV/AIDS in Southern Africa.* IMF Working Paper.

Hacker, R. Scott and Hatemi-J, Abdulnasser. 2006. "Tests for causality between integrated variables using asymptotic and bootstrap distributions: theory and application." *Applied Economics*, 38(13), 1489–1500.

IMF. (2020). *World Economic Outlook the Great Lockdown.* Washington DC: IMF Pub.

Jo, Changik. 2014. "Cost of illness studies: Concepts, scopes and methods," *Clinical and Molecular Hepatology*, 20, 327–337.

Jones, Paul W. 2002. "Interpreting thresholds for a clinically significant change in health status in asthma and COPD," European *Respiratory Journal,* 19, 398–404.

Leach, Andrew, Nic, Rivers and Blake Shaffer. 2020. "Canadian electricity markets during the COVID-19 pandemic: an initial assessment," Canadian *Public Policy*, 46, 145–159.

Lowder, Travis, Nathan, Lee and Jennifer, Leisch, E. 2020. *COVID-19 and the power sector in southeast Asia impacts and opportunities.* USAID & NREL Report.

Mahal, Ajay, Anup, Karan, Engelgau, Michael. 2010. *The economic implications of non-communicable disease for India.* HNP Discussion Paper, 52913.

Norouzi, Nima, Gerardo Zarazua de Rubens, Saeed Choupanpiesheh and Peter Enevoldsen. 2020. "When pandemics impact economies and climate change: exploring the impacts of COVID-19 on oil and electricity demand in China," *Energy Research & Social Science*, 68, 101654.

OECD. 2020. *Unit labour costs and labour productivity (employment based), total economy*, https://stats.oecd.org/Index.aspx?DataSetCode=ULC_EEQ

Omay, Tolga. 2015. "Fractional frequency flexible fourier form to approximate smooth breaks in unit root testing," Economic *Letters*, 134, 123–126.

Ouassou Hayat, Loubna, Kharchoufa, Mohamed, Bouhrim, Nour Elhouda Daoudi, Hamada, Imtara, Noureddine, Bencheikh, Amine, Elbouzidi and Mohamed Bnouham. 2020. "The pathogenesis of coronavirus disease 2019 (COVID-19): Evaluation and Prevention," *Journal of Immunology Research*, 2020, 1357983

Oxford University. 2020. *The economic impact of covid-19.* https://www.research. ox .ac.uk /Article/2020-04-07-the-economic-impact-of-covid-19.

Prol, Javier Lopez and Sungmin, O. 2020. *Impact of COVID-19 Measures on Electricity Consumption*, MPRA Paper No. 101649. file:///C:/Users/Lenovo/ Downloads/ MPRA _paper _101649.pdf.

Qarnain, Syed Shuibul, Suresh Kumar Muthuvel and Bathrinath, S. 2020. "Review on government action plans to reduce energy consumption in buildings amid COVID-19 pandemic outbreak," *Materials Today: Proceedings* https://doi.org/10.1016/j .matpr.2020.04.723

Rice, David .2000. "Cost of illness studies: what is good them," *Injury Prevention*, 6,177-179.

Ruan, Guangchun, Dongqi. Wu, Xiangtian. Zheng, Haiwang Zhong, Chonqing. Kang, Munther A. Dahleh, Sivaranjani, S. Lee Xie. 2020. "A cross-domain approach to analyzing the short-run impact of COVID-19 on the U.S. electricity sector," *Joule.* http://dx.doi.org/10.2139/ssrn.3631498.

Schwert, G. William. 1989. "Tests for unit roots: A Monte Carlo investigation," *Journal of Business and Economic Statistics*, 7, 147–160.

Sen, Amartya 1992. *Inequality Reexamined.* Cambridge: Harvard University Press.

Toda, Hiro Y. and Taku, Yamamoto. 2020. "Statistical Inference in Vector Autoregressions with Possibly Integrated Processes," *Journal of Econometrics* 66, 225–250.

Tolmasquim, Mauricio, Enrique, Chueca, Pauline, Ravillard, Michelle, Hallack and Ariel, Yepez. 2020. "Monitoring the Impact of the COVID-19 Crisis On Electricity: Lower Demand With Different Profiles." *Energia Para EL future.* https://blogs.iadb.org/energia/en/monitoring-the-impact-of-the-covid-19-crisis-on -electricity-lower-demand-with-different-profiles/.

U.N. 2020. *World Economic Situation and Prospects as of Mid-2020.* https://www.un .org/ development/desa/dpad/wpcontent/uploads/sites/45/publication/WESP2020_ MYU_Report.pdf.

WHO. 2008. *How to Put on and Take Off Personal Protective Equipment (PPE).* World Health Organization. https://apps.who.int/iris/bitstream/handle/10665/70066/ WHO_CDS_EPR_2007.8a_eng.pdf?sequence=1&isAllowed=y.

WHO. 2009. *WHO Guidelines on Hand Hygiene in Health Care.* Geneva: World Health Organization Press.

WHO. 2018. *Managing Epidemics: Key Facts About Major Deadly Diseases.* Geneva: World Health Organization.

WHO. 2019. Coronavirus Disease 2019 (COVID-19). Events as They Happen March 2020, https://www.who.int/emergencies/diseases/novel-coronavirus-2019/events -as-they-happen.

WHO. 2020. *Coronavirus Disease (COVID-19) Technical Guidance: Infection Prevention And Control / WASH March 2020.* https://www.who.int/emergencies /diseases/novel-coronavirus-2019/technical-guidance/infection-prevention-and-co ntrol.

WHO. 2020. WHO Coronavirus Disease (COVID-19) Dashboard, https://covid19 .who.int/?gclid=EAIaIQobChMIgZ6o7yQ7AIVApOyCh19vwnoEAAYASAAE gI1_vDwE.

Chapter 13

Asymmetric Impacts of Asset Purchase Program and Exchange Rate on Credit Volume in Turkey

Evidence from a Nonlinear ARDL Approach

Ahmet Usta

INTRODUCTION

The outbreak of COVID-19 has serious impacts on human life in terms of health and economy. Global economy has witnessed severe challenges. As the speed of spread increased, the global growth outlook has weakened. Negative impacts of the pandemic have caused deteriorations in the real economies and financial markets. Particularly, volume and direction of capital flows, liquidity conditions, international trade across economies, and asset prices have been affected negatively. According to the World Economic Outlook report of the IMF (2021), the global output contracted by around 3.5 percent and world trade volume declined by 9.6 percent in 2020. While output growth in advanced economies declined by 5 percent, emerging market and developing economies have experienced output contraction by 2.4 percent. In terms of trade volume, advanced economies have suffered (–10 percent) more than emerging economies (–8.9 percent).

Although the COVID-19 has been a serious global threat, its impact on the economies is not the same. Namely, each country has been affected differently and should devise policies accordingly. Dealing with the negative effects of the COVID-19 has become a global priority for countries. Therefore, governments and central banks have taken several fiscal and monetary measures against the devastating impacts of pandemic on their domestic markets.

Governments introduced fiscal policies to support households and firms with the aim of increasing demand in their economies. Central banks not only in advanced economies (AEs) but also in emerging markets economies (EMEs) have announced and started to implement various monetary policy actions. The Central Bank of Republic of Turkey (CBRT) also took various actions including interest rate cuts and bond purchases with the aim of accelerating its financial markets, enhancing cash flow of the corporate sector, and providing liquidity. Therefore, it is important to analyze the impact of monetary policy actions during the pandemic. Particularly, an evaluation of unconventional monetary policies such as asset purchase programs conducted for the first time by the central banks in the emerging market economies becomes a necessity because such programs could be added to their policy toolkit especially when the conventional policy has limited impact.

The number of studies to understand the different aspects of the COVID-19 is increasing. Among others, research made on the effect of the COVID-19 on economic and financial dimensions has been very intense recently. In a theoretical study, Eichenbaum, Rebelo, and Tranabandt (2020) developed a model to investigate the relationship between pandemics and economic decisions. The outcome of their model suggests that the severity of the pandemic can be reduced by containment policy increases that lead to decreases in the consumption and employment. Particularly, policies such as quarantines and mobility restrictions have been implemented to mitigate the spread of the pandemic. However, the outcomes of these policies are likely to be negative for the economy. For example, Sobieralski (2020) estimates a job loss approximately 7 percent to 13 percent in the airline industry due to COVID-19.

Financial market and asset prices have also been affected by the pandemic. COVID-19 has negative impact on the stock markets along with a surge in the volatility and an increase in the concern about the spread of the virus (Capelle-Blanchard and Desroziers 2020; Phan and Narayan 2020). There is a positive relationship between news reflecting a panic about the coronavirus outbreak and an increase in the equity market (Haroon and Rizvi 2020). Haddad, Moreira, and Muir (2020) studied the dynamics in the bond market during the pandemic. According to their observations, disruptions in the bond market caused CDS spread to increase and led investors to sell their liquid and safe assets to raise cash in their hands.

Rebucci, Hartley, and Jimenez (2021) analyze the impacts of thirty quantitative easing announcements on government bond yields. Regarding the classes, they consider 10 (20) announcements made by 8 (13) central banks in AEs (EMEs). By using a daily dataset over the period March 16, 2020, and April 28, 2020, they employ event study and GVAR and find that QE announcements in AEs (EMEs) have had a 13 (23) basis points single-day impact on government bond yield. Moreover, they investigate that the AEs have experienced a larger depreciation than that of the EMEs on the announcement days. Sever et al. (2020) examine the announcement effects of asset purchases on bond yields and exchange rates in the context of emerging market economies during the pandemic. They use event study and local projections methodology and find, following asset purchase program announcements, a decline in the bond yields and insignificant effects on domestic currencies and equities in EMEs. Arslan, Drehman, and Hofman (2020) assess the local currency bond purchase programs launched by the central banks in EMEs and find that the bond yields fall slightly (10 basis points) on the announcement day but strongly (50 basis points) after five days. The domestic currency against the U.S. dollar rate depreciates insignificantly. Hoffman, Shim, and Shin (2020) document the performance of exchange rates and local currency bond markets in emerging market economies during the COVID-19 pandemic. They observe a spike in the domestic currency bond spreads, a depreciation in national currencies, and an increase in capital outflows.

The applications of nonlinear models in macroeconomics have become popular and received more attention than the linear ones (Terasvirta 2018). Since the linear relationships between variables may not be sufficient to capture actual short- and long-run effect in the analyses, using the nonlinear characteristics of macroeconomic and financial time series becomes helpful (Kocaarslan and Soytas 2019). Therefore, it is important to consider nonlinear relationship between variables in econometric research (Shin, Yu and Greenwood-Nimmo 2014). Positive and negative changes in the variables may have different impacts in terms of magnitude and direction (Ahmed, Zhang, and Cary 2021). There are several studies assessing the asymmetric relationships in empirical finance and macroeconomics. The asymmetric linkages are found between yield spread and economic policy uncertainty (Wang et al. 2020), currency and equity markets (Luqman and Kouser 2018), ecology, and economic activity and financial environment (Ahmed, Zhang and Cary 2021; Pata and Caglar 2021), energy prices and economic activity (Pal and Mitra 2015; Kocaarslan and Soytas 2019; Rehman, Ali and Shahzad 2020).

In this study, we test whether there is a long-run relationship between credit volume, bond purchases, and exchange rate in Turkey by estimating a nonlinear autoregressive distributed lag (NARDL) model with weekly observations over the period between May 31, 2019, and January 22, 2021. The NARDL approach allows us to test short- and long-run asymmetric interactions between variables. The main finding of this study is as follows: while we do not observe a long-run relation among aforementioned variables through a traditional ARDL model, we find a long-run level relation by esti mating a nonlinear ARDL (NARDL).

Rest of the study is organized as follows. After providing an overview of fiscal and monetary policy measures taken against pandemic in Turkey, this study introduces data and methodology and reports empirical findings. The study is finalized with the conclusion section.

AN OVERVIEW OF FISCAL AND MONETARY MEASURES TAKEN AGAINST PANDEMIC IN TURKEY

Several measures have been implemented to slow down the spread of the virus, to sustain the well-functioning of the health system, and to reduce the deteriorations in the real economy and the financial markets in Turkey. Since the scope of this study is on the economy side, this section presents information about the economy-related measures. Fiscal and monetary policies were introduced against the negative economic and financial impacts of the pandemic.

On the fiscal side, the government unveiled an economic package including tax breaks, deferrals, credit guarantees through public banks, and delays in credit payments. Moreover, the tax rates for several services reduced. Income tax filing and payments, social security contribution payments, and public rent payments have been postponed. Credit and salary support were provided to companies. Short time working allowance was introduced. Deductions made in the amount transferred from the treasury to the municipalities were postponed, and the municipalities were funded by the central government.

On the monetary policy side, with press releases of March 17, 2020, March 31, 2020, and April 17, 2020, the CBRT has shared several measures taken against the economic and financial impacts of COVID-19 (CBRT 2020a; CBRT 2020b; CBRT 2020c). Table 13.1 summarizes the aims and policy actions taken by the CBRT to struggle with the adverse effects of the uncertain economic and financial environment led by the COVID-19 outbreak on the Turkish economy.

DATA AND METHODOLOGY

In the analysis, we employ weekly data on credit volume, monetary policy action, and exchange rate in Turkey between May 31, 2019, and January 22, 2021.

Right after the first Covid-19 case was recorded on March 11, 2020, in Turkey, the CBRT undertook several measures to deal with the negative effects of the pandemic in the economy. The CBRT made announcements on government bond purchase programs on March 31, 2020, and April 17, 2020. Moreover, we detect a break in our data on April 3, 2020, due to policy

Table 13.1   Press Releases by the Central Bank of Republic of Turkey

Date	Aim	Measures
March 17, 2020	To enhance the flexibility of banks on liquidity management	Liquidity through intraday and overnight standing facilities, Repo, and swap auctions
	To secure the credit flow of corporate sector	Decline in the FX reserve requirement ratios,
	To boost the cash flow of exporting firms	Adjustments for repayments and maturities of rediscount credits
March 31, 2020	To enhance the effectiveness of monetary transmission mechanism	Outright purchase operations, Government Domestic Debt Securities (GDDS)
	To enhance the flexibility of banks on liquidity management	Extension of collateral pool with asset-backed securities and mortgage-backed securities, swap auctions
	To boost the cash flow of exporting firms	Extension in the Turkish lira-denominated rediscount credits for export and foreign exchange earning services
April 17, 2020	To strengthen the monetary policy transmission mechanism	Increase in the maximum limit for the ratio of the open market operations portfolio nominal size to total assets of CBRT
	To maintain the market depth and to support the Primary Dealership (PD) system	Adjustment on the limits of PD for GDDS sales to the CBRT

Source: Created by author

change. In this context, our sample period covers between April 3, 2020, and January 22, 2021, for the post-COVID period. We extend our sample period back to May 31, 2019 as the pre-COVID period. All in all, final horizon for our sample is between May 31, 2019, and January 22, 2021.

In this study, we use credit volume as the dependent variable. We consider total amount of credit provided by the deposit of banks only. This item is composed of commercial and individual loans, and specialized loans including agricultural loans, loans to tradesmen and artisans, housing loans, and others. We employ asset purchases and exchange rate as the independent variables in our analysis. We use total amount of asset purchases as an unconventional monetary measure taken by the CBRT. In response to pandemic, domestic debt security purchases increased extremely to strengthen the liquidity conditions in the economy. Thus, observing the impact of asset purchases on credit volume would be important. Since the exchange rate is an important determinant of credit volume in the domestic economy, we also use selling rate in the analysis. The source of the data is the electronic data delivery system (EVDS) of the CBRT.

Methodology

Linear and symmetric models have been used to uncover long-run relationship between variables. However, ignoring asymmetric impacts may result in misleading results. Therefore, utilizing asymmetric interactions is important.

The pioneering work by Shin, Yu, and Greenwood-Nimmo (2014) is essential to investigate asymmetric correlation between variables. The nonlinear ARDL method developed by Shin, Yu, and Greenwood-Nimmo (2014) takes positive and negative partial sum of independent variables into account to uncover the dynamic asymmetric interactions between variables in the short- and long-run.

This study considers both linear and nonlinear versions of ARDL models to analyze the symmetric and asymmetric correlation between credit volume, asset purchases, and exchange rate in Turkey.

First, we estimate $\Delta CREDIT_t = c_0 + \sum_{i=1}^{p-1} c_1 \Delta CREDIT_{t-i} + \sum_{i=0}^{q-1} c_2$

$\Delta PURCHASE_{t-i} + \sum_{i=0}^{q-1} c_3 \Delta EXC_{t-i} + \gamma_1 CREDIT_{t-1} + \gamma_2 PURCHASE_{t-1} + \gamma_3$

$EXC_{t-1} + DUM_t + \varepsilon_t$, which is the error correction representation of linear ARDL. This model is useful in determining the symmetric long-run relationship between designated variables. CREDIT is the total credit supplied by deposit banks. PURCHASE is the total amount of government debt purchases by the CBRT through open market operations. EXC is the exchange rate between USD and TL. All variables are in their logarithmic form. DUM is the dummy variable to capture the break date. The dummy variable takes a value of 1 after the break date and 0 otherwise. The short-run coefficients are represented by c_1, c_2, and c_3. The long-run coefficients for the variables in the model are represented by γ_1, γ_2, and γ_3. Δ indicates the first difference of the variables. As suggested by Pesaran and Shin (1999) and Pesaran, Shin, and Smith (2001), we use bounds testing procedure to test whether there is a correlation between variables. As a decision rule, we use F-statistics to test the $H_0 = \gamma_1 = \gamma_2 = \gamma_3 = 0$, which indicates there is no correlation between variables. The decision of the test is made through the two sets of asymptotic critical lower and upper bounds, I (0) and I (1). We have three possible outcomes. First, if the F-statistics is lower than the critical value associated with the I (0) bound, we fail to reject the null hypothesis. Second, if the F-statistics is in between the lower and upper bound, we have inconclusive result. Third, if the F-statistics is greater than the critical value associated with the I (1), we reject the null and conclude that there is a long-run relationship between variables.

In case of a presence of nonlinear relationships between variables, we modify traditional ARDL model and use asymmetric ARDL model, which enables us to capture asymmetric effects among variables under consideration. As suggested by Shin et al. (2014), the nonlinear long-run correlation regression is $y_t = \beta^+ x_t^+ + \beta^- x_t^- + u_t$, where β^+ and β^- are long-run parameters, and x_t^+ and x_t^- indicate increases and decreases in independent variables as computed by the positive partial sum, $x_t^+ = \sum_{i=1}^{t} \Delta x_i^+ = \sum_{i=1}^{t} max(\Delta x_i, 0)$, and negative partial sum, $x_t^- = \sum_{i=1}^{t} \Delta x_i^- = \sum_{i=1}^{t} min(\Delta x_i, 0)$.

Second, we estimate modified ARDL model to analyze the asymmetric impacts of asset purchases, and the exchange rate on credit volume can be described as follows:

In this equation, the coefficients ϕ_1^+, ϕ_1^-, ϕ_2^+, and ϕ_2^- are the short-run coefficients of the model. ω_1^+, ω_1^-, ω_2^+, and ω_2^- refer to long-run coefficients for the variables. To investigate the short- and long-run symmetry, we conduct Wald test.

$$\Delta CREDIT_t = c_0 + \sum_{i-1}^{p-1} \tau \Delta CREDIT_{t-i} + \sum_{i=0}^{q-1} \phi_1^+ \Delta PURCHASE_{t-i}^+$$

$$+ \sum_{i=0}^{q-1} \phi_1^- \Delta PURCHASE_{t-i}^- + \sum_{i=0}^{q-1} \phi_2^+ \Delta EXC_{t-i}^+$$

$$+ \sum_{i=0}^{q-1} \phi_2^- \Delta EXC_{t-i}^- + \zeta CREDIT_{t-1} + \omega_1^+ PURCHASE_{t-1}^+$$

$$+ \omega_1^- PURCHASE_{t-1}^- + \omega_2^+ EXC_{t-1}^+ + \omega_2^- EXC_{t-1}^- + DUM_t + \varepsilon_t$$

As in the linear ARDL model, we use F-statistic to test $H_0 : \zeta = \omega_1^+ = \omega_1^- = \omega_2^+ = \omega_2^- = 0$, which indicates no symmetric correlation between variables. The decision rule is the same as described in the linear version. For the long-run symmetry, we test $H_0 : -\omega_{1(2)}^+ / \zeta = -\omega_{1(2)}^- / \zeta$ against $H_1 : -\omega_{1(2)}^+ / \zeta \neq -\omega_{1(2)}^- / \zeta$. If the p-value of the computed test statistic is less than 5 percent, we reject the H_0 and conclude this to be the evidence of long-run asymmetry. Short-run asymmetry test is carried out by Wald test again. This time, we test $H_0 : \sum_{i=0}^{q-1} \phi_{1(2)}^+ = \sum_{i=0}^{q-1} \phi_{1(2)}^-$ against the alternative, $H_1 : \sum_{i=0}^{q-1} \phi_{1(2)}^+ \neq \sum_{i=0}^{q-1} \phi_{1(2)}^-$. The decision rule is same as the long-run symmetry test. If the p-value of the test statistic is less than 5 percent, we reject the H_0 and conclude that to be the evidence on short-run asymmetry. We depict the graphs of the asymmetric cumulative dynamic multipliers, which show the pattern of the dependent variable, y_t, to a new equilibrium following a positive and negative unit change in the independent variables, x_t^+ and x_t^-, respectively.

The derivation of the cumulative dynamic multiplier effects of x_t^+ and x_t^-

on y_t are $m_h^+ = \sum_{j=0}^{h} \partial y_{t+j} / \partial x_t^+$ and $m_h^- = \sum_{j=0}^{h} \partial y_{t+j} / \partial x_t^-$, respectively. If

$h\to\infty$, then $m_h^+ \to -\omega_{1(2)}^+ / \chi$ and $m_h^- \to -\omega_{1(2)}^- / \chi$.

EMPIRICAL FINDINGS

This section presents the results of empirical tests conducted to investigate the long-run relationships between variables of interest. Particularly, we estimate a linear and a nonlinear ARDL model to analyze the symmetric and asymmetric impacts of independent variables on dependent variable.

In the first step, we investigate the stationarity characteristics of the variables. We conduct unit root tests to determine the order of integration of the variables. To serve this aim, Augmented Dickey Fuller (ADF) and Phillips–Perron (PP) are used. We observe uncertainty about the order of integration for the time series of PURCHASE. CREDIT and EXC are stationary at first differences with certainty. Given these results, we move on estimating an autoregressive distributed lag (ARDL) model suggested by Pesaran and Shin (1999) and Pesaran, Shin, and Smith (2001). Moreover, we are also allowed to estimate a nonlinear ARDL model proposed by Shin, Yu, and Greenwood-Nimmo (2014) to consider the impacts of nonlinearities.

Next, we estimate ARDL model and conduct bound test to investigate correlation between variables. The decision on the existence of correlation is made by considering lower and upper asymptotic critical bounds, which assume that all regressors are either I (0) or I (1). The optimal lag length is determined by the Akaike information criterion (AIC) for the cointegration tests. Four is the maximum lag length for the lagged values of the variables.

The F-statistic for the bound test for the linear ARDL is 2.17, which is smaller than the lower bound, 3.26. Therefore, we fail to reject the null hypothesis and conclude that there is no correlation between variables in the absence of nonlinearities. This finding leads us to examine the presence of nonlinearities for the correlation. We conduct bounds test for the NARDL model. The F-statistic, 6.98, is larger than the upper critical bound, 5.51, at 1 percent and suggests a nonlinear relationship between variables. We conclude that ignoring asymmetries may show misleading results in terms of correlation. Therefore, we proceed with NARDL model.

Table 13.2 displays the results of the NARDL model shown by Eq (1), in which the dependent variable is $\Delta CREDIT_t$. Lag order for the NARDL model is selected

Table 13.2 Estimation Results of Nonlinear ARDL (NARDL)

Variables	Coefficient	Std. Error	t-Statistic	Prob.
Panel A: Long-run coefficients				
PURCHASE$^+$	0.192081	0.065235	2.944433	0.0044
PURCHASE$^-$	−0.296598	0.191454	−1.549187	0.1260
EXC$^+$	0.262417	0.170851	1.535943	0.1293
EXC$^-$	0.499453	0.181457	2.752459	0.0076
Panel B: Short-run coefficients				
ΔCREDIT$_{t\text{-}1}$	−0.363872	0.106941	−3.402558	0.0011
ΔPURCHASE$_t^+$	0.042738	0.018557	2.303107	0.0244
ΔPURCHASE$_{t-1}^+$	−0.006427	0.011415	−0.563052	0.5753
ΔPURCHASE$_{t-2}^+$	0.028738	0.011047	2.601510	0.0114
ΔPURCHASE$_{t-3}^+$	0.018735	0.010996	1.703868	0.0930
ΔEXC$_t^+$	0.344889	0.062230	5.542135	0.0000
ΔEXC$_{t-1}^+$	−0.155481	0.066042	−2.354282	0.0215
ΔEXC$_t^-$	0.340959	0.071007	4.801773	0.0000
DUM	−0.022410	0.009214	−2.432000	0.0177
ECT$_{t\text{-}1}$	−0.135785	0.022327	−6.081786	0.0000
Panel C: Symmetry Tests				
Long-run symmetry				
	F-statistic	p-value	H$_0$	Decision
	6.837640	0.0109	No symmetry	Reject H$_0$
	0.980419	0.3254	No symmetry	Fail to Reject H$_0$
Short-run symmetry				
	−	−	−	−
	0.239231	0.6262	No symmetry	Fail to Reject H$_0$
Panel D: Diagnostics				
	Tests	p-value	H$_0$	Decision
	Breusch-Godfrey LM	0.6342	No serial correlation	Fail to Reject H$_0$
	Breusch-Pagan-Godfrey	0.5888	Homoscedasticity	Fail to Reject H$_0$
	Jarque-Bera	0.6794	Normal distribution	Fail to Reject H$_0$
	CUSUM		Parameter stability is satisfied	
	CUSUM of squares		Parameter stability is satisfied	

Source: Calculated by author

by the AIC. The appropriate lag lengths suggested by the AIC is (2,4,0,2,1). Long- and short-run coefficients of NARDL model are given in the Panel A and Panel B in table 13.2, respectively. In the same table, Panel C and Panel D display the symmetry test results and diagnostics of the model, respectively.

According to the long-run coefficients estimated from the NARDL model, a positive change in the PURCHASE has a positive and significant effect on the CREDIT. The coefficient suggests that the CREDIT increases by 0.19 percent when there is a 1percent increase in the PURCHASE. On the other hand, the CREDIT is negatively affected by a negative change in the PURCHASE, which means that the CREDIT increases by 0.29 percent when the PURCHASE decreases by 1 percent. The negative change has a greater impact on the CREDIT. However, the impact is insignificant in the long run. Moreover, our finding from the Wald test suggests us to reject null hypothesis if there is no symmetry. Namely, the impact of PURCHASE on CREDIT is asymmetric in the long run. The EXC is a positive factor on the CREDIT in the long run as demonstrated by the coefficients. The findings suggest that a 1 percent negative (positive) change in the EXC is associated with a 0.49 percent (0.26 percent) decrease (increase) in the CREDIT. While the long-run coefficient for the negative component of the EXC is statistically significant, the coefficient for the positive change is not statistically significant. A decrease in the EXC has a much more profound positive effect on the CREDIT in the long run. We do not find an asymmetric impact of EXC on the CREDIT in the long run as suggested by the Wald test result.

In addition to the long-run effects of the variables, this model enables us to analyze the short-run impacts of the variables, as well. The results are displayed in Panel B in table 13.2. Regarding the short-run effect of the PURCHASE, the results mainly demonstrate that the PURCHASE has a positive and statistically significant impact on CREDIT in the short run. Moreover, we find a positive impact of EXC on CREDIT in the short run. Both the positive and negative changes in the EXC have similar impact on the CREDIT in terms of magnitude. In the short run, CREDIT increases (decreases) by 0.34 percent when there is a 1 percent positive (negative) change in the EXC. Since the short-run coefficients are of both positive and negative changes in the EXC, we do not observe asymmetric effect of EXC on on the CREDIT in the short run.

The ECT_{t-1} is the error correction term, which is the coefficient of speed of adjustment. In our NARDL model, it is statistically significant and has expected negative sign (-0.13). The interpretation of the error correction term is as follows: the long-run equilibrium could be achieved in less than one year.

We conduct stability and diagnostic tests to see whether we achieve correct model specification. The parameter stability of the model is supported by the CUSUM and CUSUM of squares tests. Moreover, we fail to reject the null hypothesis of no serial correlation and homoscedasticity. This means that the model is free of serial correlation and there is no evidence on heteroscedasticity. The outcome of the Jarque–Bera test illustrates the normal distribution. Diagnostic test results are displayed in Panel D in table 13.2. The results of the diagnostic suggest that the model is correctly specified.

The black solid (dashed) line implies how dependent variable adjusts over the horizon due to positive (negative) shocks in the independent variables. The red dashed line is an asymmetric plot, which is the difference between the dynamic multipliers (m^+ - m^-) of positive and negative changes in the regressors. The red dotted lines, lower and upper bands are the confidence intervals (CI), which indicate the statistical significance of asymmetry. If the 0 line lies within the CI, then the asymmetric effect is insignificant at 5 percent.

Figure 13.1 displays the multipliers for EXC and PURCHASE. Regarding the effects of unitary positive and negative shocks, our findings are as follows.

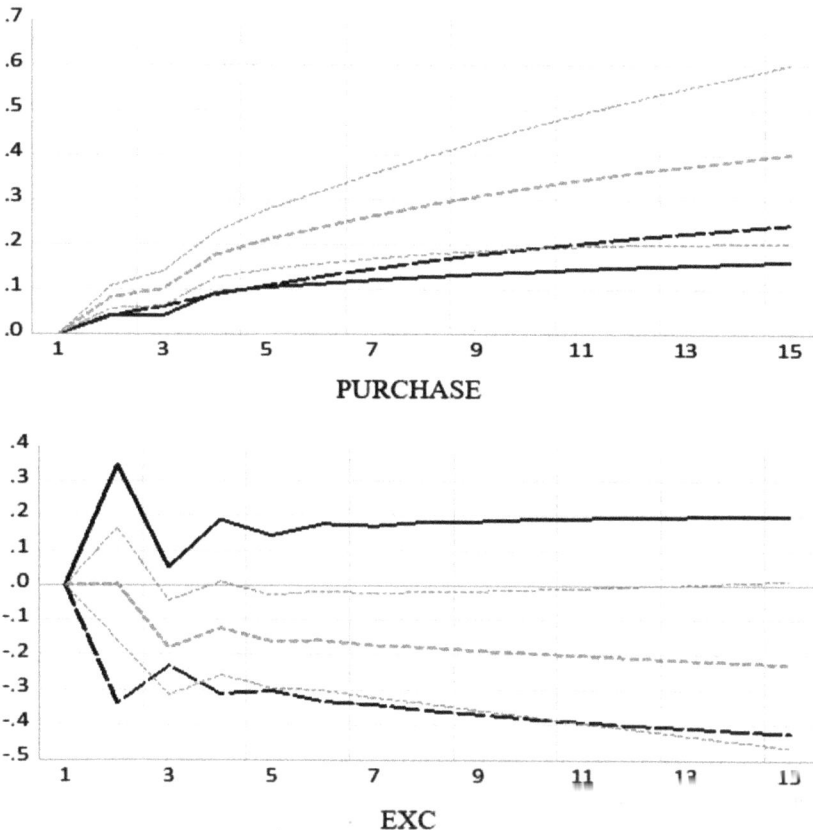

PURCHASE

EXC

Figure 13.1   Dynamic Multipliers. *Source*: Calculated by the author

Nonlinear adjustment of CREDIT to both positive (black solid line) and negative (dashed solid line) shocks in EXC and indicate that there is a direct relationship between CREDIT and EXC. The unitary negative shocks dominate the relationship between CREDIT and EXC. However, we do not observe a clear evidence on significance of the asymmetric effect of the EXC on the CREDIT. The results of dynamic multipliers for PURCHASE indicate an inverse relationship with the CREDIT in the long run. However, the unitary positive shocks dominate the relationship. According to the dashed red line between the CI, the asymmetric relationship of CREDIT with PURCHASE is significant in the long run.

CONCLUSION

The COVID-19 pandemic influenced globally. Among others, the pandemic has financial and economic consequences. The impacts of the outbreak have manifested itself in countries differently in terms of timing and intensity. Therefore, measures taken against the devastating impacts of the pandemic have been varying across countries. Both in the AEs and emerging market economies, the governments, and monetary authorities have implemented several policies to recover the functioning of the real economy and financial markets. Central banks in the AEs have been practicing large-scale asset purchase programs many times. However, unconventional monetary policy in the form of asset purchasing is a new experience for the emerging market economies. In response to pandemic shock, central banks of several emerging economies have launched bond purchase programs to prevent deteriorations in the economy and to feed the market depth. The CBRT has also implemented bond purchase program as a measure against the adverse effects of the pandemic. The stated objective of the bond purchase program by the CBRT is to strengthen the monetary transmission mechanism.

In this study, we investigate whether there are long-run relationships between total amount of bond purchases, exchange rate, and credit volume by considering nonlinearities. Therefore, we estimate a nonlinear ARDL (NARDL) with weekly data over the period between May 31, 2019, and January 22, 2021. The results reveal significant asymmetric relationship between the government bond purchases and credit volume. We find that a positive (negative) change in the purchase has a positive (negative) and significant (insignificant) effect on the credit volume. Moreover, we observe a significant asymmetric relationship between the bond purchases and the credit volume. This result points out that the increase in the credit volume has been led by the boost of the liquidity of the government bond market. Moreover, estimation results suggest that the exchange rate is a positive factor on the credit volume. This finding is consistent with Bruno and Shin (2015), who present that the borrowing by local banks from global banks increase when the local currency appreciates against the U.S. dollar.

The first experience of emerging market economies with asset purchase programs has been positive so far. Given this experience, central banks in emerging market economies such as the CBRT should consider asset purchase programs as an additional measure in its toolkit when the conventional policies do not work effectively. In addition to government bond purchases, the CBRT may also practice corporate sector purchases via corporate bonds to promote firm financing.

REFERENCES

Ahmed, Zahoor, Bin Zhang, and Michael Cary. 2021. "Linking economic globalization, economic growth, financial development, and ecological footprint: Evidence from symmetric and asymmetric ARDL." *Ecological Indicators* 121: 1–12 https://doi.org/10.1016/j.ecolind.2020.107060

Arslan, Yavuz, Mathias Drehmann, and Boris Hofmann. 2020. "Central Bank Bond Purchases in Emerging Market Economies." *BIS Bulletin* No 20, June. Retrieved from https://www.bis.org/publ/bisbull20.pdf

Bruno, Valentina, and H. Song Shin. 2015. "Capital flows and the risk-taking channel of monetary policy." *Journal of Monetary Policy* 71: 119–132. http://dx.doi.org/10.1016/j.jmoneco.2014.11.011

Capelle-Blancard, G. and Adrien Desroizers. 2020. "The stock market is not the economy? Insights from the COVID-19 Crisis" *CEPR Covid Economics.* http://dx.doi.org/10.2139/ssrn.3638208

Central Bank of Republic of Turkey. 2020a. *Press Release on the Measures Taken against the Likely Economic and Financial Impacts of the Coronavirus* [Press release]. 17 March. Retrieved from https://tcmb.gov.tr/wps/wcm/connect/EN/TCMB+EN/Main+Menu/Announcements/Press+Releases/2020/ANO2020-16

Central Bank of Republic of Turkey. 2020b. *Press Release on Additional Measures Taken against the Economic and Financial Impacts of the Coronavirus* [Press release]. 31 March. Retrieved from https://tcmb.gov.tr/wps/wcm/connect/EN/TCMB+EN/Main+Menu/Announcements/Press+Releases/2020/ANO2020-21

Central Bank of Republic of Turkey. 2020c. *Press Release on Additional Measures Taken against the Economic and Financial Impacts of the Coronavirus* [Press release]. 17 April. Retrieved from https://tcmb.gov.tr/wps/wcm/connect/EN/TCMB+EN/Main+Menu/Announcements/Press+Releases/2020/ANO2020-22

Dickey, David A., and Wayne A. Fuller. 1979. "Distribution of the estimators for autoregressive time series with a unit root." *Journal of American Statistical Association* 74 (306): 427–431. https://doi.org/10.2307/2286348

Eichenbaum, Martin S., Sergio Rebelo, and Mathias Trabandt. 2020. "The Macroeconomics of Epidemics." *NBER Working Paper*, No. 26882, April. https://doi.org/10.3386/w26882

Haddad, V., Alan Moreira, and Tyler Muir. 2020. "When Selling Becomes Viral: Disruptions in Debt Markets in the COVID-19 Crisis and the Fed's Response." *NBER Working Paper,* No. 27168, May. https://doi.org/10.3386/w27168

Haroon, O., and Syed Aun R. Rizvi. 2020. "COVID-19: Media coverage and financial markets behavior—A sectoral inquiry." *Journal of Behavioral and Experimental Finance* .https://doi.org/10.1016/j.jbef.2020.100343

Rebucci, Alessansdro, Jonathan S. Hartley, and Daniel Jimenez. 2021. "An event study of COVID-19 central bank quantitative easing in advanced and emerging economies." *NBER Working Paper*, No. 27339. February. https://doi.org/10.3386/w27339

Hofmann, Boris, Ilhyock Shim, and Hyun Song Shin. 2020. "Emerging market economy exchange rates and local currency bond markets amid the COVID-19 pandemic." *BIS Bulletin No. 5*, April. Retrieved from https://www.bis.org/publ/bisbull05.pdf

IMF. 2021. *World Economic Outlook Update.* January. Retrieved from https://www.imf.org/en/Publications/WEO/Issues/2021/01/26/2021-world-economic-outlook-update

Iyke, Bernard. N. 2020. "The disease outbreak channel of exchange rate return predictability: Evidence from COVID-19." *Emerging Markets Finance and Trade* 56(10): 2277–2297, https://doi.org/10.1080/1540496X.2020.1784718

Luqman, Rabia, and Rehana Kouser. 2018. "Asymmetrical linkages between foreign exchange and stock markets: Empirical evidence through linear and non-linear ARDL." *Journal of Risk and Financial Management*, 11(3): 1–13. https://doi.org/10.3390/jrfm11030051

Phan, Dinh H. B., and Paresh K. Narayan. 2020. "Country responses and the reaction of the stock market to COVID-19—A preliminary exposition." *Emerging Markets Finance and Trade,* 56(10): 2138–2150. https://doi.org/10.1080/1540496X.2020.1784719

Pal, Debdatta, and Subrata Kumar. 2015. "Asymmetric impact of crude price on oil product pricing in the United States: An application of multiple threshold nonlinear autoregressive distributed lad model." *Resources Policy* 51: 436–443. http://dx.doi.org/10.1016/j.econmod.2015.08.026

Pata, Ugur K., and Abdullah E. Caglar. 2021. Investigating the EKC hypothesis with renewable energy consumption, human capital, globalization and trade openness for China: Evidence from augmented ARDL approach with a structural break." *Energy* 216: 1–16. https://doi.org/10.1016/j.energy.2020.119220

Pesaran, M. Hashem, and Yongcheol Shin. 1999. *"An autoregressive distribute lag modeling approach to cointegration analysis."* In Econometrics and Economic Theory in the 20th Century: The Ragnar Frisch Centennial Symposium; Chapter 11; Strom, S., Ed.; Cambridge University Press.

Pesaran, M. Hasheem., Yongcheol Shin, and Richard J. Smith. 2001. "Bounds testing approaches to the analysis of level relationships." *Journal of Applied Econometrics* 16: 289–326. https://doi.org/10.1002/jae.616

Phillips, Peter C.B., and Pierre Perron. 1988. "Testing for a unit root in time series regression. *Biometrika* 75(2): 335–346. https://doi.org/10.1093/biomet/75.2.335

Rehman, Mobeen U., Sajid Ali and Syed Jawad H.S. 2020. "Asymmetric nonlinear impact of oil prices and inflation on residential property prices: A case of US, UK and Canada." *Journal of Real Estate Finance and Economics* 61: 39–54. https://doi.org/10.1007/s11146-019-09706-y4

Sever, Can, Rohit Goel, Dimitris Drakopoulos, and Evan Papageorgiou. 2020. "Effects of Emerging Market Asset Purchase Program Announcements on Financial Markets During the COVID-19 Pandemic." IMF Working Paper, No. 292. December. Retrieved from https://www.imf.org/en/Publications/WP/Issues/2020/12/18/Effects-of-Emerging-Market-Asset-Purchase-Program-Announcements-on-Financial-Markets-During-49967

Shin, Y., Byungchul Yu, and Matthew Greenwood-Nimmo. 2014. "Modelling Asymmetric Cointegration and Dynamic Multipliers in a Nonlinear ARDL Framework." *Festschrift in Honor of Peter Schmidt.* Springer, New York, NY. https://doi.org/10.1007/978-1-4899-8008-3_9

Sobieralski, Joseph B. 2020. "COVID-19 and airline employment: Insights from historical uncertainty shocks to the industry." *Transportation Research Interdisciplinary Perspectives* 5: 1–9. https://doi.org/10.1016/j.trip.2020.100123

Wang, Mei-Chih, Pao-Lan Kuo, Chan-Sehng Chen, Chien-Liang Chiu, and Tsangyao Chang. 2020. "Yield Spread and Economic Policy Uncertainty: Evidence from Japan." *Sustainability* 12(10): 1–14. https://doi.org/10.3390/su12104302

Chapter 14

A Qualitative Research on Adaptation of Bank Headquarters Employees to Teleworking during the COVID-19

Case of Turkey[1]

Aslan Tolga Öcal

INTRODUCTION

The quick spread of COVID-19 pandemic throughout the world had severe impacts on all aspects of life, affecting the agenda of all scientific communities. Turkey is no exception; it experienced significant changes in social and economic life. Labor market also received its own share of the impact of this situation, which comprised the focus of our study. This study shall address the inclination of white-collar workers to teleworking as a consequence of the COVID-19 pandemic. The study was conducted on employees working in the headquarters of banks. Information obtained was about the change in working conditions, compliance of employees with telework, employee efficiencies, as well as positive and negative aspects experienced by employees upon the transition to telework between March and May 2020.

Coronaviruses (CoV) are a large family of viruses that cause a host of diseases, such as common cold, as well as more serious diseases, such as Middle East Respiratory Syndrome (MERS-CoV) and Severe Acute Respiratory Syndrome (SARS-CoV). COVID-19 is a species within this family, which was discovered in China in 2019 (Açıkgöz and Günay 2020). Upon the spread of COVID-19, which is believed to have started in Wuhan, China, for the first time in December 2019, World Health Organization declared it as a pandemic on March 11, 2020.

As a result, health policies and health expense budgets became the principal agenda of worldwide public opinion, and emergency conditions, which

189

had remained on paper until then, became the main concern of all communities as a fact of life (Altınkaya, 2020). According to the statistics of WHO, while deaths related to lower respiratory tract infections ranked the first among the most prevalent causes of death in underdeveloped countries, they occupied significantly lower ranks in EU countries before 2020. Deaths related to lower respiratory tract infections, ranking the 7th in EU and the 4th worldwide in 2016 rapidly rose to 5th and 3rd ranks, respectively, following COVID-19 (WHO, [13.05.2020]).

Besides the impacts of COVID-19 on health policies, its impacts on economy, which will be manifested more clearly in the long-term, are also discussed. On the other hand, in social life, social distancing is the main topic of conversation. Social distancing was designed to minimize the interactions between people living in a large community, where individuals are potentially infected but not diagnosed yet (Suppawittaya, Yiemphat and Pratchayapong and Yasri, 2020). The concept of social distancing, which gained prominence as a result of the pandemic, brought along many social changes, particularly teleworking to ensure that white-collar office-goers do not disrupt social distancing. The concept of teleworking, which has been discussed for almost thirty years in the framework of flexibility, once again became a prominent matter during the pandemic. In this context, the purpose of this descriptive qualitative study is to examine the adaptation process experienced by the headquarters employees of a bank for the first time during COVID-19.

FLEXIBILITY AND TELEWORKING

The concept of flexibility, in the broadest sense, can be described as the ability to adapt rapidly at minimum cost and with the lowest effort in the presence of changes. Having flexibility provides businesses with the ability to preserve their competitive power in a global economy, where competition is fierce (Parlak and Özdemir, 2011). As a result of technological progress, the change in the conditions of competition led the businesses willing to adapt to new conditions to flexible production systems (Güllü, 2019). Therefore, European labor markets, which started to lose their comparative advantage against the backdrop of increasing global competition, gravitated toward flexibility practices in every aspect of working life, particularly in the 2000s (Öcal, 2014).

Although the term "flexible working" seems like a term that concerns employers, it is actually used in a broader sense covering several working models, such as reduced working hours, non-standard working hours, various forms of teleworking, and compressed working time and it encompasses working arrangements that concern employees rather than employers (Kelliher and Anderson, 2009). Even though there are many types of flexibility, this chapter will address teleworkers. (Although this concept has numerous different uses, this study will resort to using the concept "teleworkers," which is preferred by ILO. The literature also contains other uses similar to this concept, for example, telecommuters, remote workers). Teleworking is generally described as working with the assistance of remote information and communication technologies outside a main office location. Telework includes a range of working relationships: employees connected to corporate networks while working from their homes or other remote locations, such as telecenters or client offices; self-employed consultants usually working from home, or home-based business operators operating businesses from their homes; independent contractors or self-employed subcontractors who rely on ICTs in order to carry out their work; and workers, whether directly employed or outsourced, located in back offices or call centers, linked telematically to employers' central office (Gurstein, 2001). Teleworking, which is generally described as being home-based, can be performed from a satellite office, a telework center, or any other location (Verbeke et al., 2008). Although work location is important from various aspects, this study considers telework as a type of home-based work.

Initial projections regarding telework emerged in the 1980s. Chief among these are the opinions of Alvin Toffler. Toffler (1984) indicated that it was necessary to strip off the fear that telecommunication would prevent direct contact. He predicted that a low-cost workstation could be created in a house and telework could be performed by means of a computer console and teleconferencing equipment, leading to the elimination of commuting costs (Toffler, 1984). Although there are variances between the authors about the concept, telework has achieved the status of a recognized type of work in Europe and other parts of the world since mid-1990s (Vega, 2003). Among the theoreticians of the concept, Huws et al. (1997) determined four fundamental variables that could describe the concept. These are: amount of time spent in the workplace of the employer, place of work, contractual relationship with the employer, and the nature of technology being used. Toffler's predictions proved to be correct and the cost of telework decreased based on the reduction in the costs of information technology and network systems. This situation also brought along efficiency and effectiveness and led to a gradual increase in the number of teleworkers (Parlak and Özdemir, 2011).

Although the concept of telework is discussed from time to time, it became a prominent item of the agenda particularly for white-collar office workers after COVID-19 pandemic. ILO utilizes three fundamental factors as they determine the policy to fight COVID-19 based on international labor standards. These three factors are determined as (i) protecting workers in the workplace, (ii) stimulating the economy and labor demand, and (iii) protecting employment and incomes. One of the measures under the main title of protecting workers in the workplace is the adaptation of work arrangements. It means the implementation of flexible working arrangements such as telework. During this process, telework was introduced at national or business levels in many countries; for example, it was incentivized in Japan and Italy with financial supports and by simplifying processes (ILO, 2020a). In Japan, only 13 percent of companies were able to perform telework as of April 2020, while 38 percent were unable to perform telework due to a host of issues including technical problems although they were willing to engage in such work. Telework was another important measure besides the closure of schools and the cancellation of festivals and sports competitions in Japan, which invested in medical facilities to reduce the number of cases affected by the virus (Shaw, Kim and Hua, 2020). Of course, it is quite challenging to obtain telework data during COVID-19. In fact, it is challenging to obtain any data concerning labor market. ILO admits to this in its labor survey studies. Lockdown practices, social distancing, and other restrictions implemented by governments are indicated as obstacles to data collection (ILO, 2020).

Due to these special circumstances based on the pandemic, it currently seems difficult to obtain data concerning labor markets. Therefore, it is necessary to focus on qualitative studies. This study will examine changing work conditions of bank headquarters employees, working in office environments, after their transition to telework, and address positive and negative consequences of telework in terms of employees.

METHODOLOGY

This study analyzed experiences of bank headquarters employees in terms of compliance with telework during the COVID-19 process using descriptive and qualitative research methods. The study, which required the use of purposive sampling, involved difficulties in accessing participants; so snowball sampling method was used (Dawson, 2002; Hutchinson, 2004) and the findings were obtained by means of semi-structured interviews. The factors that influenced the use of qualitative research method involved the difficulty of using a quantitative method, in addition to the fact that, thanks to this method, understanding the dynamics of current issue was more important than reaching general opinions. A total of thirteen participants among headquarters employees of three separate banks, comprising seven females and six males, were interviewed, and the interviews took place between May 18 and 25, 2020. The interviews were terminated at the saturation point when the data started to become repetitive. Names of individuals and banks were kept private during the field study.

FINDINGS

Attributes of the participants are given in table 14.1.

A total of thirteen participants, comprising seven females and six males, participated in the study. Age interval of the participants ranged between thirty-one and forty-six. The fact that all the participants are married draws attention. It is seen that, among the participants, who exhibit similar characteristics in terms of their roles at work, ten are directors, two are assistant directors, and one is a manager. Among the participants, whose work experiences vary between ten and twenty-three years, work in three separate banks, respectively eight in X bank, four in Y bank, and one in Z bank.

The first matter of interest in terms of compliance with telework was whether the employees considered their jobs to be compatible with teleworking. All of the participants consider their jobs to be completely suitable for, or largely compatible with, working at home to a great extent. Two participants point out that although the job is compatible with teleworking, there might be certain drawbacks. Participant 9 expressed, "I believe it is completely suitable for routine procedures, but I do not think that meetings, where decisions to be taken for determination of a roadmap would be made, are not held very efficiently by means of remote attendance." Participant 1 stated, "If the infrastructure required to enable access to our systems and work files is implemented, there is no technical obstacle. However, my personal opinion

Table 14.1   Attributes of Participants

Participants	Age	Gender	Marital Status	Role at Work	Number of Children	Work Experience (Years)	Employer Institution
Participant 1	45	Female	Married	Department Manager	2	23	X Bank
Participant 2	42	Female	Married	Director	1	20	X Bank
Participant 3	40	Male	Married	Assistant Director	1	23	Y Bank
Participant 4	36	Female	Married	Assistant Director	---	12	Y Bank
Participant 5	45	Male	Married	Director	2	22	Y Bank
Participant 6	40	Male	Married	Director	1	14	Y Bank
Participant 7	37	Female	Married	Director	1	14	Y Bank
Participant 8	31	Female	Married	Director	1	10	Y Bank
Participant 9	41	Female	Married	Director	2	17	Y Bank
Participant 10	39	Female	Married	Director	–	14	Y Bank
Participant 11	37	Male	Married	Director	1	12	Z Bank
Participant 12	46	Male	Married	Director	2	22	X Bank
Participant 13	43	Male	Married	Director	1	20	Y Bank

Source: Created by author

is that the healthiest approach is a manner of work that should be conducted in the office with your teammates."

Second, the participants were inquired about whether they had technological infrastructure during this process, support of the workplace in this regard, and adequacy of their physical conditions at home. In general, it was seen that workplaces were inadequate in terms of technological support and most of the participants used their own internet and telephone subscriptions. As a matter of fact, Participant 10 stated, "I provided necessary technological infrastructure completely with my own means. Not only my workplace failed to provide any support, but I also would have had to work at the office until a computer was provided if I had not had a personal computer" and emphasized that the process to transition to teleworking would have been extended if they had been unable to fulfill the necessary conditions on their own. Participants 5 and 6 stated that computers were allocated to them. Only Participant 11 stated that the workplace provided all requirements, such as computer, internet connection, etc. This indicates that only Z bank was completely prepared for the whole process. Although general tendency in terms of physical conditions is that they were adequate, certain drawbacks that could influence the study were mentioned. For example, it was observed that working on the dinner table, due to absence of a desk, was not ergonomic (Participant 3) and there were certain physical issues arising from the household, such as having children at home and absence of a separate work room (Participant 2).

The participants were inquired about whether not being in the same surroundings with their co-workers influenced compliance with teleworking. All of the male participants clearly stated that it was not problematic at all. Participant 12 expressed this as "we focus on work, and we work more efficiently because there are not time-consuming requests that unnecessarily block us." Female participants predominantly stated that such situation did not raise any issue, while there were participants that stated otherwise (Participants 1–2) and that emphasized the presence of certain disadvantages although there was no major issue (Participants 9–10). Accordingly, issues such as higher effectiveness and understandability of direct dialogue than telephone or e-mail communication (Participants 1–2), having general awareness about general situation and developments in the workplace (Participants 1–10), extended process and misunderstandings in terms of matters that should be negotiated before making a decision (Participants 9–10) are attributed to the lack of direct communication with co-workers. Another finding obtained from the interviews was that e-mail, telephone calls, WhatsApp application, and intra-bank communication systems were used to facilitate communications.

The participants were inquired about whether they had difficulties in accessing documents, records, sources, signatures, etc. It was observed that there were no significant issues other than the matter of original signature. In consideration of the issues in this regard, the issue of original signature varies between institutions. In X bank, previously received documents are signed as an employee goes to the office once a week. In Y Bank, it was decided to sign the documents later in the process. However, there are also other situations that draw attention, such as sending documents by courier for original signatures (Participant 8) or visitation by a notary public to have the participant sign documents at home (Participant 10). Besides these, different issues are pointed out, such as obtaining approvals by e-mail due to the lack of e-signature infrastructure (Participant 3), difficulties in reviewing documents due to the failure to print at home (Participants 2–7), occasional delays in opening documents due to slow operation and freezing of the system (Participant 9), and expectation of a more clear understanding of the situation in the future due to unavailability of issues depending on reduced work load as a result of the postponement of debt enforcement proceedings (Participant 5).

While general tendency was positive in terms of whether they received adequate feedback on current practices, objectives, and new arrangements of the workplace during the pandemic, different answers were given as well. Participants 2 and 3 expressed that they could not get feedback. Participant 2, who indicated that they could not get feedback, stated, "we are trying to stay informed about the process with hearsay information." On the other hand, Participant 4 stated that they received feedback on some matters, while there was no feedback on some others: "Notifications are made about arrangements (dining hall, shuttle buses, etc.) to be implemented in terms of health and hygiene. However, no information has been shared yet about planning in terms of either logistics matters such as hygiene and layout plan within the building, or whether there will be changes in human resources and personnel rights with respect to objectives and future collective working processes." These statements draw attention to the fact that feedback is rather related to ancillary matters; however, also in consideration of the pandemic, feedback on more important matters is unavailable.

In terms of whether taking initiative about work went through any change during the pandemic, responses of the participants predominantly indicate that there was no change. For example, Participant 6 stated, "There was no change, I need to be in continuous contact with my direct superior due to the balances in my line of work" and indicated that there could be no difference in the structure of performed work. On the contrary, Participant 9, who pointed out that their initiative on the work increased, stated, "Yes, there was. I started to take more initiative in my personal decisions as we experience the pandemic at the same time as teleworking and the pandemic impacts all aspects of life, particularly economy." Participant 9 thus stated with reference to economy in general that the pandemic impacted all aspects of life, and that pandemic played a role in making decisions about their work. Initiatives taken in respect of decisions to be made are also accepted by the management. On the other hand, Participant 2 claimed that they started to take less initiative. They stated that they could use more initiative at the workplace. They indicate that their director asked them to withdraw e-mails, containing decisions made by taking initiative during the telework process, or that they were warned not to take initiative without consulting the director.

Another matter of interest was the manner of change in work hours and overtime. Although it was predominantly stated that overtime work increased, it should be mentioned that there are dissenting opinions in this regard. Participants 4 and 6 stated that they did overtime at the workplace, but there was no overtime during telework, while Participant 7 stated that their working hours did not change. Participant 5 stated that they did half an hour overtime upon elimination of commuting time, and Participant 9 indicated that there was a slight increase amounting to half an hour per day. The grounds for complaints of other participants were matters such as intertwinement of business and family lives, extension of working time, abuse of working hours, the need to engage in work even during the weekend. Participant 10 responded to this question with: "Although I try to make this distinction as much as possible, there are factors that cause shifting in working hours, such as untimely e-mails and telephone calls received as the managers are aware that I am at home all day, or video conferences starting near the end of working hours. If this process turns out to be permanent, I believe that this will increase further as the managers get concerned that they are losing control" and shared their concern that the issues would increase further upon extension of the process. Another interesting statement was expressed by Participant 12. "We certainly spend more time in front of PC in comparison with the office. With the impact of the lockdown, we are expected to work even in the weekend as we cannot leave the house. They even send us on a compulsory leave and demand us to work during that leave." In consideration of the statements "Managers abuse the concepts of working hours and days" by Participant 3 and "The notion of working time put aside and a structure that serves 24/7 was implemented" by Participant 2, in addition to the preceding statement, some participants had the perception that their right were violated by the workplace, and they were forced to work excessively overtime.

The participants gave different responses to whether they would prefer to telework or working at office. The participants, who were asked to indicate positive and negative aspects of telework, mentioned a host of different positive and negative aspects. These positive and negative attributes, indicated by the participants, can be seen in table 14.2.

Table 14.2, prepared with reference to the responses given by the participants, shows conflicting positive and negative aspects. This is related to the

Table 14.2   Positive and Negative Aspects of Telework

Positive Aspects	Negative Aspects
Saving time spent during commuting (Participants 1-2-4-6-7-8-9-10-12)	Increase in domestic disputes, issues with children and concentration problems (Participants 1-7-8-9)
Being able to wear casual clothing, reduction in expenses such as clothing and makeup (Participants 1-10-12)	Discomfort experienced due to the lack of ergonomics at home (Participants 1-3)
The advantage of being at home in case of various needs or sickness, comfort (Participants 10-12)	Physical and psychological problems experienced due to general immobility or isolation (Participants 1-4-7)
Working in more sterile and calmer surroundings (Participants 1-3-4-7-12)	Time losses that might occur due to communication problems (Participants 1-7-11)
Finding it easier to concentrate on work at home (Participant 4)	Intertwinement of business and family lives (Participants 5-10)
Reduction in overtime work (Participant 6)	Disregard for working hours (Participants 2-8-10)
	Measurement of efficiency with the duration of remaining online (Participant 3)
	Additional cost due to the use of telephone, electricity, and personal computer (Participant 4)

Source: Created by author

different perspectives of individuals in terms of their preferences between telework and working at office during and after the pandemic. In this context, it was asked which manner of working they would prefer. While Participants 4, 6, 8, 10, 12 preferred to telework, Participants 1, 2, 5, 11 preferred to work at office. Besides, Participant 2 stated that, while making this decision, their preference to work at the office was influenced by malpractices such as the failure to protect social rights and the increase in overtime work during teleworking; otherwise, they could accept teleworking. However, certain participants did not consider it adequate to prefer only one of these two manners of working. Participants 3, 7, 9, 13 stated that they would prefer a hybrid system where both manners of working would be implemented in combination.

The participants were asked to evaluate efficiency differences between telework and work at office from their perspective. The participants predominantly stated that there was an increase in efficiency or, at least, they did not experience a decline in efficiency. However, participants 1, 2, 9 think that they experienced a decline in efficiency. In this regard, issues experienced by particularly female employees with young children due to social gender gains importance. Female participants have some complaints in this regard.

The words of Participant 12, a male employee, are quite important in terms of understanding the situation. Accordingly, Participant 12 states, "If factors such as child and babysitter in the house are convenient, work environment is certainly more efficient than the office. I have not experienced any compliance issues as our babysitter does the daily chores and takes care of the children. I have heard of mothers without babysitters and with young children at home, who got felt under burden at home. This issue will be resolved when the schools open."

DISCUSSION

After diagnosis of the first coronavirus case in Turkey, we entered the process called "the new normal" regarding business and life as a consequence of practices such as social distancing, lockdowns, travel restrictions, closure of institutions and workplaces, flexible working hours, distance education, and telework (Zeybekoğlu-Akbaş and Dursun, 2020). During this period, the pandemic process was brought up for discussion throughout the world in many aspects such as social, psychological, economic, and particularly medical studies. One of the matters of discussion during this process is telework, depending on flexible working.

Precautions taken to restrict movement for the purpose of slowing down the spread of the pandemic and measures taken to implement social distancing in the private sector made telework more feasible than before. While only a certain minority within the labor force used to work from home before the pandemic, it is observed that the pandemic increased the rate of people working from home. However, it is impossible to perform every occupation and job with telework. Professional, scientific and technical services, company and business management, educational services, and jobs in fields such as finance and insurance are the most suitable jobs for telework (Kara, 2020). During the survey conducted by Webrazzi Insights in Turkey between March 27 and 30, 2020, with 2,849 users of Webrazzi Insight (1,677 of which were employed) to measure the perspective on the coronavirus epidemic, working arrangement circumstances of employees during the pandemic were inquired. Among participants that answered this question, 43.5 percent reported that they continued to go to their workplaces, 38 percent reported that they were teleworking, 11.4 percent reported that they were on paid leave, and 7 percent reported that they were sent to unpaid leave or dismissed (Webrazzi Insights, 2020).

There are studies conducted during the pandemic process on the extent of jobs that are suitable for telework. According to the differential classification conducted by Dingel and Neiman (2004) by means of O*NET program supported by U.S. Ministry of Labor, it was found out that 37 percent of the jobs in the United States could be performed with teleworking. This is a high rate. While determination of these jobs assists the economy to perform well particularly during the pandemic, it also gives an idea about whether telework will continue in terms of efficiency after the pandemic.

Again, according to another study conducted on EU countries, the rate of jobs that could be performed with telework was determined as 23.9 percent in Italy, 28.2 percent in France, 28.7 in Germany, 25.4 percent in Spain, 30.7 percent in Sweden, and 31.4 percent in England (Boeri et al., 2020). It can be said that, during the pandemic, those employed in jobs compatible with telework are luckier than those employed in jobs that are not compatible. In another study conducted in the United States, it was seen that those with jobs compatible with telework were impacted less by the pandemic, and their risk of losing their jobs was lower than those working in jobs that were not compatible with telework (Béland, Wright and Brodeur, 2020).

Besides compatibility of jobs with telework, telework also has issues specific to the pandemic and the concept of telework itself. Findings of the survey conducted by KPMG between April 2 and 12, 2020, based on data collected from 102 professionals in human resources, finance/financial affairs, and strategy/business development departments, 45 percent of which are senior executives, include data on telework, efficiency, and work-life balance (KPMG, 2020). Upon evaluation of these findings, which indicate the challenges of telework during the pandemic, in percentages, results are as follows: sustaining the motivation to work (65.85 percent), follow-up and feedback concerning work performance (63.41 percent), ensuring balance between business and private lives (59.76 percent), creating a suitable work environment at home (43.90 percent), clarification of tasks with time schedules (32.93 percent), ability to work alone (20.73 percent) (KPMG, 2020).

Findings obtained as a result of the interviews indicate that the issue regarding motivation and efficiency in the banking sector does not have a high correlation with the KPMG study. However, mentioned issues are in correlation with both this study in general, and the questions used to measure the impact of telework on employees and the issues encountered in answers.

Pandemic process brings along certain issues. There are fundamental differences between telework in this process and telework performed before the pandemic. The most fundamental difference is that telework is combined with childcare depending on the closure of places such as schools and kindergartens. Accordingly, there is a transformation particularly in work-life balances of parenting employees. Rice (2017) indicates that flexible working may have both positive and negative consequences in terms of stress and work-life balance, and this relationship is led by factors such as motivations, preference, location, and organizational norms. Gajendran and Harrrison (2007), who reviewed studies conducted before the pandemic, indicate that telework has small but beneficial effects on autonomy and work-family conflict, and it also has beneficial effects in terms of job satisfaction, stress, and performance. In another study, it was revealed that employees had higher levels of work performance and job satisfaction, and their performances increased during telework (Vega et al., 2015).

These positive data belong to the pre-pandemic period and it is also worth reviewing studies conducting during the pandemic. According to the outcome of a survey conducted on 14,005 Flemish workers, 64.6 percent of the participants considered that telework improved the balance between work and life, while almost half of the participants believed that telework assisted in minimizing both work-related stress (48.4 percent) and burnout potential (47.6 percent). Again, 56.3 percent of the participants claimed that telework increased their efficiency and 50.7 percent claimed that it increased their concentration during working. During the study, it was seen that women had more positive opinions than men. Based on traditional gender roles, women have more difficulties in establishing a work-life balance. Telework is beneficial in combining responsibilities imposed on women by gender roles and responsibilities imposed by work life. In workplaces that receive a lot of feedbacks, employees working under other people report fewer positive opinions. This situation, which creates a coordination issue, is a negative aspect of telework. Employees that are used to receiving heavy feedback have concerns of receiving lower feedbacks due to telework, and the decrease of face-to-face communication reduces feedbacks and appreciation (Baert et al., 2020). Similarly, our study also encountered concerns about the decrease of face-to-face communication. However, although face-to-face work displays better performance than virtual groups in creative teamwork assignments, working away from office increases focus on individualized assignments (Guyot and Sawhill, 2020).

These results indicate that telework still has positive impacts in prevention of stress and burnout and ensuring improvement in work-life balance, efficiency, and concentration even during the pandemic, although not very prominently. Although it was not possible to make an evaluation in percentages during our study, it can be said that women were impacted more negatively due to social gender roles. This is caused by social gender rather than telework itself. Nevertheless, the thought that telework still can facilitate work-life balance makes women incline more to telework.

Similar to our area of study, findings of a study conducted in Turkey during the pandemic with executives in the Business Sustainability Commission in banking and finance sectors indicated that digital infrastructures of banks were ready for telework, telework culture was established in these institutions, and therefore no compliance issues were experienced (Aydın Göktepe, 2020). These findings make us consider that executives of banks that previously engaged in teleworking were interviewed, unlike our study. However, such a practice was unavailable before in the banks within the scope of our study. Another difference might be that executives in the Business Sustainability Commission could be more optimistic about compliance as they were in charge of the process. Besides, although they had employees compatible with telework, even they stated that they experienced problems with business sustainability in the presence of sudden or intensive increases in online activities during the pandemic (Aydın Göktepe, 2020). In the study, it was stated that arrangements were made in performance and compensation plans, as well as benefits such as leave, private health insurance, and lunch and travel allowance due to telework. Besides these, it is indicated that new payments such as internet quota and telephone bill support, which is almost non-existent in our study, were defined (Aydın Göktepe, 2020). In this study, we observed that the employees were able to work in compliance with telework mostly with their own means. This difference suggests two possibilities. The first one is that there might be scale differences between studied banks. It is possible that while certain banks in the sector previously ensured telework compliance, certain banks engaged in telework during the pandemic. A second possibility is that executives of the Business Sustainability Commission, which is in charge of this process, attempted to represent the situation better than it was. As mentioned above, even if it is stated that there is no issue regarding compliance, online activities due to the pandemic lead to various issues.

It is also a matter of discussion whether telework will continue after the pandemic. From the perspective of employees, conflicts in respect of work and family needs will decline when kindergartens and schools open after this process. Thereafter, it is expected that parents may benefit from telework upon cultural transformations of companies and adoption of new technologies by parents (Arntz, 2020). One of the results of the study by Baert et al. (2020) is that 85 percent of survey participants believed that telework was permanent despite their concerns such as reduced promotion opportunities or weakening of their bonds with their employers or colleagues. According to the results of a study conducted in the United States in April 2020, it was stated that finding out new ways of telework and reorganization of businesses could create more permanent impacts on work organization in case of a hysteria effect (Brynjolfsson et al. 2020).

RESULT

It is seen that interviewed participants attempted to adjust to telework practices during the pandemic. The participants, who have certain concerns and hesitations due to either private circumstances at home or issues of work-places to adapt to the process, are generally inclined to transition to telework or, at least a hybrid manner of work in case issues are resolved. In consid-eration of literature discussion, telework would be even more possible upon both elimination of deficiencies by workplace management and elimination of the issues of female employees who experience challenges due to social gender after schools and kindergartens open during the period following the pandemic.

Upon alleviation of negative impacts of telework during the pandemic, it could be predicted without doubt that performance of telework would continue, but it is difficult to estimate the extent of such outcome. The dis-cussions made so far have emphasized benefits and feasibility of telework in terms of employees rather than cost and other calculations of employers. To be able to have a clearer picture of the continuation of this process, there is also a need for studies analyzing the matter in terms of the employer. This study addresses the matter from the perspective of employees. The fact that the matter is evaluated only from the perspective of employees and only a small number of participants in a certain sector constitutes the constraint of the study. It is our hope that this study contributes to new academic dis-cussions aimed at teleworking during and after the period called "the new normal."

NOTE

1. This book chapter is a revised and expanded version of an abstract paper entitled "Covid-19 Sürecinde Banka Genel Müdürlük Çalışanlarının Uzaktan Çalışmaya Uyumu Üzerine Nitel Bir Araştırma" presented at Online International Conference of COVID-19 (CONCOVID), June 12, 13, 14, 2020, in Istanbul, Turkey.

REFERENCES

Açıkgöz, Ömer and Aslı Günay. 2020. "The Early Impact of The COVID-19 Pandemic on the Global and Turkish Economy." *Turkish Journal of Medical Sciences 50*: 520–26.

Altınkaya, Zelha. 2020. "2020 Koronavirus Pandemisinde Avrupa Birliği Sağlık Politikaları ve Neoliberalism: İtalya örneği." *Yalova Sosyal Bilimler Dergisi* 10 (20): 1–31.

Arntz, Melanie, Sarra Ben Yahmed, and Francesco Berlingieri. 2020. "Working from Home and COVID-19: The Chances and Risks for Gender Gaps." *ZEW ExpertBrief 20-09*: 1–12. Accessed July 9, 2020. http://ftp.zew.de/pub/zew-docs/ZEWKurzexpertisen/EN/ZEW_Shortreport2009.pdf

Aydın Göktepe, Esra. 2020. "Kriz Döneminde İş Sürdürülebilirliğine Yönelik Yönetim Uygulamaları; COVID-19 Pandemi Araştırması." *Journal of Social, Humanities and Administrative Sciences* 6 (26): 630–38.

Baert, Stijn, Louis Lippens, Eline Moens, Philippe Sterkens, and Johannes Weytjens. 2020. "The COVID-19 Crisis and Telework: A Research Survey on Experiences, Expectations and Hopes." GLO Discussion Paper, No:532, Essen. Accessed July 28, 2020. https://ideas.repec.org/p/zbw/glodps/532.html.

Béland, Louis-Philippe, Abel Brodeur, and Taylor Wright. 2020. "The Short-Term Economic Consequences of COVID-19: Exposure to Disease, Remote Work and Government Response." Discussion Paper Series, *IZA DP* No. 13159. Accessed July 8, 2020. https://www.iza.org/publications/dp/13159/the-short-term-economic-consequences-of-COVID-19-exposure-to-disease-remote-work-and-government-response.

Boeri, Tito, Alessandro Caiumi, and Marco Paccagnella. 2020. "Mitigating The Work-Security Trade-Off While Rebooting the Economy." 9 April, Accessed July 9, 2020. https://voxeu.org/article/mitigating-work-security-trade.

Brynjolfsson, Erik, John J. Horton, Adam Ozimek, Daniel Rock, Garima Sharma, and Hong-Yi TuYe. 2020. "COVID-19 and Remote Work: An Early Look at US Data." *NBER* Working Paper, No:27944. Accessed July 9, 2020. https://ideas.repec.org/p/nbr/nberwo/27344.html.

Dawson, Catherine. 2002. *Practical Research Methods: A User-Friendly Guide to Mastering Research.* United Kingdom: How To Books Ltd.

Dingel, Jonathan, and Brent Neiman. 2020. "How Many Jobs Can Be Done at Home?" *NBER White Paper*, Becker Friedman Institute, Chicago. Accessed June 30, 2020. https://bfi.uchicago.edu/working-paper/how-many-jobs-can-be-done-at-home/.

Gajendron, Ravi S., and David A. Harrison. 2007. "The Good, the Bad, and the Unknown About Telecommuting: Meta-Analysis of Psychological Mediators and Individual Consequences." *Journal of Applied Psychology* 92 (6): 1524–541.

Gurstein, Penny. 2001. *Wired to the World, Chained to the Home: Telework in Daily Life.* Toronto: UBC Press.

Guyot, Katherine, and Isabel V. Sawhill. 2020. "Telecommuting Will Likely Continue Long After the Pandemic." Accessed July 2, 2020. https://www.brooking s.edu/blog/up-front/2020/04/06/telecommuting-will-likely-continue-long-after-the-pandemic/.

Güllü, Gökhan. 2019. 'Yeni Teknolojiler, Değişen Endüstri İlişkileri ve İşçi Sendikalarındaki Dönüşüm." *Marmara Üniversitesi İktisadi ve İdari Bilimler Dergisi* 41 (2): 432–52.

Hutchinson, Susan R. 2004. "Survey Research." In *Foundations for Research: Methods of Inquiry Education and Social Sciences*, edited by Kathleen B. deMarrais, and Stephen D. Lapan, 283–301. Mahwah: Lawrence Erlbaum Associates Inc.

Huws, Ursula, Niolt Jagger, and Siobhan O'Regan. 1999. "Teleworking and Globalisation." *IES*, Report 358, Brighton. Accessed June 13, 2020. https://www .employment-studies.co.uk/system/files/resources/files/358.pdf.

ILO. 2020a. "COVID-19 and the World of Work: Impact and Policy Responses." ILO Monitor 1st Edition, 18 March 2020. Accessed June 10, 2020. https://www.ilo .org/wcmsp5/groups/public/---dgreports/---dcomm/documents/briefingnote/wcms _738753.pdf.

ILO. 2020b. "COVID-19: Guidance for Labour Statistics Data Collection." ILO Technical Note, April 30, 2020. Accessed June 10, 2020. https://ilo.org/wcmsp5/gr oups/public/---dgreports/---stat/documents/publication/wcms_745658.pdf.

Kara, Elif. 2020. "COVID-19 Pandemisi: İşgücü Üzerindeki Etkileri ve İstihdam Tedbirleri." *Avrasya Sosyal ve Ekonomi Araştırmaları Dergisi (Eurasian Journal of Researches in Social and Economics)* 7 (5): 269–82.

Kelliher, Clare, and Deirdre Anderson. 2009. "Doing More Withless? Flexible Working Practices and the Intensification of Work." *Human Relations* 63 (1): 83–106.

KPMG. 2020. "COVID-19 ile Çalışma Hayatındaki Yeni Uygulamalar Anket Raporu." Accessed June, 13 2020. https://assets.kpmg/content/dam/kpmg/tr/pdf/2 020/04/covid19-calisma-hayatindaki-yeni-uygulamalar.pdf.

Öcal, Aslan Tolga. 2014. "Güvenceli Esneklik Gündemi: 2008 Mali Krizi Sonrası Danimarka İşgücü Piyasası." *Sosyal Güvenlik Dergisi* 4 (1): 59–86.

Parlak, Zeki, and Süleyman Özdemir. 2011. "Esneklik Kavramı ve Emek Piyasalarında Esneklik." *Sosyal Siyaset Konferansları* 60 (1): 1–60.

Rice, Ronald E., 2017. "Flexwork, Work–Family Boundaries, and Information and Communication Technologies." In *The Wiley Blackwell Handbook of the Psychology of the Internet at Work,* edited by Guido Hertel, Dianna L. Stone, Ricard D. Johnson, and Jonathan Passmore, 175–193. London: Wiley Blackwell.

Shaw, Rajib, Yong-kyun Kim, and Jinling Hua. 2020. "Governance Technology and Citizenship Behavior in Pandemic: Lessons from COVID-19 in East Asia.' *Progress in Disaster Science* 6 (April 2020): 1–11.

Suppawittaya, Piwat, Pakara Yiemphat, and Pratchayapong Yasri. 2020. "Effects of Social Distancing, Self-Quarantine and Self-Isolation During the COVID-19 Pandemic on People's Well-Being, and How to Cope with It." *International Journal of Science and Healthcare Research* 5 (2): 12–20.

Toffler, Alvin. 1980. *The Third Way.* United States of America: William Morrow & Co. Inc.

Vega, Ronald P., Amanda J. Anderson, and Seth A. Kaplan. 2015. "A Within-Person Examination of the Effects of Telework." *Journal of Business and Psychology* 30 (2): 313–23.

Vega, Gina. 2003. *Managing Teleworkers and Telecommuting Strategies.* 1st published. United States of America: Praeger Publishers.

Verbeke, Alain, Robert Schulz, Nathan Greidanus, and Laura Hambley. 2008. *Growing the Virtual Workplace: The Integrative Value Proposition for Telework.* UK: Edward Elgar Cheltenham.

Webrazzi Insights. 2020. "Coronavirüs Salgınına Bakış Açısı." Accessed June 19, 2020. https://webrazzi.com/2020/04/02/corona-virus-salginina-bakis-acisi/.

WHO. 2020. "Top 10 Causes of Death: Situation and Trends." Accessed Mai 13, 2020. https://www.who.int/gho/mortality_burden_disease/causes_death/top_10/en/.

Zeybekoğlu Akbaş, Özge, and Cansu Dursun. 2020. "Koronavirüs (COVID-19) Pandemisi Sürecinde Özel Alanına Kamusal Alanı Sığdıran Çalışan Anneler." *Avrasya Sosyal ve Ekonomi Araştırmaları Dergisi (Eurasian Journal of Researches in Social and Economics)* 7 (5): 78–94.

Index

About the Contributors

Çağatay Başarır is an associate professor of finance in Bandirma Onyedi Eylul University, Faculty of Application Sciences on International Trade and Logistics Department. He received his undergraduate degree (BA) in business administration from the Ege University in 2003. He earned his MA in 2006 and his PhD in business administration in 2016 from Balikesir University. He has studied about financial markets, stock exchange markets, commodity markets, and precious metals in the field of time series analyses, multicriteria decision analysis, and performance measurement. He teaches financial management, financial analysis, financial markets, international finance, and portfolio management lessons both in graduate and undergraduate degree courses. He is the editor of *Bandırma Onyedi Eylül University Social Sciences Research Journal*. In addition to many published articles, book chapters, and reviews, he is the editor of five international books.

Burak Darıcı is a professor and deputy head of Department of Economics; director of Continuing Education Center and also E-sports and Economics Application Research Center at Bandirma Onyedi Eylül University. His expertise includes financial economy, financial stability, labor market, and unemployment. He is the editor of both the *Journal of Management and Economics Research* and the *Journal of Applied Economics and Social Sciences*. In addition to many published articles, book chapters, and reviews, he is the editor of six international books.

Mustafa Kevser was born in 1983 in Selçuk, İzmir, Turkey. He got his bachelor's degree in public finance, Anadolu University in 2005; master's degree in business administration in Dokuz Eylul University in 2007; and PhD in international trade and finance in Yalova University in 2018. He is a certified public accountant and the member of Union Chambers of Certified Public Accountants of Turkey. Before his academic life, he worked as an independent CPA. After that Mustafa Kevser worked as a financial analyst and portfolio manager in banking sector for about ten years. He is an assistant professor at Bandırma Onyedi Eylul University since June 2019 in Turkey. His main research areas include financial markets and institutions, financial performance, banking, and corporate governance.

Mustafa Bilik did his primary, secondary, and high school education in Bursa. He completed his university education at Dokuz Eylül University, Department of Economics between 2008 and 2012. He earned his master's degree at Dokuz Eylül University, Department of Economics in 2015. He completed his doctorate degree in the same department in 2020. He worked as a research assistant at Dokuz Eylül University between 2014 and 2020. He continues his academic studies especially in microeconomics, international economics, and applied economics.

Üzeyir Aydın was born in 1980 in Manisa, Gördes. After his secondary education at Salihli Trade Vocational High School, he did his undergraduate education in the field of economics at Dokuz Eylül University, Faculty of Economics and Administrative Sciences, Department of Economics in 2000. He earned his master's degree at Dokuz Eylül University, Institute of Social Sciences, Department of Economics in 2003. In the same department, he received his PhD degree with the thesis titled "Comparative Organizational Efficiency in the Finance Industry: The Case of Turkey" in 2010. Aydın, who teaches microeconomics, financial economics, behavioral finance, behavioral economics, advanced microeconomics, mathematical economics, introduction to economics at the undergraduate, no and doctoral levels, His main research areas include, financial efficiency,monetary policy, microfinance, economic theory, behavioral economics, and behavioral finance. Aydın is married with two children.

Dr. İnci Merve Altan graduated from the Ondokuz Mayıs University, Department of Mathematic, and completed her master's degree in mathematics from Department of Karabuk University, doctorate in business from Department of Karabuk University. She is currently working as assistant professor at Bandırma Onyedi Eylül University, Bandırma Vacotional School, Department of Accounting and Tax.

Metin Kılıç, who is a graduate of Muğla Sıtkı Koçman University, Faculty of Economics and Administrative Sciences, Department of Business Administration, completed his master's degree in Muğla University Social

Sciences Institute and completed his PhD in accounting at Anadolu University, Institute of Social Sciences, Bandirma Onyedi Eylül University, faculty of economics and administrative sciences, Business Administration Department. As an associate professor, he conducts various academic researches. He is also the rector's advisor in quality activities.

Ramazan Ekinci is an assistant professor of economics at Faculty of Economics and Administrative Sciences, Izmir Bakircay University, Turkey. He received his undergraduate degree (BA) in economics from the Atatürk University in 2010 winning the top student award from Faculty of Economics and Administrative Sciences. Dr. Ekinci earned his MA in 2013; and his PhD in economics in 2018 from Dokuz Eylul University. Dr. Ekinci, who has many articles published in academic journals, was awarded with the Turkish Economic Association Awards for his master thesis in 2013; best paper award from International Conference on Eurasian Economies in 2018. Dr. Ekinci's research interests include the financial economics; banking and finance; efficiency and productivity analysis; time series analysis; and applied econometrics.

İbrahim Külünk was born on the seashore in November 1983. He completed his undergraduate, graduate, and doctorate degrees in economics. He has conducts studies on economic growth. He started working at Düzce University as an assistant professor in November 2018. He still teaches economics and finance at the Faculty of Business Administration of the same university.

Arzu Alvan Bozdereli completed her undergraduate education on business administration. She completed her master's and doctoral studies on economics. Her master's thesis topic is a critical analysis of the relationship between monetary policy and inflation in Turkey after 1980. Her doctoral dissertation topic was advised by Queens University and Eastern Mediterranean University faculty member Prof. Dr. Glen P. JENKINS. Her doctoral dissertation subject is sources of growth at Turkish manufacturing industry: two-deflator growth accounting approach. The two-deflator growth accounting method was applied for the first time in Turkey. Both his master's and doctoral theses have been published by international publishing houses. Her areas of expertise are economic growth and development, world economy and finance, political economy, innovation and transformation economics. She has various academic studies in these fields. She is still a faculty member in the Department of Business Administration at Cyprus Science University. She is the vice dean of the Faculty of Economics, Administrative, and Social Sciences. She is the assistant director of the Graduate Education and Research Institute.

Lale Aslan was born in Istanbul in 1983. She completed the MBA program at Yildiz Technical University in 2007. She worked in the finance sector between 2006 and 2016 as auditor and head of compliance in top international companies, such as KPMG, Credit Agricole Cheuvreux, and Yapi Kredi. She completed her PhD degree in business (Track: Accounting and Finance) from Yeditepe University in 2014 at the top of the class, while she was working in the finance sector. She has been teaching accounting and finance in Istanbul Yeni Yuzyil University as assistant professor since 2017. Her academic work focuses on auditing and corporate governance. She has Level 3 and Derivatives Licenses of Capital Markets Board of Turkey and CRMA (Certificate of Risk Management) of the IIA (Institute of Internal Auditors). She is an active member of TIDE (IIA Turkey).

Cem Berk is an experienced university lecturer with a demonstrated history of working in the higher education industry as well as in private industry. Prof. Berk is a full-time finance professor in Kirklareli University. Prof. Berk is a staunch academician with a PhD in accounting and finance from Marmara University and a bachelor of science degree from Bogazici University. Primary research fields of Prof. Berk are international finance, energy finance, and real estate finance. Prof. Berk has teaching experience of accounting and finance courses in PhD, MBA, and undergraduate programs.

Tuba Gülcemal received her PhD in 2016 from Erciyes University, Institute of Social Sciences, Department of Business Administration, Accounting and Finance. Dr. GÜLCEMAL has published articles in international peer-reviewed journals, presented at international scientific meetings and in the proceedings and also published book chapters with international publishing houses.

Ünay Tamgac Tezcan is an assistant professor in the Department of Economics at TOBB University of Economics and Technology. Her research fields are open economy macroeconomics and international finance. She works on applied macro-financial topics in international economies, such as financial crises, exchange rate regimes, capital flows, and financial markets. Her research focus is on emerging economies and Turkey. Her other research areas include housing cycles, consumption-saving behavior, peer effects. Dr. Tamgac received her MA and PhD in economics from the University of California, Santa Cruz (UCSC). She holds an MBA from Middle East Technical University and a B.S. in industrial engineering from Bilkent University, Turkey. Originally from Turkey, she is fluent in English and German.

İhsan Erdem Kayral was born in Ankara in 1987, associate professor İhsan Erdem Kayral graduated from the Department of Economics at Hacettepe University as the top student of faculty and department. He received his MSc and PhD degrees in the field of finance in the Department of Business Administration from the same university. After completing his studies, İhsan Erdem Kayral started to work in TUBITAK (The Scientific and Technological Research Council of Turkey) as a chief expert in 2010, and he served there for over 8 years. Currently, he works in the Department of Economics in Konya Food and Agriculture University. He has written several papers and book chapters on finance. İhsan Erdem Kayral has received lots of awards in various fields. He also gets "National Tubitak Master's Degree Scholarship" and received "Turkish Economics Association Achievement Grant" in his bachelor's degree.

Pınar Koç is an assistant professor in the Department of Economics at Gümüşhane University. Her research fields are open macroeconomics, econometric and health economics. She works on applied macroeconomics in international economies, such as unemployment, exchange rates and financial markets, the macroeconomic costs of illness. She has a focus on advanced economies and Turkey. Her other research areas include environmental economics. He received her MA and PhD in economics from the University of Sakarya.

Ahmet Gülmez is an associate professor in the Department of Economics at Sakarya University. His research fields are open macroeconomics and economic growth. He works on applied macro-financial topics in international economies, such as convergence hypothesis, international trade. He has a focus on advanced economies and Turkey. His other research areas include environmental economics and health economics. He received her MA and PhD in economics from the University of Sakarya.

Ahmet Usta received his undergraduate degree in economics from Uludağ University, Bursa–Turkey in 2008. He got two master's degrees in economics from University of Illinois at Urbana–Champaign, IL–USA, and from Bilkent University, Ankara–Turkey in 2014. He started his PhD studies at Özyeğin University, İstanbul–Turkey in 2014. He attended PhD program in finance and obtained his PhD degree with a thesis titled "Essays in Macro-Finance" in 2020. During his PhD studies at Özyeğin, he visited University of Vienna and spent the 2015–2016 academic year in PhD program in economics. His issue of research is at the intersection of macroeconomics and finance. Particularly, he is interested in monetary policies, global liquidity conditions and their effects on the real economy and financial markets, financialization, and asset prices. Since 2012, he has served in the Department of Economics at Recep Tayyip Erdoğan University, Rize–Turkey.

Aslan Tolga Öcal was born in Istanbul in 1978. He completed his middle and high school education in Saint Michel French high school and his undergraduate education in the Department of Labour Economics and Industrial Relations at Istanbul University. He completed his master's degree and doctorate at the Institute of Social Sciences at Istanbul University and earned his PhD on "Change in Industrial Relations and Corporate Social Responsibility." He was awarded the title of Associate Professor in 2017 and has been working in the Department of Labour Economics and Industrial Relations at Marmara University since 2001. His interests include labor markets, social policy, business ethics, corporate social responsibility, and industrial relations.

www.ingramcontent.com/pod-product-compliance
Lightning Source LLC
Chambersburg PA
CBHW050646280326
41932CB00015B/2794